EMBODYING BORDERS

EASA Series

Published in Association with the European Association of Social Anthropologists (EASA)

Series Editors: Jelena Tošić, University of St. Gallen; Sabine Strasser, University of Bern; Annika Lems, Max Planck Institute for Social Anthropology, Halle

Social anthropology in Europe is growing, and the variety of work being done is expanding. This series is intended to present the best of the work produced by members of the EASA, both in monographs and in edited collections. The studies in this series describe societies, processes and institutions around the world and are intended for both scholarly and student readership.

Recent volumes:

41. EMBODYING BORDERS
A Migrant's Right to Health, Universal Rights and Local Policies
Edited by Laura Ferrero, Chiara Quagliariello and Ana Cristina Vargas

40. THE SEA COMMANDS
Community and Perception of the Environment in a Portuguese Fishing Village
Paulo Mendes

39. CAN ACADEMICS CHANGE THE WORLD?
An Israeli Anthropologist's Testimony on the Rise and Fall of a Protest Movement on Campus
Moshe Shokeid

38. INSTITUTIONALISED DREAMS
The Art of Managing Foreign Aid
Elżbieta Drążkiewicz

37. NON-HUMANS IN AMERINDIAN SOUTH AMERICA
Ethnographies of Indigenous Cosmologies, Rituals and Songs
Edited by Juan Javier Rivera Andía

36. ECONOMY, CRIME AND WRONG IN A NEOLIBERAL ERA
Edited by James G. Carrier

35. BEING-HERE
Placemaking in a World of Movement
Annika Lems

34. EXPERIMENTAL COLLABORATIONS
Ethnography through Fieldwork Devices
Edited by Adolfo Estalella and Tomás Sánchez Criado

33. BACK TO THE POSTINDUSTRIAL FUTURE
An Ethnography of Germany's Fastest-Shrinking City
Felix Ringel

32. MESSY EUROPE
Crisis, Race and Nation-State in a Postcolonial World
Edited by Kristín Loftsdóttir, Andrea L. Smith and Brigitte Hipfl

For a full volume listing, please see the series page on our website:
https://www.berghahnbooks.com/series/easa

EMBODYING BORDERS

A Migrant's Right to Health,
Universal Rights and Local Policies

*Edited by Laura Ferrero,
Chiara Quagliariello and Ana Cristina Vargas*

berghahn
NEW YORK • OXFORD
www.berghahnbooks.com

First published in 2021 by
Berghahn Books
www.berghahnbooks.com

© 2021, 2024 Laura Ferrero, Chiara Quagliariello and
Ana Cristina Vargas
First paperback edition published 2024

All rights reserved. Except for the quotation of short passages for the purposes of criticism and review, no part of this book may be reproduced in any form or by any means, electronic or mechanical, including photocopying, recording, or any information storage and retrieval system now known or to be invented, without written permission of the publisher.

Library of Congress Cataloging-in-Publication Data

Names: Ferrero, Laura, editor. | Quagliariello, Chiara, editor. | Vargas, Ana Cristina, editor.
Title: Embodying borders : a migrant's right to health, universal rights and local policies / edited by Laura Ferrero, Chiara Quagliariello and Ana Cristina Vargas.
Description: New York : Berghahn, 2021. | Series: EASA series ; 41 | Includes bibliographical references and index.
Identifiers: LCCN 2020041639 (print) | LCCN 2020041640 (ebook) | ISBN 9781789209259 (hardback) | ISBN 9781789209266 (ebook)
Subjects: LCSH: Immigrants--Medical care. | Emigration and immigration--Health aspects. | Right to health. | Health services accessibility. | Medical policy.
Classification: LCC RA408.M5 E53 2021 (print) | LCC RA408.M5 (ebook) | DDC 362.1086/912--dc23
LC record available at https://lccn.loc.gov/2020041639
LC ebook record available at https://lccn.loc.gov/2020041640

British Library Cataloguing in Publication Data

A catalogue record for this book is available from the British Library

ISBN 978-1-78920-925-9 hardback
ISBN 978-1-80539-331-3 paperback
ISBN 978-1-80539-442-6 epub
ISBN 978-1-78920-926-6 web pdf

https://doi.org/10.3167/9781789209259

Contents

Introduction
    Laura Ferrero, Chiara Quagliariello and Ana Cristina Vargas   1

PART I. Borders and Inequalities

Chapter 1. Framing Deservingness in Health Care: Media Constructions of Unauthorized Youth in the United States
    Anahí Viladrich   35

Chapter 2. Constructing the Undeserving Citizen: The Embodied Consequences of Immigration Enforcement in the US South
    Nolan Kline   60

Chapter 3. Structural Violence, Tuberculosis and Health-Care Processes: Bolivian Immigrants in Buenos Aires and São Paulo
    Alejandro Goldberg, Cássio Silveira, Tatiane Barbosa and Denise Martin   80

Chapter 4. Women, Migration and Health: An Inquiry into Gender-Based Violence and the Limits of Maternity Care Services in Southern Europe's Borderlands
    Chiara Quagliariello   102

PART II. From the Individual to the Community

Chapter 5. Roma and the Right to Health: A Transnational Approach to Structural Vulnerability
    Pietro Cingolani   127

Chapter 6. Mental Health as Politics: Exploring Mental Health
  Services among Syrian Refugees in Lebanon
  Hala Kerbage and Filippo Marranconi   152

Chapter 7. Intercultural Mediation in the Italian Health-Care
  System
  Ana Cristina Vargas   182

Chapter 8. 'Community Welfare': Community-Based
  Networks as Migrant Health Promoters
  Laura Ferrero   209

Afterword. Forced Migration, State Violence and the
  Right to Health
  Daniela DeBono   235

Index   249

Introduction

Laura Ferrero, Chiara Quagliariello and Ana Cristina Vargas

Medical Anthropology, Human Rights and Migration

On 10 June 2018, Matteo Salvini, minister of the interior of Italy and political leader of the Lega Nord, announced the refusal to allow the ship *Aquarius*, of the non-governmental organization (NGO) SOS Méditerranée to berth in any Italian port, as she was carrying 629 refugees who had been rescued from the waters of the Mediterranean. The minister's decision was accompanied by numerous tweets that had the tone of a declaration of war: 'As of today even Italy will begin to say NO to the trafficking of human beings, NO to the business of illegal immigration'. After days of political clashes, uncertainties and tensions, Spain declared itself willing to welcome the refugees and *Aquarius* sailed to the port of Valencia. Salvini, still on Twitter, gloated, writing: 'VICTORY! 629 immigrants on board the Aquarius ship in the direction of #Spain, first goal achieved! #chiudiamoiporti'.

Salvini's words are an eloquent example of the climate that has developed in recent years around the theme of immigration and the political manipulation of the so-called 'migration crisis'. Migration phenomena are certainly not new to European countries; however, between 2012 and 2016, crossings to Europe by sea steadily increased, and in 2014–2015 there was also a significant increase in arrivals by land. This trend, which began to reverse in 2017, has been described and managed as an emergency. In many contexts, the so-called 'migration crisis' has been accompanied by the rise of nationalist political movements, openly hostile to immigration, which do not hesitate to adopt xenophobic or, in the most serious cases, explicitly racist language.

The increase in migratory flows has overlapped in part with an economic recession and a widespread lack of confidence in the future of the European Union. As Holmes and Castañeda write, 'how displaced people are framed reveals a great deal about anxieties in Europe regarding diversity and change within a paradigm of limited good ... informed by debt, austerity, and neoliberal disassembling of social systems' (Holmes and Castañeda 2016: 13). From the point of view of migration policies, the European Union has responded with increasingly restrictive regulations and with targeted strategies that create differentiated, and often discriminating, access conditions for migrants (Altin and Sanò 2017). In the last ten years the legal channels of arrival have been severely limited, and the favoured policies have been those that contain arrivals and strengthen security, with interventions aimed at the integration and protection of migrants.

A similar situation is observed in the United States. After an electoral campaign dominated by rhetoric strongly opposed to immigration, President Donald Trump adopted a policy of 'zero tolerance' towards migrants, which has led to a significant number of people, mainly from Mexico and other parts of Latin America, being detained and remanded for criminal trial. Trump's 'hard-line' approach has had a serious impact on minors, such that in the months of May, June and July 2018, the entire world saw the dramatic images of thousands of children, some less than a year old, being forcibly separated from their parents and detained, first in facilities unsuitable for their initial reception (the Customs and Border Protection facilities), and then in Immigrant Children's Shelters, places where they are accommodated for longer periods, without any certainty about their future or even about the possibility of reuniting with their families.

The situation is critical in other countries as well, and it is not surprising that many anthropologists – among other observers – have described these as 'dark times' (Sorgoni 2011; Fassin 2011; Pinelli 2013; Ben-Yehoyada 2015; De Genova 2017).

The images we have chosen to evoke in this Introduction are representative of the historical-political context in which the life experience of migrants unfolds and where the reflections contained in this volume are developed. In the following pages we will return in more detail to current migration scenarios; for the moment, it seems important to emphasize that, in our opinion, the choice to address the issue of the health of migrants from a perspective of interdisciplinary dialogue between medical anthropology and human rights, in addition to being effective on a conceptual level, also represents a political stance. We believe, as Willen, Mulligan and Castañeda (2011) have stated, that medical anthropology should play an active role in public debate on the issue of migrants' right to health, and has a responsibility towards the construction of more inclusive health systems. More than twenty years have passed since Merrill Singer (1995) called for a deeply committed and participatory position on the processes of social change; and more than a decade since Mark Nichter, then president of the American Society of Medical Anthropology (SMA), invited anthropologists to 'take a stand' in the field of public health protection policies (see Inhorn 2007). The words of these authors are more central than ever for our discipline.

Given the historical complexity of the relationship between anthropology and human rights, we must offer some brief preliminary reflections. Although today there is a fruitful dialogue between these two disciplinary fields, until relatively recently the relationship between human rights and anthropology has been ambivalent and critical. In 1947, a year before the publication of the Universal Declaration of Human Rights, the Statement on Human Rights was published, signed by the Executive Board of the American Anthropological Association (AAA). The document was drafted by Melville Herskovits,[1] and moved from serious criticism to the assumption of universality that was at the core of the declaration: elevating a system of principles and values that are the fruit of a specific culture to the rank of universal truth risked establishing the hegemonic superiority of this system with respect to others, thus creating 'a legal smokescreen for the oppression of one group of human beings by another' (AAA 1947: 542). Furthermore, colonialism and the many forms of oppression, including racial discrimination, which existed within the signatory states, were far from the ideals the declaration wanted to promote. 'There cannot be individual liberty,' Herskovits declared accordingly, 'if the social group with which the individual identifies is not free' (ibid.: 543).

Herskovits's concerns were not in fact unfounded. In more recent years, authors such as Ahmed An-Na'im (1992) and Talal Asad (1997) have highlighted the ethnocentrism of some of the most important concepts on which the declaration is based, and Lila Abu-Lughod (2013), following the war in Afghanistan, denounced the political use of references to democracy and human rights (especially those of women) to justify the American intervention.

Meanwhile, new generations of rights have been added to the first:[2] humanitarian law has been progressively imposed as a social language with broad international recognition and has been increasingly used by native populations and minorities as a tool for political action. In field research, anthropologists encounter language and practices that focus on human rights, and it has become necessary to reconcile a critical approach to the hegemonic implications of this juridical-value system with awareness of the social (and important) role that it plays in each of the analysed contexts. Attention has therefore focused on the 'practice of human rights' (Engle Merry and Goodale 2007), which calls for the researcher to contend with complex, transnational processes, in which reality and rhetoric are inseparably intertwined.

In the field of migrants' health, the language of human rights is one of the most important tools for the protection of the individuals involved (health workers, policymakers, associations, NGOs, patients, activists and others). Health is in fact recognized as a fundamental right in international documents and agreements: from a legal point of view, this implies a positive obligation for the states that have signed the commitments in question, which have a duty to guarantee adequate access to medical care, even to irregular migrants or those living in poverty.

Furthermore, the right to health is conceptualized as an inclusive right; health protection should therefore include both access to adequate medical care and attention to the social determinants of health, or, in other words, all factors of a social, economic, environmental, cultural and political nature that affect the health and wellbeing of the individual. From this perspective, medical anthropology and human rights can help researchers to understand and respond to issues of health, illness and treatment, taking into account 'the interaction between the macrolevel of political economy, the national level of political and class structure, the institutional level of the healthcare system, the community level of popular and folk beliefs and actions, the microlevel of illness experience, behavior, and meaning, human physiology, and environmental factors' (Singer 1995: 81).

We believe that this attention to local contexts and the way in which body, health and illness intertwine in the life experience of migrants and their life stories, is the most interesting contribution that medical anthropology can offer to the interaction, with a perspective based on transversal and universalist principles such as human rights.

Migration and Health

Migration phenomena, as explained in the opening of the recent World Migration Report 2018 by the International Organization for Migration (IOM), include 'a wide variety of movements and situations involving people of all walks of life and backgrounds' (IOM 2017a: 2). Defining migrants, then, is not simple: this expression, in fact, groups together people with different legal statuses and migratory histories; with variable levels of social capital for coping with the adversities of emigration; and with different cultural backgrounds, beliefs and worldviews. One of the cross-cutting elements is the distinction between regular migrants and irregular migrants, two categories often sharply demarcated: on the one hand the 'good', who 'deserve' access to public assistance; on the other, the 'illegal', who do not contribute to the growth of the nation and therefore do not 'deserve' to be recipients of the resources of the community. Although most people tend to move within the borders of their own nation, there are currently around 244 million people globally who have left their country of origin to look elsewhere for a new life.[3] This is about 3.3 per cent of the world's population, a figure that has increased significantly in recent years as a result of the increase in global economic inequalities, the growing economic and political interconnectedness of the world system, and the still widespread phenomena of violence, conflict and war. While in some cases migration can represent an opportunity for personal growth and can be a constructive experience, in many other cases it is the result of the need to escape intolerable living conditions or situations that endanger survival itself.

On many occasions, the migratory journey is itself a trauma. In dealing with dangerous routes often controlled by organized crime, migrants – especially if irregular – are subject to numerous forms of violence, discrimination and exploitation (Freedman 2016).[4] Things do not always improve upon arrival: even in host countries, human rights violations are the order of the day. Reception systems are often lacking, or are unable to cope with complex needs that are simultaneously social, psychological and health-related.

The path of assimilation is also fraught with difficulty. The migratory experience is often associated with poverty, unfavourable housing conditions, poor social recognition, exploitation and dependency. Some of the elements that can characterize a foreigner's everyday life are: linguistic challenges; the difficult task of inserting oneself into a new and often hostile situation; the loss of the relational and affective networks of the country of origin; the need to cope with a different culture; and being permanently placed in a hybrid, uncertain and marginal position. Added to this is the existential fatigue of migration, which has to do with a complex reorganization of the horizons of meaning, which is expressed in what Abdelmalek Sayad called the 'double absence of the migrant' (Sayad 1999).

One of the factors influencing the living and welfare conditions of migrants is their legal status. While maintaining some features of homogeneity, the legal categories associated with migratory phenomena vary significantly from one country to another and are closely linked to factors of a political, historical, economic and geographical nature. This volume clearly demonstrates the heterogeneity of local immigration regulations, as well as the strong contradiction between the universal (and universalistic) character that fundamental rights should have, and restrictive laws that drastically reduce the possibility of regularization of newcomers and, consequently, their ability to access adequate health protection.

At the same time, the volume shows to what extent the distinction between regular and irregular migrants is much less clear than it appears. As underscored by the International Organization for Migration itself,

> a person's immigration status can be fluid and change quickly, arising from circumstances and legal-policy settings. For example, many international migrants who may be described as 'undocumented' or 'irregular' enter countries on valid visas and then stay in contravention of one or more visa conditions. In fact, there are many paths to irregularity, such as crossing borders without authorization, unlawfully overstaying a visa period, working in contravention of visa conditions, being born into irregularity, or remaining after a negative decision on an asylum application has been made. (IOM 2017b: 20)

However, as Anahi Viladrich and Nolan Kline explain in detail in this volume, this distinction is often used in public discourse to legitimize inequalities in access to the health system.

Finally, a particularly important reflection is on refugees and asylum seekers. This theme, dealt with in this volume in the chapters by Chiara Quagliariello and by Hala Kerbage and Filippo Marranconi, is vast and has been the subject of numerous reflections in the field of anthropology, of which we cannot offer an adequate overview here.[5] It is worth remembering, however, that one of the issues that has characterized the debate in recent years is the difficulty in making a clear distinction between asylum seekers and economic migrants. This difference, inevitable on the legal level, does not reflect the emic perspective. As Barbara Sorgoni writes,

> for individual migrants it may be impossible, or even meaningless, to distinguish and separate economic and political aspects from the motives behind their movements, or measure the degree of voluntariness of their choice to travel or flee, within the complex migratory trajectories often driven by several factors. (Sorgoni 2011: 15)

The juxtaposition between those who are 'entitled' to international protection and economic migrants, represented as 'less' worthy, has been used in public discourse not only with regard to the right to asylum, but also to legitimize/delegitimize access to welfare and health systems, disregarding the universal character of the right to health.

Borders and Boundaries

In recent years, the desire to build walls, gates and military zones that mark the separation between nation states has become one of the main political concerns in many countries worldwide. These trends clash with the idea of a 'global village', introduced in 1968 by Marshall McLuhan (MacLuhan and Fiore 1968). Although the wide circulation of objects, commodities, raw materials and information highlights the reduction of geographical distances between one part of the world and another (Appadurai 1996; Amselle 2000), the interconnected dimension of the global space does not affect the movement of human beings in the same way. The latter is more and more often allowed or denied according to national, economic, cultural and racial criteria. As pointed out by the anthropologist Didier Fassin (2011), the deployment of increasingly sophisticated military devices to stem global migratory flows highlights a 'return' to the idea of a nation state in which the presence of the foreigner is understood as a threat to the local population (Shryock 2012).

In the current context, the critique advanced by so-called border studies (Donnan and Wilson 1999, 2016) regarding the introduction of increasingly visible borders appears particularly pertinent. Authors such as Nicholas De Genova (2017) highlight how the 'rhetoric of invasion' supported by the nationalist parties in many countries of the so-called Global North has no correlation with global migratory flows. Consistent with these theories, the case studies collected in this volume show the extent to which migrations from the southern to the northern hemisphere represent only a part of global migratory movements. At the same time, authors such as Goldberg, Silveira, Barbosa and Martin in this volume emphasize how the functioning of neoliberal national economies rests in large part on the contribution of a labour force composed of migrants. Finally, the selection criteria and the limitations imposed for border crossings clash with the principles defended by the convention for the protection of human rights, such as the idea that all human beings are entitled to freedom of movement. On the contrary, as shown in the chapters by Viladrich, Kline and Quagliariello, the 'invention' of different categories of human being, each with different degrees of right to move from one country to another, has become increasingly evident in recent years.

The variability of the concept of border is a theme that encompasses the anthropological studies and reflections proposed in this volume. The border as a line of separation between adjacent territories or states is a category that is only applicable to some forms of border control (Cuttitta 2015). An example is the border between Mexico and the United States, previously evoked, where any attempted entry into the North American territory by migrants is enforced by physical rejection (Heyman 2016). In other cases, the border corresponds to a more complex and structured control system. The so-called Schengen area in Europe, where there is a 'double movement' of borders, concurrently facing inwards and outwards, is emblematic in this regard. On the one hand, there is collaboration between Euro currency members that, for a number of years, have decided to use a single currency and to abolish national borders to facilitate international mobility and economic exchanges. On the other hand, EU states members share the policy of 'blocking borders' to non-Schengen citizens, such as international migrants and asylum seekers. In particular, the Dublin III agreement signed in 2013 following the Libyan crisis of 2011 has produced a spatial separation between territories trying to function as a *unicum*, leading to a new juxtaposition between countries in southern Europe, which are directly involved in the phenomenon of migrations by sea, and countries that are geographically more distant from the Mediterranean. At the same time, the process of externalizing the borders through the restrictions on visas required for entry into Europe by people coming from other parts of the world has extended the borders of the old continent beyond the territories belonging to this geographical area (Menjívar 2014; Casas-Cortes, Cobarubbias and Pickles 2015; De Genova 2017). The control policies exercised 'at a distance' in the migrants' countries of origin, such as those of the sub-Saharan Africa area, underscore the extent to which the border is a 'mobile apparatus', and not something connected to a 'fixed' territory. This apparatus not only moves within areas and territories that are geographically ascribed – such as the European Union area – but can also assume a deterritorialized dimension, depending on the geopolitical interests of certain countries with respect to others. This is how the border apparatus can cover a larger space than that suggested by national boundaries, even involving two or more continents. The agreements established by the European Union with some sub-Saharan African countries and North Africa for the 'limitation' of migratory movements towards the Mediterranean are an example of the transfer of European borders to the African continent. The same goes for the agreements drawn up in 2016 between the European Union and Turkey, the purpose of which was to limit the arrivals of Syrian refugees fleeing to Europe through the territories of Greece (Christopoulos 2017).

If a border can therefore correspond to a space that extends beyond a national border, the chapters presented in this volume underscore the presence of numerous physical, social and symbolic limits – all of which have been summarized by several anthropologists in the category of *boundaries* (Fassin 2011; Bramilla et al. 2015) within national borders. The increasing number of migrants and political refugees arriving in the countries of southern Europe and in some areas of the Middle East, such as Lebanon, have led to the introduction of spaces set aside for these groups. The fact that migrants and asylum seekers are considered to be 'passing through' the national territories is reflected in the fact that these people have to live, sometimes for years, in tents, sheds, containers and buildings that are temporary, and some can even be dismantled and transported from one place to another. Likewise, the transformation of geographically isolated locations, such as the island of Lesbos in Greece or the island of Lampedusa in Italy, into legal-bureaucratic 'waiting areas' is representative of the desire to make migrant populations 'invisible' and keep them as much as possible 'at a distance' from the local inhabitants. Consistent with this type of approach, most refugee camps and migrant reception centres in Europe and the Middle East, are located on the outskirts of urban areas or in extra-urban areas that are poorly connected to public transport. As pointed out by the anthropologist Barbara Pinelli (2017), the decision to make newcomers reside in isolated places that are physically separated from those dedicated to local populations reinforces the separation between migrant and non-migrant people, often creating an irreducible distance between these two populations. The prohibition for the local population to enter the refugee camps, and the low investment in integrating migrant people into the local communities, feeds divisions between the 'native' and 'alien' populations who sometimes reside side by side, but who are forced to lead completely parallel lives. As highlighted in this volume, the condition of physical isolation and social marginality experienced by migrants and asylum seekers reflects a more widespread situation, which also involves other foreigners and minority groups. The physical separation from the local population represents, for example, a 'structural condition of life' for the Roma living in the camps located on the outskirts of the cities of Europe. The same situation of isolation is found, on the other side of the Atlantic, among Bolivian migrants living and working in the capitals of other South American countries, where life for them takes place inside industrial warehouses for the production of clothing items that will be exported abroad. A final example is the living conditions of Latin American migrants in the city of Atlanta, Georgia, where the presence of checkpoints for the inspection of documents limits migrants' movement within the urban space.

Embodying Borders, Migrant Bodies

Migratory experiences, and migration laws and policies have an impact on the bodies of immigrants. The social, political and cultural dimensions of the human body are one of the 'classical' themes of medical anthropology. Authors such as Nancy Scheper-Hughes and Margaret Lock (1987), Thomas J. Csordas (1990) and Mariella Pandolfi (1993) describe the human body as the main physical support of the person, but also as a material support upon which the collective and individual experiences are registered. The category of 'incorporation', introduced in 1990 by Csordas in accordance with the tradition of phenomenological studies, sums up the centrality of the body in the process of identity building, but also in the 'stratification' of successive events in the biography of each human being. The uses of the body change, furthermore, from one cultural context to another (Godelier and Panoff 1998). Critical medical anthropology emphasizes the link between cultural representations of the human body and the experiences of health and illness (Kleinman 1980, 1981; Good and Del Vecchio Good 1980; Augé and Herzlich 1984). From a bio-political point of view, the body is the main arena of control over human life for the institutions that regulate the functioning of societies (Foucault 1976), including legal and medical institutions (Fassin and Memmi 2004).

The thesis supported in this book is that it is possible to talk about the inscription of boundaries onto the body, or the incorporation of borders, on several levels. A first level is the onset of diseases, and other forms of illness, related to the strengthening of borders and the processes of externalization of the borders described above. As highlighted by various international agencies (Amnesty International 2016; IOM 2017b), the difficult travel conditions and physical deprivation experienced along migratory routes have an impact on the health of those who choose to leave. Lack of hygiene, malnutrition and severe dehydration are some of the conditions experienced by migrants during the Mediterranean crossing and their stay in countries such as Libya, where respect for the right to health, and to human rights more generally, is not guaranteed.

The incorporation of borders also takes other forms in the migratory experiences. Migrants' bodies can be defined as physical supports that carry the weight of borders upon themselves. These are bodies that, starting from a tangible otherness – for example, in terms of skin colour – make the borders visible. As was also revealed during the period of Western colonialism (Fanon 1952), encountering bodies with physical characteristics different from those of the local population often leads to the idea that migrants are dangerous entities and possible bearers of epidemics. The need to keep society's immunization high translates into a systematic implementation of health checks at the border (Redfield 2005). As was the case in the past for sea voyages by European migrants to the countries of North America and Latin America, health professionals are among the first representatives of the receiving state that migrants and asylum seekers meet today in Mediterranean harbours. The use of gloves and masks during medical checks at the border also reflects the consideration of migrant bodies as a possible threat to public health and national security. The need for the state to make sure that the bodies entering the national territory are healthy and 'non-contaminating' underscores the extent to which the assessment of the 'quality' of individual migrants takes place primarily on the physical level. The policies aimed at the immunization of society also emerge in health checks carried out in the United States on South American citizens, or in the disease-prevention campaigns carried out in Europe against Roma populations. As highlighted in this volume, the association between the presence of foreigners from disadvantaged socio-economic backgrounds and the possible spread of diseases is a discriminatory phenomenon that has a national and international scope.

Another given highlighted in this volume is that, in some cases, individuals endowed with healthy bodies at the time of the migratory project became people with sick bodies during their stay abroad. The harsh working conditions faced by migrants, especially if they do not have a residence permit, can be at the root of diseases (Marmot 2005; Marmot and Wilkinson 2006; Fassin 2009; Aiach 2010). The same applies to housing conditions, which often scarcely guarantee respect for the right to health. The high tuberculosis rates among Bolivian migrants living and working in industrial warehouses located in the capitals of other Latin American countries is an example. Others are the high presence of allergies and respiratory diseases among Roma populations, and the numerous symptoms of illness among newly arrived migrants and asylum seekers residing in shelters and refugee camps in Europe and the Middle East. As Kerbage and Marranconi highlight in their chapter on the case of Syrian refugees in Lebanon, the response provided by the state to the pathologies manifested by this population – such as eating disorders, frequent headaches, insomnia, forms of anxiety and depression – is an exclusively biomedical interpretation of these symptoms. Consistent with the theories proposed by the anthropologist Liisa Malkki (1995), this volume shows that the systematic tendency towards medicalization and psychiatrization of forms of suffering connected to traumatic experiences represents a form of depoliticization of the symptoms presented by migrants and asylum seekers. Reduction of different types of illness expressed through body language to a simple medical or psychiatric problem means not taking into consideration the subjective experiences or the difficult living conditions experienced by migrants in reception centres or refugee camps where daily life is often reduced to 'mere biological life' (Agamben 1998), and people are 'bodies to be kept alive' by guaranteeing basic needs, such as eating and sleeping.

Vulnerability and Structural Violence

In the contexts analysed throughout the various chapters, indirect, invisible and institutionalized violence, which takes forms such as racism, discrimination, stigmatization, economic exploitation and poverty, can be observed across the board. Health inequalities are, in many ways, 'a mirror of inequalities in material conditions and in social and political structures within a society' (WHO 2013). The cases analysed in this volume by Goldberg, Silveira, Barbosa and Martin, and by Cingolani, highlight the pervasive nature of the connection between 'structural violence' (Farmer 1996, 2005), social marginality and health, which is expressed in the diseases of poverty, but also, more indirectly, in the incorporated forms of suffering and discomfort.

Economic inequalities, discrimination and marginalization produce 'bodies on the margins': 'other' bodies, in which the health consequences of the absence of real social inclusion clearly manifest themselves. This marginalization is reinforced by negative social images of migrants, which strongly influence self-perception. An inconvenient figure, the alien can be represented as an invader, as a potential terrorist or dangerous criminal, as someone who puts the nation's identity and values at risk, as an undesired and illegitimate competitor who takes resources away from the natives in times of difficulty. These negative images act as a mirror for the individuals, and lead to a complex imbalance in the sense of self: how one is perceived by others deeply impacts how one represents oneself and, consequently, influences individual agency.

The multiple asymmetries that characterize the relationship between the migrant and the host society place the foreigner in a position of 'structural vulnerability' (Quesada, Hart and Bourgois 2011). This concept was proposed by James Quesada, Laurie Hart and Philippe Bourgois with the aim of bringing attention to, in addition to the political and economic aspects that characterize the analysis of structural violence, the cultural and subjective dynamics that can be a source of suffering. The structural vulnerability category, therefore, has as its focal point the intersection between medical pathology, autobiographical experience and social suffering. This category, which we hope will become an instrument that is concretely applicable in the clinic, allows us to approach the health of migrants and other socially marginalized groups, not as the result of purely biological processes, but starting from the intersection of historical-cultural processes and life stories. The concepts of 'structural violence' and 'structural vulnerability' are therefore both essential in order to capture the multiple ways in which social forces shape the body, health and well-being of migrants.

Access to Healthcare

Some of the effects related to the primacy of the biomedical approach to migrants and asylum seekers' health include little consideration of the phenomena of violence and structural vulnerability described above, and the reduction of these people to organisms to be cared for through the 'classic' patterns of medicine and/or psychiatry (Kleinman 1987). A hierarchy of health needs implemented by medical staff itself sustains these tendencies in many cases. Contrary to the logic behind humanitarian and human rights, according to providers the bodies of (im)migrants do not all have the same value, and the needs registered in these bodies are not all considered equivalent. In this regard, one of the theses defended in this book is that the hierarchization of migrants' bodies and health needs is a phenomenon linked to the greater or lesser importance of clinical situations, but also to numerous other factors such as their gender identity, nationality, 'race', and even age. It is also on the basis of these elements that some migrants are considered more deserving than others of receiving medical assistance. As suggested by the theories of intersectionality (Crenshaw 1991), the interweaving of positive or negative forms of discrimination, linked to gender, race, class and generation is a particularly useful reading tool for reflecting on the inequalities within the fundamental right to health. An example is given by the importance attached internationally to the protection of maternal and child health. If, within migratory flows, female bodies are considered less dangerous and more vulnerable than male bodies, the case of pregnant migrants and asylum seekers is particularly exemplary from this point of view (Grotti et al. 2017, 2018). The latter, in fact, appear to be particularly deserving of medical assistance because of their physical condition. A second example is young migrants and asylum seekers, who are likewise considered to be more vulnerable than adult (especially male) migrants and thus more deserving of medical treatment. As highlighted by Viladrich in the case of the United States, from a cost–benefit perspective, assistance provided to young migrants is often considered a form of investment in the future of the nation.

Another element that characterizes medical assistance provided to migrants and asylum seekers is an emergency-based approach to the right to health. This type of approach usually ensures that essential care and assistance are guaranteed in situations where human lives are in danger. Access to long-term care and specialized treatments – for example, when confronting chronic diseases – is more complex and nuanced. As highlighted in this volume, the opposition between *universalized* access to primary care and *selective* access to secondary care depends on the (more or less inclusive) functioning of national health systems, but also on the classification of health problems according to urgency. The situation described in Quagliariello's chapter on Lampedusa, where the immediate assistance provided to recently pregnant migrants who have miscarried is contrasted with the long waits experienced by migrants who request a voluntary interruption of pregnancy, highlights the extent to which what qualifies as a 'health emergency' depends on the point of view of the professionals rather than on the clinical needs of the patients.

As mentioned earlier, legal status is another factor that determines access to health care or, conversely, contributes to migrants' decisions to reject medical treatments. This dichotomy is particularly evident in the case of the United States, where the difficulties for foreign patients to enter the insurance system severely limits their access to medical treatment. As other case studies proposed in this volume show, having a regular residence permit or a temporary residence permit, however, does not automatically guarantee the right to care. At the same time, with regard to assistance to (im)migrants, asylum seekers and other foreigners, the need to respond to complex needs, which go beyond simple access to health services, clearly emerges. The lack of autonomy and/or the frequent mobility of foreign patients, which restricts the continuity of care, as well as the physical distance between the places of residence and places of care, are some of the fundamental problems that arise in case studies described in this volume. Furthermore, the economic cuts linked to austerity policies have reduced public investment in services for foreign populations over time (Knight and Stewart 2016). One of the situations that emerges in the contexts touched by the so-called 'migration crisis', such as the Middle East and South European countries, is the outsourcing of certain medical services to the humanitarian sector. The psychological support services NGOs offer in reception centres and refugee camps are an example of a model of integrated care in which the choice to delegate to health professionals working outside the hospital world fills the gaps of the public health system.

Another of the responses to the limits of health-care systems encountered abroad is migrants' search for care in their country of origin or in third countries. This choice may also be linked to the need to integrate different healing models, such as 'modern' and 'traditional' ones. As will be highlighted in this volume, the transnational dimension of models of care carried out by migrant people presents multiple forms. In accordance with other spheres of daily life, therapeutic paths chosen by some groups of migrants and foreign populations – such as Roma groups living in Europe – go beyond a system of localized care whose limits correspond to geographical boundaries. The literature on medical tourism and medical travels (Kangas 2010) especially focuses on the situations of populations who belong to economically developed areas of the world but who turn to countries with weaker economies for the purchase of drugs and access to medical treatments – for example, those related to reproductive health problems – that may not be authorized or so readily available in their countries of origin (Whittaker and Speier 2010). Migrants, asylum seekers and foreign minority groups' search for and construction of 'therapeutic connections' in different places of the world is a less studied topic. As argued in the book, this form of 'transnational therapeutic syncretism' – a concept that differs from the category of medical pluralism, which mainly concerns the provision of care (Benoist 1996; Baer 2011) – is an integral part of the right to care and the right to health.

Beyond the Individual Level

In this volume, health inequalities are dissected and analysed as both a product of precise historical and political conditions and as a result of discrimination that affects specific groups. In both cases, observation leads the anthropologists who discuss health and illness to divert attention from pure biomedical data and to consider social, economic and political issues that influence the health of individuals. This means contextually shifting attention from a single individual to the group that shares certain characteristics with him or her, whether they be cultural, values-based or social.

The second part of the volume strongly emphasizes that dealing with health and migration means not only dealing with migrants as individuals, but also as groups. This means thinking about groups as agents of health; it means reiterating that health capital is both individual and collective, and it ultimately means thinking about groups as social subjects.

Considering that groups have their own health capital and describing the structural conditions that lead them to lose this health capital inevitably leads to thinking about the meaning and the possibility of a community approach to treatment – that is, to treatment that takes into account both the collective dimensions of suffering and the social group as a resource for health.

A *community-based approach* to health and care contains both great risks and great potential. The chapter by Cingolani, analysing the case of the Roma minority in Italy, clearly shows how ad hoc interventions for specific migrant populations can reinforce stereotypes and increase social exclusion instead of enabling access to medical care and, in general, the exercise of their rights. The same chapter shows, starting from ethnographic examples, the risks that occur when health professionals think of the subjects as representatives of a social group, and consequently relate to them based on what they already know (or think they know) about their group of origin, thus depriving the patient of his or her subjectivity. The attitudes of the professionals identified by Cingolani are summarized as expulsive, re-educational, generalizing and culturalist. These approaches can also be found in the way in which the professionals described by Quagliariello relate to Nigerian women who are pregnant when they disembark at the island of Lampedusa and also in the way in which health providers perceive and relate to Syrian refugees, as described by Kerbage and Marranconi, who demonstrate either a widespread ignorance among professionals regarding the Syrian context or stereotyping towards patients. The authors note among the health-care providers a widespread representation of refugees as people who must be educated in relation to mental health, and as people who cannot independently evaluate their situations.

These cases highlight the presence of stereotypes and prejudices among health professionals. In order to understand the life contexts or the horizons of meaning within which people represent and recognize illness and psychological discomfort, much less attention is paid to the underlying representations of body, health and disease. The complexity of the meeting between health professionals and individuals from cultural contexts in which there are other visions of the body, health and illness opens up the question of the cultural competencies necessary to guarantee the right to treatment for foreign patients (Kleinman and Benson 2006). Misunderstandings related to the application of Western models to people who uphold other interpretative categories emphasize the need on the part of professionals to broaden their knowledge. As highlighted by Vargas in this volume, the integration of fundamental figures in hospital services, such as linguistic-cultural mediators, is a first step in this direction. At the same time, the analyses proposed by Vargas underline how the concept of 'cultural competence' of health-care providers has great potential, but also risks oversimplification, generalization and negation of individual agency. One of the dangers is the excessive use of the category of culture, or the reduction of any behaviour or choice by foreigners to reasons that have to do with the culture of origin. The need to take into consideration other elements that make up the individual identity of each foreign patient is described in this volume as a possible remedy for the numerous forms of discrimination and racialization, often summarized in the category of clinical racism for these patients (Bridges 2011).

Obviously the migrant doctor–patient relationship does not occur in a social vacuum, but in specific contexts characterized by open or closed climates. As Viladrich reminds us, the role of the media is fundamental in the construction of a collective discourse on migrants, and is often linked both to the circulation of stereotypes and to changes in terms of policies. Finally, it should be noted there is a risk that the widespread rhetoric, public speech and stereotypes of professionals will spread to patients and create a feeling of non-legitimacy about seeking health-care assistance. As Kline points out, the outcome of a stigmatizing discourse on migrants may be that the immigrants internalize sentiments of not belonging and of being undeserving of social services.

After briefly summarizing the risks associated with a collective approach to health and disease issues, we want to return to the aspects that make this approach necessary. From a reading of the contributions in this book it is clear that eliminating the collective aspect from an interpretation of the pathologies of migrants means depoliticizing suffering. In contrast, restoring centrality to the political aspect of pathologies and of psychological distress gives centrality to a suffering that is collective before being individual.

We therefore believe that a transition from the individual to the community with regard to health and illness is necessary both in order to recognize the political dimension of the disease, and to enhance the role that social networks can play for care and welfare in the broadest sense. To say that health capital is collective is to recognize the role of social networks in its maintenance and also to define the absence of social networks as a risk factor for health (Kawachi 1999).

The presence of social networks can be a factor for reducing health-related risk and can facilitate access to treatment and understanding – both linguistic and symbolic – in the relationship between doctor and patient.

Agency, Resistance and Transformation

As pointed out earlier, over several years in various contexts we have witnessed the withdrawal of the state from welfare services (Ferrera and Maino 2011) and the appearance of entities of a different nature that provide additional services. The health arena is certainly an interesting field of analysis for observing the interaction between the public and private sectors, as well as observing new forms of welfare. The coexistence of different actors involved in health care emerges from different contributions in this volume and pushes towards the adoption of a *systemic approach* – that is, an analysis that takes into account the different contexts where treatment takes place. Among the non-governmental bodies that deal with various types of health, the examples in the volume include both formal organizations, such as NGOs and international bodies, and informal entities, such as the associations that advocate the rights of migrants described by Kline, the groups of volunteer doctors mentioned by Cingolani and the migrant associations that are the focus of attention in the chapter by Ferrero. Especially in some urban environments, these entities integrate with the public sector (Biglino and Olmo 2014: 10) and are sometimes perceived by users as more welcoming and more dedicated to protecting the health of migrants.

Here we are particularly concerned with overturning the logic of assistance and looking at examples that see migrants not in the role of people who need help, but in the position of active subjects who become social actors capable of triggering change in the contexts in which they live. This possibility emerges above all when one swaps the logic of emergencies for one of rootedness, and then observes the possible consequences of the integration path. To do this it is necessary to expand the concept of migration – and consequently that of migrants – to phases following the arrival, and thereby return this temporal dimension to the process. The images of the landings and the rhetoric of reception that have dominated over the last few years have quashed any discussion of migration in the early stages after arrival, detracting attention from what happens next, to the processes of settlement and inclusion. Restoring the element of process to the reading of migration removes foreigners from the category of victims, and returns to their bodies the social and political dimension of which they had been deprived (Agamben 1998).

From the temporality of the migratory process comes the development of the ability to resist. In terms of health protection this means that migrants themselves can become resources, recovering both an individual and a collective agency. The chapter by Vargas on cultural mediators, and that by Ferrero on the associations of foreigners, clearly show how foreigners can play an active role in improving existing services and in supporting newly arrived compatriots who are less able to manoeuvre in the context of arrival on the path to approaching these services.

The role of mediators and associations, however, is not limited to this. Vargas defines the mediator as a resource for humanizing care, while Ferrero defines migrant associations as entities that can fill the gap between caring and curing. This shows, on the one hand, how the presence of social networks can be a factor for reducing health-related risks, and on the other, how having social networks can facilitate access to treatment and understanding – both linguistic and symbolic – in the relationship between doctor and patient. Migrants' associations can therefore represent a tool for increasing access to services but also for implementing the right to health when they establish themselves as people who possess a cultural capital that they make available to others – for example, to newly arrived compatriots or people who do not speak the language of the host country.

In Part I of the volume it is stressed that the right to health is not something universal, but an abstraction that takes shape in precise local contexts. The same applies to the resources activated by migrants. Vargas points out that, far from being a neutral process, mediation is a social process situated within an area of non-neutral sociopolitical forces. Likewise, Ferrero's chapter, describing the associations that the author has observed, contextualizes the results of her research in a specific urban milieu.

The presence of mediators in services and the role of foreign associations break the dichotomy between universal services and services dedicated only to foreigners, representing instruments in which a universalistic service can adapt to heterogeneous users and thus become more welcoming. In particular, networking reformulates the relationship between supply and demand, bringing it to a more equal level, and increases the social capital of immigrants (Tognetti Bordogna 2008). Above all, the relationship between migrants and welfare reveals the gap between holding and exercising rights that also occurs in inclusive systems. To be entitled to a right does not necessarily mean being able to enjoy it, and the existence of self-organized and community forms of protection can give back to the migrants part of that agency that has been undermined by the migratory process.

These reflections appear to be a useful tool to counteract the rhetoric describing migrants simply as individuals who burden the welfare systems of the host countries. To make some reflections that go beyond the emergency it is essential to divert attention from the moment of arrival and to turn to the possible integration paths that demonstrate how foreigners can play an active role in improving services aimed at the migrant populations and, therefore, ultimately be crucial actors on a path towards more inclusive and welcoming services. These resources, increasing the degree of health literacy of the communities, contribute to spreading a more conscious use of health services – a process that will benefit the entire population, and not just the migrants. In conclusion, it seems that viewing migrants as people who are able to speak for themselves and making changes to standardized care systems helps us to think about health literacy, not as a one-way process that involves passing information from doctors to users, but as a two-way exchange that includes both an increase in awareness and an increase in cultural competency.

Structure of the Book

This volume has as its starting point a multidisciplinary research project on migrants' right to health in Turin (Italy) with the Fundamental Rights Laboratory (LDF).[6] The chapters included in the volume are a selection of papers based on the findings of this research project, integrated with other contributions relevant to the topic.

The protagonists of this volume are people who fall within the category of 'migrant', but whose life paths are marked by experiences very different from each other: some have moved by choice for reasons of work or family reunification; others have moved by necessity as asylum seekers or refugees. In some cases these people are from historical minorities, like Latinos in the United States and the Roma in Italy, while others have taken part in more recent flows, as in the case of Syrians in Lebanon. Among the cases analysed in the volume we find some with regular residence permits, some with temporary visas and others who remain in a state in an illegal situation. Thus, one of the volume's primary tasks is to show, beginning with descriptions of the local contexts, the complexity of the 'migrant' category. Moreover, our contributions demonstrate how the theme of global health is intertwined with health systems and rules on accessing services that are rooted in national and local contexts. These settings are characterized by different legislation or a different social fabric that can either favour or hinder the entitlement to a right and the effective possibility of exercising this right. These local contexts are found in spaces that can geographically be very distant from each other. Pursuing the objective of enhancing the plurality of perspectives within the same discipline, the volume attempts to remedy an often Eurocentric view of the migratory phenomenon by including contributions on the United States, Latin America and the Middle East.

The concepts of 'migrant' and the 'right to health' are thus categories used by the authors, according to what they mean in the contexts qualitatively investigated in their chapters. Ethnographic methodology and in-depth observation are characteristic of each contribution, but it is interesting to note immediately the presence of different facets that show the richness and the heterogeneity of the research on health in the anthropological field. In the volume we find an ethnography of the media in the chapter by Viladrich; the figure of the activist researcher in Kline's contribution; a regional comparative perspective in the work of Goldberg, Silveira, Barbosa and Martin; an interdisciplinary angle in the chapter by Kerbage and Marranconi; and the multi-sited methodology of Cingolani. In our opinion this clearly indicates the number of ways available to achieve the 'thick description' (Geertz 1973) that is typical of the anthropological approach, and allows us to bring attention to the anthropologist as a field-maker, or as an individual who actively chooses the portion or portions of reality that he or she intends to study, reducing the initial indeterminacy of reality (Candea 2009: 27) and modulating the qualitative methodology according to that decision.

The volume is divided into two parts. The first is titled *Borders and Inequalities*, and focuses on the intersection between the concepts of frontier and structural vulnerability. Observing how migrants embody the 'border' – according to the meaning that the volume intends to give this term – means describing how people incorporate social and political inequalities that vary from context to context. However, similarities between the cases allow general conclusions to be drawn on the effects that vulnerability has on the health of people who often live in conditions of social, economic and housing marginality. In the first chapter, Anahi Viladrich describes the passage of DACA (Deferred Action for Childhood Arrivals) in 2012, which granted temporary protection status to unauthorized youth and barred them from inclusion in Obama's health-care reform. The chapter examines US mainstream media constructions of deservingness after the passage of the US Affordable Care Act. In the second chapter, Nolan Kline continues to reflect on the concepts of 'deservingness' and 'undeservingness'. Drawing from a year of ethnographic fieldwork in Atlanta, Georgia, the author shows how immigrant policing can result in some immigrants internalizing sentiments of being undeserving of social services and, ultimately, how policy efforts may be used to maintain social hierarchies based on categories such as race and immigration status. With the contribution of Alejandro Goldberg and colleagues, we move from an analysis of policies to that of working conditions. These anthropologists created a multifocal ethnography in Buenos Aires (Argentina) and São Paulo (Brazil) through which they compared the health status of Bolivian immigrants employed in the textile industry. In this case the tuberculosis many Bolivians suffer from is analysed as a side effect of precarious and dangerous working conditions, and becomes, in the last instance, an incorporation of structural violence that the authors describe in terms of neo-slavery. In the fourth chapter, Chiara Quagliariello focuses on a border that has often been at the centre of the news in recent years: reaching the Italian island of Lampedusa does not, in fact, mean just entering the island but entering Italy and Europe too, and that is why the context of this chapter can be widely described as the Southern Europe borderlands. She introduces gender, intersectionality and maternal and child health into the discussion, analysing gender-based violence against women during the migratory journey from the African continent to Europe. The difficulties women face in order to access 'voluntary termination of pregnancy' (VTP) and the impact of living conditions in the Italian reception system on their overall health lead the author to argue that the structural violence and discrimination that pregnant African women are subjected to continues after their arrival in Europe.

The second part of the book is entitled *From the Individual to the Community*, and aims to reflect on the issue of health from a collective perspective. The concept of structural violence, extensively described in the early part of the text, leads the discussion on health to conditions that are purely biological and, therefore, individual, and to the observation of the health status of individuals as a symptom of social, political and economic conditions. Given that these conditions are often shared by a certain category of people or a group, moving from the individual to the collective dimension, we emphasize the social and political dimension of many health problems. This concept is clearly expressed in the contributions by Pietro Cingolani and by Hala Kerbage and Filippo Marranconi.

Cingolani's chapter deals with the Roma, one of the groups with the worst health conditions and with whom medical professionals have strong relational difficulties. The concept of 'cultural difference' is often used to explain these difficulties, while the author places at the core of his analysis the social exclusion that this group has experienced over decades. In addition to illustrating the relationship between doctors and Roma patients, the author highlights how social exclusion can be reproduced and perpetuated along transnational paths, underscoring how transnational treatment paths can be the answer to an exclusion that is experienced as much in the context of departure as in that of arrival.

The sixth chapter, by Kerbage and Marranconi, focuses on the mental health of the Syrian population in Lebanon. The context of displacement in a post-war setting as well as the social adversity that refugees are exposed to have been associated with mental health problems, mainly depression, anxiety and post-traumatic stress disorder (PTSD). Beyond these diagnostic categories, qualitative studies in this context revealed that refugees may suffer from the loss of role and social networks, isolation, feelings of helplessness and hopelessness, loss of a sense of meaning and purpose, and an inability to imagine a future. Mental health services might pathologize ordinary human suffering in reaction to horrifying events and hinder important aspects like social history and political justice; on the other hand, restoring the collective aspect of suffering can re-politicize the mental health discourse of Syrian refugees in Lebanon.

The final two contributions continue the reflection on migrant communities by shifting attention from the conditions that generate marginality and health inequalities to resources that can be activated by migrants themselves in order to support access to and proper use of health services by other migrants. Ana Cristina Vargas describes intercultural mediation in the Italian context, one of the strategies promoted by the European Union. After an overview of the figure of the mediator, the author describes the contexts in which this figure participates in the social and health services setting. Mediation is usually represented as a neutral technique, whereas the author describes intercultural mediation as a social process within an area of non-neutral sociopolitical forces.

While Vargas highlights the limits and potential of the presence of mediators in the health sector, Laura Ferrero in the last chapter describes how migrant associations can sometimes informally play the role of mediators between services and compatriots living in situations of marginality. Through observations conducted at five associations of foreigners active in the city of Turin (Italy), the author shows how the obligations of these entities can be transformed into an element that facilitates both access to and the success of the medical encounter.

Laura Ferrero obtained her PhD in anthropology and has been a postdoctoral fellow at Turin University, where she teaches Anthropology of the Middle East; she is also research fellow at the Fundamental Rights Laboratory, Turin. She has conducted research in Italy, Egypt and Palestine. Her main research interests are: migration studies; migrants' access to health and housing; as well as gender and family in Arab-Muslim societies.

Chiara Quagliariello is currently working as Marie Skłodowska-Curie postdoctoral fellow at the Ecole des Hautes Etudes en Sciences Sociales in Paris and the City University of New York within the Global Individual Fellowship 'Racialization in Reproduction: Maternal Health Crisis among Black Women in Europe and the US.' She has had study and research experiences at the Fundamental Rights Laboratory in Turin, the European University Institute in Florence, University College London and the Max Planck Institute of Social Anthropology. She has a long experience in field research in Italy, France and Senegal. Her research interests include medical anthropology, particularly childbirth models; reproductive rights; social and health inequalities; gender, class and ethnicity; intercultural medicine; and medical challenges in migrant patients' health care.

Ana Cristina Vargas, PhD in anthropological sciences, is Adjunct Professor of Cultural Anthropology at the University of Turin. Since 2012 she has been the scientific director of the Ariodante Fabretti Foundation, and is also research fellow at the Fundamental Rights Laboratory, a research unit of the European Human Rights Research Network. Her main research and publication topics include Colombian armed conflict, intercultural communication, human rights, medical anthropology and fundamental rights.

Notes

This introduction is based on the three authors' shared work. Parts 1, 2 and 4 were written by Ana Cristina Vargas; parts 3, 5 and 6 by Chiara Quagliariello; and parts 7, 8 and 9 by Laura Ferrero.

1. The document was the result of a request from UNESCO to Herskovits for his opinion, as president of the Committee on International Cooperation in Anthropology of the US National Research Council. Once the document was drawn up, Herskovits submitted it to the AAA board, which elected to endorse it.
2. In addition to civil and political rights, also called 'first generation' rights, economic and social rights, or 'second generation' rights to which the individual is entitled, are particularly relevant in the field of the right to health. In more recent years a 'third generation' of rights has developed, which, unlike the first two, has a collective character, because the holders of these rights are not individuals but communities.
3. We will not dwell here on the phenomenon of displacement, but it is worth noting that the latest estimate by the UN has found a figure of 740 million migrants and internally displaced persons.
4. United Nations General Assembly, 'Report of the Special Rapporteur on the Human Rights of Migrants', Doc. A/69/302, 11 August 2014.
5. See *The Oxford Handbook of Refugee and Forced Migration Studies* (Fiddian-Qasmiyeh et al. 2014).
6. The Fundamental Rights Laboratory is a research centre that investigates social and health inequalities and other forms of social injustice associated with the implementation of human rights in the Italian and other European contexts. It is member of the Comitato per la promozione e protezione dei diritti umani and of the European Human Rights Research Network. The Fundamental Rights Laboratory is made up of legal scholars and social scientists who carry out research work together in an applied and interdisciplinary perspective.

References

Abu-Lughod, L. 2013. *Do Muslim Women Need Saving?* Cambridge: Harvard University Press.
Agamben, G. 1998. *Homo Sacer: Sovereign Power and Bare Life*. Stanford, CA: Stanford University Press.
Aiach, P. 2010. *Les inégalités sociales de santé*. Paris: Economica.
Altin, R., and G. Sanò. 2017. 'Richiedenti asilo e sapere antropologico. Una introduzione'. *Antropologia Pubblica* 3(1): 7–34.
American Anthropological Association (AAA). 1947. 'Statement on Human Rights'. *American Anthropologist* 49: 539–43.

Amnesty International. 2016. 'Refugees and Migrants Fleeing Sexual Violence, Abuse and Exploitation in Libya'. Retrieved 24 September 2018 from https://www.amnesty.org/en/latest/news/2016/07/refugees-and-migrants-fleeing-sexual-violence-abuse-and-exploitation-in-libya/.

Amselle, J.L. 2000. 'La globalisation: "Grand partage" ou mauvais cadrage?' *L'Homme* 156: 207– 26.

An-Na'im, A. 1992. 'Toward a Cross-Cultural Approach to Defining International Standards of Human Rights: The Meaning of Cruel, Inhuman or Degrading Treatment or Punishment', in A. An-Na'im (ed.), *Human Rights in Cross-Cultural Perspectives: A Quest for Consensus*. Philadelphia: University of Pennsylvania Press, pp. 19–43.

Appadurai, A. 1996. *Modernity at Large: Cultural Dimensions of Globalization*. Minneapolis: University of Minnesota Press.

Asad, T. 1997. 'On Torture, or Cruel, Inhumane, and Degrading Treatment', in A. Kleinman, V. Das and M. Lock (eds), *Social Suffering*. Berkeley: University of California Press, pp. 285–308.

Augé, M., and C. Herzlich. 1984. *Le sens du mal: Anthropologie, histoire, sociologie de la maladie*. Paris: l'Harmattan.

Baer, H.A. 2011. 'Medical Pluralism: An Evolving and Contested Concept in Medical Anthropology', in M. Singer and P.I. Erickson (eds), *A Companion to Medical Anthropology*. Hoboken, NJ: Wiley-Blackwell, pp. 405–23.

Benoist, J. 1996. *Soigner au pluriel: Essais sur le pluralisme médical*. Paris: Karthala.

Ben-Yehoyada, N. 2015. '"Follow Me, and I Will Make you Fishers of Men': The Moral and Political Scales of Migration in the Central Mediterranean'. *Journal of the Royal Anthropological Institute* 22(1): 183–202.

Biglino, I., and A. Olmo. 2014. *La salute come diritto fondamentale: una ricerca sui migranti a Torino*. Bologna: Il Mulino.

Brambilla, C., et al. 2015. *Borderscaping: Imaginations and Practices of Border Making*. Farnham, UK: Ashgate.

Bridges, K. 2011. *Reproducing Race: An Ethnography of Pregnancy as a Site of Racialization*. Berkeley: University of California Press.

Brown, C., et al. 2013. 'Governance for Health Equity: Taking Forward the Equity Values and Goals of Health 2020 in the WHO European Region'. World Health Organization, Regional Office for Europe.

Candea, M. 2009, 'Arbitrary Locations: In Defence of the Bounded Field-Site', in M.A. Falzon (ed.), *Multi-sited Ethnography Theory, Praxis and Locality in Contemporary Research*. Farnham, UK: Ashgate, pp. 25–46.

Casas-Cortes, M., S. Cobarubbias and J. Pickles. 2015. 'Riding Routes and Itinerant Borders: Autonomy of Migration and Border Externalization'. *Antipode* 47(4): 894–914.

Christopoulos, D. 2017. 'Human Rights in a State of Perpetual Emergency', *Open Democracy*, 5 January. Retrieved 24 September 2018 from https://

www.opendemocracy.net/can-europe-make-it/dimitris-christopoulos/human-rights-in-state-of-perpetual-emergency.

Crenshaw, K.W. 1991. 'Mapping the Margins: Intersectionality, Identity Politics, and Violence against Women of Color'. *Stanford Law Review* 43(4): 1241–99.

Csordas, T.J. 1990. 'Embodiment as a Paradigm for Anthropology'. *Ethos* 18(1): 5–47.

Cuttitta, P. 2015. 'Humanitarianism and Migration in the Mediterranean Borderscape: The Italian–North African Border between Sea Patrols and Integration Measures', in C. Brambilla et al. (eds), *Borderscaping: Imaginations and Practices of Border Making*. Farnham, UK: Ashgate, pp. 131–40.

De Genova, N. 2017. *The Borders of 'Europe': Autonomy of Migration, Tactics of Bordering*. Durham, NC: Duke University Press.

Donnan, H., and T.M. Wilson. 1999. *Borders: Frontiers of Identity, Nation and State*. London: Hardback Books.

———. 2016. *A Companion to Border Studies*. Hoboken, NJ: Wiley-Blackwell.

Engle Merry, S., and M. Goodale (eds). 2007. *The Practice of Human Rights: Tracking Law between the Global and the Local*. Cambridge: Cambridge University Press.

Fanon, F. 1952. *Peau noire, masques blancs*. Paris: Éditions de Seuil.

Farmer, P. 1996. 'On Suffering and Structural Violence: A View from Below'. *Daedalus* 125(1): 261–83.

———. 2005. *Pathologies of Power: Health, Human Rights, and the New War on the Poor*. Berkeley: University of California Press.

Fassin, D. 2009. *Inégalités et santé*. Paris: La documentation Française.

———. 2010. 'Inequality of Lives, Hierarchies of Humanity: Moral Commitments and Ethical Dilemmas of Humanitarianism', in I. Feldman and M. Ticktin (eds), *In the Name of Humanity: The Government of Threat and Care*. Durham, NC: Duke University Press: 238–55.

———. 2011. 'Policing Borders, Producing Boundaries: The Governmentality of Immigration in Dark Times'. *Annual Review of Anthropology* 40: 213–26.

Fassin, D., and D. Memmi. 2004. *Le gouvernement des corps*. Paris: Edition de l'EHESS.

Ferrera, M., and F. Maino. 2011. 'Il "secondo welfare" in Italia: sfide e prospettive'. *Italianieuropei* 3: 17–22.

Fiddian-Qasmiyeh, E., et al. 2014. *The Oxford Handbook of Refugee and Forced Migration Studies*. Oxford: Oxford University Press.

Foucault, M. 1976. *Histoire de la sexualité. Vol. I. La volonté de savoir*. Paris: Gallimard.

Freedman, J. 2016. 'Sexual and Gender-Based Violence against Refugee Women: A Hidden Aspect of the Refugee "Crisis"'. *Reproductive Health Matters* 24(47): 18–26.

Geertz, C. 1973. *The Interpretation of Cultures: Selected Essays*. New York: Basic Books.

Godelier, M., and M. Panoff. 1998. *La production du corps: Approches anthropologiques et historiques*. Amsterdam: Éditions des archives contemporaines.

Good, B., and M.J. Del Vecchio Good. 1980. 'The Meaning of Symptoms: A Cultural Hermeneutic Model for Clinical Practice', in L. Eisenberg and A. Kleinman (eds), *The Relevance of Social Science for Medicine*. Dordrecht: D. Reidel Publishing Company, pp. 165–96.

Grotti, V., et al. 2017. 'Pregnant Crossings: A Political Economy of Care on Europe's External Borders', in S. Shekhawat and D. Aurobinda (eds), *Women and Borders: Refugees, Migrants and Communities*. London: I.B. Tauris, pp. 63–85.

———. 2018. 'Shifting Vulnerabilities: Gender and Reproductive Care on the Migrant Trail to Europe'. *Comparative Migration Studies* 6(1): 23.

Heyman, J. McC. 2016. 'Discussion of Frontiers of Fear: Immigration and Insecurity in the United States and Europe'. *Journal of Ethnic and Migration Studies* 42(4): 693–96.

Holmes, S.M., and H. Castañeda. 2016. 'Representing the "European Refugee Crisis" in Germany and Beyond: Deservingness and Difference, Life and Death'. *American Ethnologist* 43(1): 12–24.

Inhorn, M. 2007. 'Medical Anthropology at the Intersections'. *Medical Anthropology Quarterly* 21(3): 249–55.

International Organization for Migration (IOM). 2017a. 'World Migration Report 2018'. Retrieved 24 September 2018 from https://publications.iom.int/system/files/pdf/wmr_2018_en.pdf.

———. 2017b. 'The Central Mediterranean Route: Migrant Fatalities'. Retrieved 24 September 2018 from https://missingmigrants.iom.int/central-mediterranean-route-migrant-fatalities-january-2014-july-2017.

Kangas, B. 2010. 'Traveling for Medical Care in a Global World'. *Medical Anthropology* 29(4): 344–62.

Kawachi, I. 1999. 'Social Capital and Community Effects in Population and Individual Health'. *Annals of the New York Academy of Sciences* 896: 120–30.

Kleinman, A. 1980. *Patients and Healers in the Context of Culture: An Exploration of the Borderland between Anthropology, Medicine and Psychiatry*. Berkeley: University of California Press.

———. 1981. 'The Meaning Context of Illness and Care: Reflections on a Central Theme in the Anthropology of Medicine', in E. Mendelsohn and Y. Elkana (eds), *Sciences and Cultures: Sociology of Sciences*, vol. 5 Dordrecht: D. Reidel Publishing Company, pp. 161–76.

———. 1987. 'Culture and Clinical Reality: Commentary on Culture-Bound Syndromes and International Disease Classifications'. *Culture, Medicine and Psychiatry* 11: 49–52.

Kleinman, A., and P. Benson. 2006. 'Anthropology in the Clinic: The Problem of Cultural Competency and How to Fix It'. *PLoS Med* 3(10): 294.

Kleinman, A., V. Das and M. Lock. 1997. *Social Suffering*. Berkeley: University of California Press.
Knight, D.M., and C. Stewart. 2016. 'Ethnographies of Austerity: Temporality, Crisis and Affect in Southern Europe'. *History and Anthropology* 27(1): 1–18.
MacLuhan, M., and Q. Fiore. 1968. *War and Peace in the Global Village*. New York: Bantam Books.
Malkki, L. 1995. 'Refugees and Exile: From "Refugee Studies" to the National Order of Things'. *Annual Review of Anthropology* 24: 495–523.
Marmot, M. 2005. 'Social Determinants of Health Inequalities'. *Lancet* 365(9464): 1099–1104.
Marmot, M., and R.G. Wilkinson. 2006. *Social Determinants of Health*. Oxford: Oxford University Press.
Menjívar, C. 2014. 'Immigration Law beyond Borders: Externalizing and Internalizing Border Controls in an Era of Securitization'. *Annual Review of Law and Social Science* 10: 353–69.
Pandolfi, M. 1993. 'Le self, le corps, la "crise de la présence"'. *Anthropologie et Société* 17(1–2): 57–77.
Pinelli, B. 2013. 'Migrare verso l'Italia: Violenza, discorsi, soggettività'. *Antropologia* 15: 7–20.
———. 2017. 'Borders, Politics and Subjects: Introductory Notes on Refugee Research in Europe'. *Etnografia e Ricerca Qualitativa* 1: 5–24.
Quesada, J., L.K. Hart and P. Bourgois. 2011. 'Structural Vulnerability and Health: Latino Migrant Laborers in the United States'. *Medical Anthropology* 30(4): 339–62.
Redfield, P. 2005. 'Doctors, Borders, and Life in Crisis'. *Cultural Anthropology* 20(3): 328–61.
Sayad, A. 1999. *La double absence: Des illusions de l'émigré aux souffrances de l'immigré*. Paris: Éditions du Seuil.
Scheper-Hughes, N., and M. Lock. 1987. 'The Mindful Body: A Prolegomenon to Future Work in Medical Anthropology'. *Medical Anthropology Quarterly* 1(1): 6–41.
Shryock, A. 2012. 'Breaking Hospitality Apart: Bad Hosts, Bad Guests, and the Problem of Sovereignty'. *Journal of the Royal Anthropological Institute* 18: S20–S33.
Singer, M. 1995. 'Beyond the Ivory Tower: Critical Praxis in Medical Anthropology'. *Medical Anthropology Quarterly – New Series* 9(1): 80–106.
Sorgoni, B. 2011. 'Pratiche ordinarie per presenze straordinarie: Accoglienza, controllo e soggettivita nei Centri per richiedenti asilo in Europa'. *Lares* 78(1): 15–22.
Tognetti Bordogna, M. 2008. *Disuguaglianze di salute e immigrazione*. Milan: Franco Angeli.

Whittaker, A., and A. Speier. 2010. '"Cycling Overseas": Care, Commodification and Stratification in Cross-Border Reproductive Travel'. *Medical Anthropology* 29(4): 363–83.

Willen, S.S., J. Mulligan and H. Castañeda. 2011. 'How Can Medical Anthropologists Contribute to Contemporary Conversations on "Illegal" Im/migration and Health?' *Medical Anthropological Quarterly* 25(3): 331–56.

World Health Organization (WHO). 2013. 'Governance for Health Equity: Taking Forward the Equity Values and Goals of Health 2020 in the WHO European Region'. Copenhagen: WHO Regional Office for Europe.

Part I
Borders and Inequalities

1

Framing Deservingness in Health Care

Media Constructions of Unauthorized Youth in the United States

Anahí Viladrich

Introduction: Framing Health-Care Reform

The US government's prerogative for health services to unauthorized immigrants has fuelled heated debates in recent years, with human rights frameworks embracing the notion of universal access to health care, and neoliberal positions arguing for individual responsibility and self-sustainability as the basis of deservingness. While the latter stance has traditionally been mainstream in the United States, the current presence of almost twelve million unauthorized immigrants has given rise to more controversy. Furthermore, even though federal law mandates that US hospitals treat anyone entering the emergency room, this principle does not translate into long-term free medical care for those in need (Kullgren 2003; Viladrich 2019).

Human rights approaches to health care, inspired by universal health paradigms and international law, argue that all human beings – regardless of their legal status – should have access not only to adequate and efficient medical services, but also to suitable living conditions conducive to optimal health outcomes (Willen et al. 2017). The current health and migration policies in the United States have traditionally been at odds with such principles, including the equal right to health that has been upheld by international organizations, including the UN Convention on the Rights of the Child (IOM 2013).

In the United States, the Patient Protection and Affordable Care Act (Health Reform or ACA) was signed into law in 2010, under President Obama's administration, with the explicit purpose of providing accessible and affordable health-care coverage to the formerly uninsured population. Rather than framing health care as 'a right', ACA mandated an expansion of the insured population on the basis of a market-driven model in which the uninsured would receive incentives to buy health insurance through health subsidies and low-rate health plans. Although its original intention was to inclusively transform the private insurance system by providing universal health care, ACA excluded all unauthorized immigrants – including undocumented youth – from being eligible for federally subsidized health insurance (Sanchez et al. 2011).[1] As a result, ACA left out some 11.5 million unauthorized foreign born, 76 per cent being Latino, mostly (59 per cent) from Mexico (ibid.).

At the time of ACA's passage, much of the debate in the US media revolved around the exclusion of unauthorized immigrants from public and federally subsidized health and social programmes (Viladrich 2019, 2012; Menjívar and Kanstroom 2013). As of today, little is known about the policy arguments – and related media images – that supported the foreign-born's inclusion into ACA. The provision of health benefits to specific groups among undocumented immigrants begs the question of how the media construct, and disseminate, positive messages on unauthorized immigrants aimed at enlisting public support and policy inclusion on their behalf. Despite the fact that unauthorized immigrants' exclusion from government-sponsored health insurance (and the concomitant denial of their right to health care) has been recognized as the most widespread consequence of Health Reform, more studies are needed to understand the media framing instruments deployed to support their entitlement to medical services.

As of today, most research has focused on the rhetorical ways through which immigrants have been negatively portrayed by the media literature (McConnell 2011; Brown 2013; Sohoni and Bickham Mendez 2014). This body of work has largely addressed the 'problem setting', or the process through which conflicting social issues are constructed by the press, as in the case of immigrants being portrayed as freeloaders or criminals (O'Brien 2003). Given the importance of the US media in shaping public opinion, learning about the arguments (and ideological underpinnings) utilized on behalf of the undocumented is key towards understanding the ultimate direction of immigrant and health policies (Chavez 2001).

A recently growing body of work has shown the coming of age of unauthorized youth activists who have empowered themselves by 'coming out' of the shadows while engaging in anti-deportation activism (Gonzales 2011; Holling and Calafell 2011; De la Torre and Germano 2014; Negrón-Gonzales 2014; Lukes 2015). In this vein, this paper examines media representations of the unauthorized youth, who have gained visibility in the United States in recent years while becoming the centre of controversies regarding the role of the government in granting them health rights (Gonzales, Terriquez and Ruszczyk 2014; Marrow and Joseph 2015).

The point of departure for this chapter weaves together two moments in US history: the passage of Health Reform in 2010 and the Deferred Action for Childhood Arrivals (DACA) in 2012. These policies offer an ideal lens through which to explore the direction of current media framing in shaping public opinion regarding immigrants' rights to health care. Rather than a language of human rights, journalistic accounts elicit positive stands towards particular groups of needy individuals – mostly the hard-working immigrant that is portrayed as a deserving one.

Based on a qualitative approach to media analysis – mostly newspaper articles published between 2010 and 2017 – this chapter analyses the framing of the unauthorized youth's inclusion into the US health safety net. The following questions are asked: What media frames have been deployed to advance the public agenda for the inclusion of young unauthorized immigrants into the government-sponsored health safety net? What are the main arguments shaping the agenda that supports these youths' deservingness of health insurance coverage? The chapter will discuss the following media frames drawn from the analysis. Firstly, the 'effortful immigrant' features young immigrants' industriousness and their blamelessness with respect to the conditions that led to their unauthorized status. Secondly, a 'cost-effective' frame (i.e. the benefits outweigh the costs) works in tandem with a 'cost-saving' frame (i.e. preventive care reduces costs in the long run), making the undocumented youth ideal candidates for government-sponsored coverage.[2] The insurance premiums paid by undocumented but, in general, healthy youths would help to reduce health care costs for everyone else in the United States, and thus would be 'cost-effective'. Preventive measures, including vaccinations and screening tests, are depicted by the media as a rational means for preventing the use of emergency services while curbing the spread of infectious disease and costly long-term care, and is therefore deemed as 'cost-saving'.

This study ultimately aims to advance the understanding of the 'selective inclusion' frame, which, within a meritocratic and neoliberal paradigm, protects special groups of immigrants. Towards this end, this chapter shows how these frames objectify a neoliberal assertion of the unauthorized youth as responsible subjects who are imminently worthy of receiving government-sponsored health insurance.

Framing Legislation to Protect the Undocumented Population in the United States

In the aftermath of ACA's passing, politicians and immigrant stakeholders devised new ways to extend – and gain public support for – health insurance to unauthorized populations, including pregnant women and children, in tandem with initiatives proposed by individual states to craft their own responses to unresolved immigration issues at the federal level. Under ACA's new provisions, Medicare (insurance for senior populations) and Medicaid (government-financed health insurance for the poor and disabled) were expanded, along with the creation of state-run insurance exchanges aimed at helping the public buy private insurance at lower prices. Each state was also tasked with drafting its own laws and health programmes to serve vulnerable uninsured groups.

Partly due to criticisms of the US government's inability to launch and support progressive immigration policy, on 15 June 2012 President Barack Obama issued the Deferred Action for Childhood Arrivals (DACA) executive order.[3] A temporary step on a path to legalization for undocumented immigrants, DACA offered a renewable two-year permit to remain in the United States, as well as work authorizations for undocumented youths who had entered the country before the age of 16 (either with an adult or unaccompanied). They should have (a) been in the country for five consecutive years; (b) been under the age of 31 as of 15 June 2012; (c) had no criminal record; and (d) been enrolled in school or had a high school diploma. These young people, who in many cases also had undocumented parents, became known as 'Dreamers' – named after the DREAM Act proposals upon which DACA was built.[4]

As of today, close to eight hundred thousand Dreamers have been granted DACA status, with a 92 per cent approval rate out of all submitted applications. A majority of DACA recipients are Latino (79 per cent of whom came from Mexico) and are between 16 and

35 years old. Among DACA recipients, the most common age at the time of entry was three, with a median age of six (Wong 2017). Despite the fact that DACA granted temporary protected status to eligible unauthorized youth, it also barred them from inclusion in the Affordable Care Act. Under DACA, this population has continued to remain ineligible for all forms of federal-based public assistance. At the time of writing, DACA was still in place even despite President Trump's hostile stance towards immigrants.

In order to compensate for ACA's and DACA's restrictions, about half of the states have passed bills that support either low-cost or free comprehensive health insurance to eligible youth. The law of the land in the United States, which excludes the undocumented from all forms of government-sponsored services, has been mitigated by the discretional inclusion of unauthorized youths into state and municipal initiatives that somehow bypass (and contradict) US federal policy. For example, the states of New York and California have ratified legislation that provides Medicaid coverage to undocumented youth, as well as pregnant women and children (Sommers 2013; Sundaram 2013). In California, DACA recipients are also eligible for state-funded health programmes, including Medi-Cal (the state version of the Medicaid programme), which provides health insurance and services to low-income families, people with disabilities, seniors and pregnant women (California Immigrant Policy Center 2014). Many of these state-run health initiatives also include newcomers suspected of carrying infectious diseases (Patler and Cabrera 2015). Furthermore, community-based clinics in almost every state have continued to serve those unable to afford health care, regardless of their legal status (Fernández-Kelly 2012; Sommers 2013).

Conceptual Tools: Defining the Frames

The term 'frames' is used in this chapter to identify semiotic constructs aimed at summarizing a standpoint argument by reinforcing the presumed qualities, both positive and negative, of a particular subject. The media create, reformulate and disseminate frames (e.g. scripts, metaphors, representations) that reinforce preconceived notions regarding certain vulnerable groups – for example, when asserting that immigrants are responsible for either spreading disease or are a health burden (Briggs 2005; Newton 2009). As widely noted in the literature on media coverage (Chavez 2013; Freeman, Hansen and Leal 2013; Thorbjørnsrud 2015), news framing has the power to shape public opinion, leading to either progressive or regressive public policy, and thus fuel both pro- and anti-immigrant social movements.

Media framing involves many disparate actors, including publicists and marketing strategists, lobbyists, think tank representatives, politicians, reputed academics and public figures, all of whom engage in discursive battles in a process that restructures public opinion on controversial topics (Ryan, Carragee and Meinhofer 2001; Carragee and Roefs 2004). The ability of frames to dominate the news depends upon the sponsor's economic and cultural resources and on the topic's resonance with broader mainstream cultural values (Ryan, Carragee and Meinhofer 2001). For each mainstream frame, there is at least one counter-frame, which is defined as a differing stance on an issue that is constructed through a relational process (Yoo 2001).

The literature on media framing has produced an extensive body of work in recent years (Lakoff 2006; Newton 2009; Kim et al. 2011) by focusing on the complex, interrelated ways in which the media define and construct a problem, diagnose its causes and provide solutions to it. On the basis of deploying particular labels, the media prompt audiences to align with a specific vision on a controversial topic – as when supporting a humanitarian approach (e.g. immigrants deserve compassion) or posing a threat (e.g. immigrants are dangerous, Viladrich 2012). Lakoff (2006) observes the US media's ubiquitous use of the term 'illegal aliens' – rather than 'irregular' or 'unauthorized' – in order to label immigrants as alleged criminals.

The analysis of media framing can offer unique clues to our understanding of the direction of public opinion and policy regarding immigrants' entitlement to government services (Fryberg et al. 2012). Media frames that portray immigrants as 'abnormal' or 'dangerous' have concrete consequences in terms of policy, as in the case of curtailing prenatal services to Latina women or denying free health services to farm workers. Furthermore, there exists a close relationship between framing and labelling (Knoll, Sanborn and Redlawsk 2011), as the use of certain key words and short phrases has a strong impact on the audience's emotional and intellectual evaluation of a given theme (Ommundsen et al. 2014). As a tool of political scientists and public opinion agencies, framing analysis is also key in shaping the public image of social movements and community groups (Ryan, Carragee and Meinhofer 2001).

When it comes to the health field, the popularized frame of immigrants as a 'burden' has stressed their alleged abuse of public services (including hospitals, jails and schools). Furthermore, the 'threat' frame mostly portrays immigrants as a menace to public health, typically as vectors of disease, such as Ebola, HIV or H1N1 (Fryberg et al. 2012; Viladrich 2012). The idea of immigrants as a 'moral hazard' suggests they purposely take advantage of health and social services in developed nations, a frame that has persistently been contested by social science research (Konczal and Varga 2012; Portes, Fernández-Kelly and Light 2012; Chavez 2013). Furthermore, media frames tend to conflate all immigrants, regardless of their citizenship status, into one amorphous group (McGuire and Canales 2010).

In recent years, new nativist discourses have been overhauled, particularly after the attacks on the World Trade Center in New York City on 11 September 2001, and, more recently, with the election of Donald Trump as president of the United States. Rising anti-immigrant stances – both in public policy and mainstream media – are currently in tune with prevailing neoliberal paradigms that leave it up to the market to organize social life. On this line, economic and health affairs have been widely reshaped, no longer as the realm of the state, but as the result of self-regulating economic forces that ultimately make citizens responsible for their own health care and welfare.

Methods

This chapter follows a turn in media analysis that aligns with a paradigm shift from quantitative to qualitative studies on the study of news frames (Wodak and Busch 2004; Viladrich 2012). This project examined the most significant inclusionary frames found in the print-media literature in the United States. By 'inclusionary frames', I refer to the concepts (images and representations) that support the undocumented youth's entitlement to health services on the basis of being worthy of permission to legally remain in the country. The time span (articles published between 2010 and 2017) includes the passage of Health Reform in 2010 and of DACA in 2012, followed by contemporary debates concerning the federal exclusion of unauthorized immigrants from health policy.

The following search engines were used to find the articles: Lexis/Nexis (via Queens College, CUNY); ProQuest and Factiva (via Columbia University); Google; and online archives of the *New York Daily News* and the *New York Times*. Search words included, in alphabetical order, the following terms: 'DACA', 'Dreamers', 'immigrants', 'illegal', 'Health Act', 'Health Care', 'Health Reform', 'Latino', 'Students', 'Unauthorized', 'Undocumented' and 'Uninsured'. The open-ended, mass-media corpus consisted of close to two hundred articles from over fifty sources, gathered via media searches and culled from a total of more than fifteen hundred articles, based on topic relevance and order of appearance in reference lists. Within the corpus, some 40 per cent of articles were published in mainstream metropolitan newspapers, including the *New York Times*, *Los Angeles Times*, *Chicago Tribune*, *Boston Globe* and *Washington Post*, and the websites of major news companies, such as CNN, while 60 per cent appeared in smaller local papers and tabloids.

After the corpus was assembled, the chosen articles were closely read and frames extrapolated. The analysis was done manually by recording quotations and inferring specific frames; the ones that ultimately emerged were drawn from an open assessment of the articles. As has been the case with other framing studies (Boycoff and Laschever 2011; McKay, Thomas and Warwick Blood 2011), this study is based on a critical-constructivist and qualitative content analysis in which articles were read multiple times in order to identify recurring themes throughout the media corpus.

While some articles relied on one single frame, most included two or more frames; nonetheless, a single dominant frame was identified in each of the articles for the final sample. Rather than quantifying the frequency of the appearance of each frame, this qualitative research piece focuses on the meaning of the most salient frames identified in the corpus. The study results highlight the dominance of the 'effortful immigrant' frame as shown by news narratives that describe the unauthorized foreign-born youth, and often their families, as hard-working, talented and devoted students and models for their communities – a depiction that aligns with the image of the 'super citizen' (Aptekar 2015).[5]

A second overarching frame combines 'cost-saving' and 'cost-effective' accounts, which support financially minded arguments for providing health care to uninsured immigrants. Although these two frames often appeared together, they have different meanings. The 'cost-saving' frame supports the prevention of disease towards improving health outcomes and ultimately leading to healthier and longer lives (Goodell, Cohen and Neumann 2009). For example, counselling on healthy eating and childhood immunizations are considered cost-saving interventions. On the other hand, a health programme is considered 'cost effective' when the anticipated benefits are more than worth its expected costs, even if it does not save actual money in the short term (Teutsch 2006).

The following sections focus on deconstructing the meanings of the frames summarized above in the context of the media corpus selected for the analysis.

The Deserving Other: Effort Pays Off

This study's media analysis revealed the preeminence of images that feature a hard-working undocumented young immigrant whose contributions to US society are yet to unfold. Personal stories of industrious undocumented children who experience an array of health conditions, from minor cuts to chronic asthma, are rich in accounts of their families' struggles with astronomical medical bills, and the resultant fear of losing their chance to become legalized because of unpaid debts and bad credit ratings. The media reinforce the 'effortful immigrant' frame by underscoring the fact that the undocumented contribute generously to the US economy but receive little in return (Viladrich 2012). This frame also works by counteracting the 'liability' tale, which portrays immigrants as freeloaders and lawbreakers who greedily suck up American tax dollars. The youths' contributions to American society are particularly invoked in support of their inclusion in the US government health safety net. For instance, in an article published in the *New York Times*, Robert Pear quotes a health analyst to support his claims:

> Jennifer M. Ng'andu, a health policy specialist at the National Council of La Raza, a Hispanic rights group, said: 'We do not understand why the administration decided to do this. It's providing immigration relief to children and young adults so they can be fully integrated into society. At the same time, it's shutting them out of the health care system so they cannot become productive members of society'. (Pear 2012)

In another story, Itzel (a DACA grantee who eventually received Medi-Cal) is portrayed as the eldest daughter of a poor family of farmworkers in California. Although Itzel's medical condition was not life threatening (she fell in her family's kitchen and split her lip on the counter), the news report highlights the hospital's financial harassment in order to get its bills paid. Quoting an immigrant advocate, the article's moral predicament is clear: 'That's why a lot of older immigrant kids won't go to see a doctor when they fall sick, because they are afraid that if they don't pay up their medical bills it will mess up their credit rating' (New America Media 2013). Providing health insurance to unauthorized youth – and offering them low-cost regular health care – is depicted as a rational investment rather than a liability to the nation's future. As in the case of those suffering from chronic diseases (e.g. diabetes or asthma) a youth's illnesses may curb her academic aspirations in the medium and long term (ibid.). Hence, having insurance coverage would allow these young people to overcome their health problems and, thereafter, embark on a promising path to success.

The 'effortful immigrant' frame is often found in combination with an 'innocence' stand, which points out that the immigrant youth did not choose the conditions that led to their becoming undocumented in the United States. The general understanding is that this young population did not make the decision to enter and remain in the country illegally, as they are usually assumed to have been brought in by their parents at a very young age. The 'effortful immigrant' frame becomes even stronger with accounts that portray the extreme challenges (both situational and emotional) experienced by the immigrant youth on a daily basis. The media address these issues by showing how the high hopes for these young immigrants' futures – graduate education and high-skill jobs – are invariably shattered by the grim reality of their undocumented status, which prevents them from realizing their own version of the 'American dream'.

Scholars who have followed the lives of undocumented children over time (Gonzales 2011; Suárez-Orozco et al. 2011) describe the feelings of depression, anxiety, inadequacy and stigmatization that they regularly experience. A poignant example of this is illustrated by an article in the *Washington Post* on 12 February 2017, in which Dr James Gordon describes the psychological consequences of having to live 'in the shadows' because of the threat of being deported and/or having a loved one who is in that position:

> Undocumented immigrants, who have long lived in fear of deportation, are probably the most profoundly affected. Among them are the 800,000 'dreamers', the young people who came to the United States as undocumented children and are now all but indistinguishable from U.S. citizens in high schools and colleges, as they serve in the military and work and marry and raise their own children. In 2012 when President Barack Obama created the Deferred Action for Childhood Arrivals Program, he granted them a measure of relief, allowing them to apply every two years for continuing permission to stay in the United States. These dreamers know that the platform Trump ran on contains a differing kind of promise: to 'immediately terminate' their status. (Gordon 2017)

Gordon's remarks point out the similarity between the Dreamers and those rightfully born in the United States. Not only are young immigrants victims of conditions for which they are not responsible, but they are also mistreated by a biomedical system that does not allow them to remain healthy and eventually fulfil their lofty academic and professional aspirations. It is precisely the Dreamer, whom the media has mostly framed as being innocent of trespassing into US territory, who pays the price of a broken immigration and health system. Even when they play by the rules, study hard and excel academically, their hopes for success are shattered by the 'legal ceiling' of their undocumented status.

Earlier in 2017, Trump's outspoken position in support of DACA (despite the promises he made during his presidential campaign) ruffled a few feathers among his conservative base – a turn of events that received ample media coverage. In an article by the *New York Times*, the writers reflect on Trump's sudden support for DACA:

> But once in office, Mr Trump faced a new reality: the political risks of targeting for deportation a group of people who are viewed sympathetically by many Americans. In some cases, the immigrants did not know they were in the country illegally. Many had attended American schools from the time they were in kindergarten. (Shear and Yee 2017)

The mainstream portrayal of the unauthorized youth as 'effortful immigrants' has led to the unintended consequence of making invisible those, including some undocumented activists, who do not identify with such framing (Zimmerman 2012; Nicholls 2013; Lauby 2016). The ambitious undocumented girl who hopes to pave a path of upward mobility is described as experiencing anxiety, helplessness and a loss of motivation. Ultimately, owing to her 'illegal' status, she will be unable to complete her education at a prestigious university. And the boy who finds that his dreams of becoming an engineer, doctor or lawyer have been dashed is the one upon whom the media has built a justification of worth, framing the injustice tale in terms of not being granted the health and social services that he properly deserves.

In tune with this paper's results, research shows that representing the Dreamers as 'model immigrants' has become a successful strategy largely deployed by grass-roots organizations and immigrant groups for the purpose of gaining political leverage on migration reform (Nicholls 2013; Yukich 2013; Fernandes 2015). In a sense, the Dreamers' movement has been shaped around the idea of 'framing the frames' (Viladrich and Percal 2015), which has inspired a plethora of storytelling with a view to gaining long-term political capital. Widely portrayed as well adjusted to US culture and values, the Dreamers' alleged 'Americanness' has made them the poster children for the immigrant movement. By the same token, the positive mainstream portrait of the Dreamers has somehow overshadowed the not-so-lucky and not-so-talented undocumented youth who have neither outstanding academic credentials nor a promising professional trajectory waiting to unfold.

Capitalizing on Immigrant Youth

As informed by framing theory, building support for undocumented youth requires narratives of worth that must appeal to the general public. In this vein, saving tax dollars and maximizing the contributions that the Dreamers bring to the United States, as discussed in the previous section, have become the progressive media's battle cry in recent years. Additionally, cost-saving frames used in support of the youth's entitlement to health care rest on the fact that access to health insurance will reduce government spending by billions of dollars. Timely preventive health services – including regular visits to a doctor for check-ups, vaccinations and screening tests – will result in optimal health outcomes and less total spending by the US government and society at large. For instance, an article by CNN quotes Alvaro Huerta, staff attorney for the National Immigration Law Center, as follows: 'It makes financial and practical sense to include DACA grantees in the ACA', Huerta said. 'It would increase the pool that's eligible for exchanges by adding generally young, healthy immigrants, and that would decrease health insurance costs for all of us' (Rodriguez and Hurtado 2014).

On a complementary side, the cost-effective frame emphasizes the importance of prior investments in immigrant youth to whom taxpayers have already bestowed countless resources (health, social and educational) from early childhood through to adulthood. The media talk about the returns that the United States can expect to get by providing health care to the youth, while portraying immigrants as a strategic (and financially sound) investment. The fact that the undocumented youth (and their parents) are also taxpayers enhances this argument, as in the following editorial: 'These students grew up here, went to school here, and paid taxes here, and we want them to be able to succeed here… Giving these students a fair shot means giving them the same access to our state financial aid programs that other students get. All of our children deserve the chance to fulfil the American Dream' (HeraldNet 2013).

In an article by CNBC, the journalist quotes Dr Julia Koehler, a paediatrician at Boston Children's Hospital, who presents a compelling cost-saving frame aimed at protecting the health of US-born individuals – with arguments that are also part of the 'population health frame' (Viladrich 2012):

> Even an immigrant going without a flu shot because of lack of insurance can lead to significant costs for others, she said. 'If you don't have health insurance and you have low income, it is very unlikely that you will come up with the money to buy a flu shot', Koehler said. 'So the unimmunized person will then possibly expose other vulnerable people, perhaps asthmatics, young infants, older people. ... Health insurance should be available regardless of immigration status, because, again, it goes beyond the health of the affected individuals, and it goes to the health of the whole family and the whole community', she said. (Mangan 2014)

The projected economic benefits obtained from higher salaried, better-educated adults are pictured as a cost-effective frame that justifies the expense of underwriting immigrant students' health insurance. It is important to note that even undocumented immigrants in the United States are able to obtain health coverage as long as they have enough money to pay for it. Correspondingly, prohibitive cost is often cited as a main argument to explain why health insurance is often out of reach for undocumented youth. Adding to future gains, in state and federal income taxes collected from healthy individuals, cost-effective arguments project efficiency savings in government expenditures on the welfare, aid and incarceration of poorly educated immigrants.

A basic postulate in insurance law contends that the larger the number of healthy and young individuals entering the pool, the lower the risks and overall coverage costs (Ku 2009). In this vein, unauthorized youth are presented as ideal recruits. Young, employable and healthy, their joining the health insurance system would help to lessen the pool risks for everyone and increase the number of collected premiums. An editorial in the *Washington Post* titled 'Let Illegal Immigrants Buy into Health Plans', makes a persuasive argument on the Dreamers' behalf:

> In fact, allowing such [health insurance] purchases would benefit everyone. First, the more the ranks of the uninsured are reduced, the less the

burden on hospitals and other parts of the health-care system to provide uncompensated care, the costs of which are passed on to other consumers in the form of higher prices and premiums. Second, illegal immigrants to this country tend to be relatively young and healthy. The more such individuals purchase insurance, the healthier – and less costly – the risk pool. (*Washington Post* 2009)

The burden of uncompensated health care, defined as hospitals' provision of services for which no payment is made, would be counterbalanced by the benefits of allowing healthy young immigrants to buy their own medical insurance. Their premiums would help to pay for sick US citizens who are ageing at higher rates than non-US citizens. Ultimately, the cost-effective frame considers the advantages of counting on an insured immigrant labour force able to inject their own resources into the system, thus leading to major savings in uncompensated and emergency care while ultimately lowering the insurance pool risks.

To summarize, cost-effective and cost-saving frames underline the expected returns to be drawn from having a healthy (and insured) population in the United States, regardless of immigration status. Under the spell of economic-based frames, the US media steer tropes – based on national pride and accountability – that highlight the benefits of providing government-sponsored health insurance to foreigners who, despite their 'illegal' status, are called upon to become contributors to 'America's greatness'. As per the media frames analysed here, investing in health care for deserving immigrant youth will have a beneficial spillover effect in the US economy as a whole.

Reframing the 'Emergency Room'

Hospitals' emergency departments offer both a symbolic and a physical site where the media frames highlighting immigrants' prerogatives for health care ultimately converge. By stressing the undocumented population's use of emergency rooms – contrary to public health evidence and medical records – the media help build an inclusive rationale based on an effective investment of resources. The literature reveals that, contrary to public beliefs, unauthorized immigrants use fewer services (including emergency services) than natives and legal immigrants (Ortega et al. 2007; Stimpson, Wilson and Dejun 2013). Furthermore, the overarching emergency room frame reveals how cost-effective and cost-saving frames work in tandem, as typically illustrated by quotes from health policy experts, medical providers and politicians. In an article published by PBS, Nadereh Pourat, a health expert, is quoted as follows:

> I have to acknowledge that nothing comes for free. But it's a question of whether we're spending our money wisely. A single emergency room visit or a single hospitalization is many times more than two to five doctors' visits. From a fiscal, economic perspective, you could spend a little bit more and get far better results than wait for people to show up in emergency rooms and hospitals and then spend thousands of the public's funds. If you bring people into primary care, they may be able to contribute a little bit, whether it's through paying premiums or copays. Or you can wait until they come into the hospital uninsured, and they pay nothing and you pay thousands. (Tam 2014)

Another news article describes the state of California's Medi-Cal programme, which covers eligible undocumented youth. The article quotes Republican Michelle Lujan Grishman, who introduced a bill that would make DACA grantees immediately eligible for health insurance: 'This lack of access leads to more visits to emergency rooms, where immigrants are forced to pay as much as $1,200 to treat common ailments like the flu and upper respiratory infections' (Rodriguez and Hurtado 2014). A similar approach is presented by the Chicago Business Report, which quotes Stephani Becker, a policy specialist at the Sargent Shriver National Center on poverty law: 'Any sort of state-only effort that would help cover those individuals would be huge. It's over 100,000 (undocumented) people (in Illinois) going to ERs and having chronic conditions that aren't being seen … It's a drain on the public health sector and eventually on the taxpayers, too' (Marotti 2015).

Finally, a 'chain reaction effect' paints the emergency room as a de facto depot used to treat the undocumented. According to this frame, immigrants' barriers to health services – and their lack of health insurance – would typically lead to delays in medical care until the problem ends up being very serious, and therefore too expensive for emergency departments to treat.[6] Waiting until an emergency arises would inevitably result in higher costs for the US economy and, particularly, its citizens. In due course, insuring undocumented youth would represent a common-sense financial measure, since letting threatening health conditions go untreated will ultimately lead to emergency services that are mostly paid for with the US-born population's tax dollars.

Discussion: Constructing the Deserving Immigrant Youth

This chapter has examined US media representations that support the inclusion of unauthorized youth into the government health safety net after passage of ACA and DACA, two major pieces of legislation that drove plenty of media coverage concerning undocumented immigrants' entitlement to health care. The chapter has aimed to answer the question, already posed by social scientists, regarding the different – and complementary – ways in which health-related deservingness is publicly constructed (Park 2011; Willen, Mulligan and Castañeda 2011; Viladrich 2012; Willen 2012; Menjívar and Kanstroom 2013; Vanthuyne et al. 2013).

The conceptual scaffolding of this study, supported by framing theory, has informed the scholarly interest for a deeper understanding of the social construction of immigrants' entitlement to health care. As a result, three main frames have been analysed here. A first frame – the 'effortful immigrant' – features the undocumented youths' industriousness and their blamelessness concerning the conditions by which they came to be unauthorized immigrants. Narratives within this frame involve the youths' contributions to the economy and their hard-working values, along with the situations under which they were brought to the United States. Furthermore, a 'cost-effective' frame (i.e. benefits are worth the costs) was also identified in tandem with a 'cost-saving' one (i.e. preventive care reduces long-term costs). These combined frames were drawn from narratives that portray the undocumented as mostly young and healthy individuals. Moreover, their insurance premiums would help to reduce health care costs for everyone in the country. Preventive measures, including vaccinations and screening tests, are ultimately seen as rational means for curbing both the spread of infectious diseases and costly long-term care.

In the past, the US media were adamant about eliciting compassion for foreigners by relying on the figure of the guiltless individual – such as the infirm grandparent or the undocumented child (Fujiwara 2005; Viladrich 2019). Given the current anti-immigration environment in the United States, the 'right to have rights' would not be effective in devising a sound ideological platform for building support for unauthorized young immigrants' entitlement to health services. In today's political environment, the framing of positive stands towards the undocumented requires more than sympathetic metaphors based on need or frailty. In order to be effective, media framing must set young immigrants apart from other less praiseworthy subjects (e.g. those deemed as welfare dependents and disadvantaged immigrants), while underscoring the beneficial impact that the former will bring to the US economy.

In sum, this study's findings reveal a turn in media framing: from a compassionate approach to the construction of deserving individuals who will contribute to the national greatness on the basis of their cultural assimilation and hard work. The US media has successfully carved a place where the unauthorized youth are no longer associated with the welfare dependent that 'illegally' migrated to drain (and abuse) the US economy. Instead, media narratives stress the benefits of counting on a healthy, albeit undocumented, labour force that will lead to increasing consumption, more jobs and a growing tax base (Hinojosa-Ojeda 2010). In the end, having a sickly immigrant labour force – and denying access to health care to deserving youth – is not only deemed as counterproductive but also as politically and financially heedless.

Conclusions: Revisiting Health Care as a Universal Human Right

The United States has progressively moved away from an approach that conceives immigrants as global citizens and rights-holders (WHO 2003) to one that portrays them as intruders liable for their actions, with some exceptions as in the case of the meritorious foreign-born youth. However, the United States is not alone in this matter. In recent years, countries as disparate as Canada and Spain have intensified their policies towards excluding the undocumented from public health services, a trend that reveals the gap between these nation states' loose commitment to international human rights law and the incongruent, poor delivery of health care to vulnerable populations, including children (Rousseau et al. 2008; Ruiz-Casares et al. 2010). Contrary to dominant policy models, which in the end criminalize migrants' free worldwide circulation, social science scholars have been challenging the construction of illegality as the flip side of a connected world in which human beings are denied basic necessities, including access to primary health care (Schrecker et al. 2010; Menjívar and Abrego 2012).[7]

The passage of US Health Reform in 2010 reiterated to the public the existence of a 'universal' health system that rests upon its commoditized power: a business contract that demands that its customers prove, time and again, their worth and their ability to pay for medical services. As in the case of several countries within the European

Union that grant health care access to select undocumented populations (Spencer 2016), ACA's and DACA's passage reveal an uneven geography of entitlement of public services at the local and state levels (Drevdahl and Dorcy 2007). Given the widely held opinion in the United States of the notion of health care as a market-based formula, the support for select groups of meritorious immigrants – in this case, undocumented youth – dovetails well with the notion of lending incremental access to health care to valued uninsured populations. This view is in tune with neoliberal assertions of deservingness that frame the undocumented youth as a responsible and productive worker who promises not to become a public burden to the US government. Furthermore, the young immigrant's conditional inclusion in the country demonstrates a limited meaning of deservingness that is contingent on his or her ability to prove civic and moral values (Flores 2016). At last, it is not a language of rights but rather a meritocratic ethos that paves the entry of the immigrant youth into the US safety net.

This chapter has aimed to deepen our scholarly understanding of the role of the media in shaping the public language that both supports and restricts immigrants' health rights. Informed by framing theory as an enlightened conceptual and methodological tool, this research piece has intended to shed light on an ongoing paradigm shift against the conceptualization of health as a human right. Likewise, future framing research should expand the formulation of comprehensive theoretical frameworks able to account for both the production of discourses of deservingness, and their socially shared (and experiential) effects on the lives of vulnerable – unauthorized and uninsured – immigrants. Novel alternative framings are needed to address, and further understand, the de facto construction of health benefits among vulnerable immigrants in specific contexts and in complex, even contradictory, political landscapes.

Acknowledgements

Anahí Viladrich is extremely thankful to the book's editors and the anonymous reviewers whose constructive comments greatly helped improve the contents of this chapter. Malka Percal provided pivotal assistance during the data collection stages and analysis. Slava Faybysh offered invaluable editorial advice during the editing process. Financial support for this study came from two PSC-CUNY Awards.

Anahí Viladrich is a sociologist and medical anthropologist who received higher education degrees from Argentina (her birth country) and the United States (PhD from Columbia University). Her numerous research projects and publications intertwine the fields of international migration, health, gender and culture. Viladrich's latest book, titled *More Than Two to Tango: Argentine Tango Immigrants in New York City*, received an award from the Association of Latina and Latino Anthropologists of the American Anthropological Association. Dr Viladrich is currently full professor in the Departments of Sociology (with a courtesy appointment in the Anthropology Department) at Queens College of the City University of New York (CUNY). She is also affiliated with the Department of Sociology at the Graduate Center and the Graduate School of Public Health and Health Policy, CUNY.

Notes

1. The passing of the Patient Protection and Affordable Care Act of 2010 (Public Law 111-152, 2010, ACA) mandated that most US citizens and legal permanent residents must have health insurance coverage or pay a fine. Through the creation of state-based health exchanges, ACA would help individuals and small businesses to purchase coverage with (or without) subsidies. It would also give states the option to expand Medicaid to a larger pool of individuals.
2. As noted in a report by the Robert Wood Johnson Foundation (2009), 'cost-saving' and 'cost-effective' are not synonymous, although they are often used interchangeably. For instance, an intervention is 'cost-effective' if its benefits are considered to be greater than its costs, whereas preventive care, such as screening and many childhood immunizations, is 'cost saving'.
3. The official DACA memorandum can be found at http://www.whitehouse.gov/blog/2012/08/15/deferred-action-childhood-arrivals-who-can-be-considered.
4. The DREAM Act was first introduced as a proposal in 2001 as a bipartisan effort by Senator Orin Hatch (R-Utah) and Senator Dick Durbin (D-Illinois); a dozen years later, on 6 June 2013, the House of Representatives rejected the bill, after several failed attempts at passage.
5. The 'effortful' frame speaks to the notion of the 'model immigrant' embodied by the unauthorized youth as members of an outstanding minority, and as 'super-students', whose contribution to the United States even exceeds that of US natives. In this way, Dreamers are portrayed as the cream of the crop of recent immigrants (Viladrich and Percal 2016).
6. Emergency services are mostly funded by tax dollars as public hospitals are forced to pay for non-reimbursable services (Nandi, Loue and Galea 2009).

7. Human rights approaches have called for attention to immigrants' structural vulnerability and their universal right to health care, regardless of nationality, race/ethnicity or migrant status (Schrecker et al. 2010; Willen 2012; Castañeda et al. 2015).

References

Aptekar, S. 2015. *The Road to Citizenship: What Naturalization Means for Immigrants and the United States*. New Brunswick, NJ: Rutgers University Press.

Boykoff, J., and E. Laschever. 2011. 'The Tea Party Movement, Framing, and the US Media'. *Social Movement Studies* 10(4): 341–66.

Briggs, C.L. 2005. 'Communicability, Racial Discourse, and Disease'. *Annual Review of Anthropology* 34: 269–91.

Brown, H.E. 2013. 'Race, Legality, and the Social Policy Consequences of Anti-Immigration Mobilization'. *American Sociological Review* 78(2): 290–314.

California Immigrant Policy Center (CIPC). 2014. 'Your Health, Your Future: Making DACA Work for You in the Golden State'. Retrieved on 24 August 2014 from http://www.caimmigrant.org/wp-content/uploads/2014/10/DACAReport2-YourHealthYourFuture.pdf.

Carragee, K.M., and W. Roefs. 2004. 'The Neglect of Power in Recent Framing Research'. *Journal of Communication* 54: 214–33.

Castañeda, H., et al. 2015. 'Immigration as a Social Determinant of Health. *Annual Review of Public Health* 36: 375–92.

Chavez, L.R. 2001. *Covering Immigration: Popular Images and the Politics of the Nation*. Berkeley: University of California Press.

———. 2013. *The Latino Threat: Constructing Immigrants, Citizens, and the Nation*. Stanford, CA: Stanford University Press.

De la Torre, P., and R. Germano. 2014. 'Out of the Shadows: DREAMer Identity in the Immigrant Youth Movement. *Latino Studies* 12(3): 449–67.

Drevdahl, D.J., and K.S. Dorcy. 2007. 'Exclusive Inclusion: The Violation of Human Rights and US Immigration Policy'. *Advances in Nursing Science* 30: 290–302.

Fernandes, S. 2015. 'The Making of the Dreamer: Storytelling Trainings and the Electoral Turn'. Eastern Sociological Society Annual Meeting, New York City, 26 February – 1 March. New York City: Eastern Sociological Society.

Fernández-Kelly, P. 2012. 'Rethinking the Deserving Body: Altruism, Markets, and Political Action in Health Care Provision'. *Ethnic and Racial Studies* 35(1): 56–71.

Flores, A. 2016. 'Forms of Exclusion: Undocumented Students Navigating Financial Aid and Inclusion in the United States'. *American Ethnologist* 43(3): 540–54.

Freeman, G.P., R. Hansen and D.L. Leal. 2013. 'Immigration and Public Opinion in Liberal Democracies', in G.P. Freeman, R. Hansen and D.L. Leal (eds), *Introduction: Immigration and Public Opinion*. New York: Routledge, pp. 1–20.

Fryberg, S.A., et al. 2012. 'How the Media Frames the Immigration Debate: The Critical Role of Location and Politics'. *Analyses of Social Issues and Public Policy* 12: 96–112.

Fujiwara, L.H. 2005. 'Immigrant Rights are Human Rights: The Reframing of Immigrant Entitlement and Welfare'. *Social Problems* 52: 79–101.

Gonzales, R.G. 2011. 'Learning to be Illegal: Undocumented Youth and Shifting Legal Contexts in the Transition to Adulthood'. *American Sociological Review* 76: 602–19.

Gonzales, R.G., V. Terriquez and S.P. Ruszczyk. 2014. 'Becoming DACAmented: Assessing the Short-Term Benefits of Deferred Action for Childhood Arrivals (DACA)'. *American Behavioral Scientist* 58(14): 1852–72.

Goodell, S, J.T. Cohen and P.J. Neumann. 2009. 'Cost Savings and Cost-Effectiveness of Clinical Preventive Care: The Synthesis Project. Robert Wood Johnson Foundation'. Retrieved on 20 August 2020 from http://www.rwjf.org/en/library/research/2009/09/cost-savings-and-cost-effectiveness-of-clinical-preventive-care.html.

Gordon, J. 2017. 'Living in Fear of Deportation is Terrible for Your Health', *Washington Post*, 17 February. Retrieved on 20 August 2020 from https://www.washingtonpost.com/posteverything/wp/2017/02/10/living-in-fear-as-a-refugee-in-the-u-s-is-terrible-for-your-health/?utm_term=.1205f525a699.

HeraldNet. 2013. 'Keep the "Dream Act" Alive'. Editorial, 3 April. Retrieved on 20 August 2020 from http://www.heraldnet.com/opinion/keep-the-dream-act-alive/.

Hinojosa-Ojeda, R. 2010. 'Raising the Floor for American Workers: The Economic Benefits of Comprehensive Immigration Reform'. Washington, DC: Center for American Progress, Immigration Policy Center.

Holling, M.A., and B. Calafell. 2011. *Latina/o Discourse in Vernacular Spaces: Somos de Una Voz?*. Plymouth UK: Lexington Books.

International Organization for Migration (IOM). 2013. *International migration, health and human rights*. International Organization for Migration (IOM).

Kim, S.H., et al. 2011. 'The View of the Border: News Framing of the Definition, Causes, and Solutions to Illegal Immigration'. *Mass Communication and Society* 14(3): 292–314.

Knoll, B.R., H. Sanborn and D. Redlawsk. 2011. 'Framing Labels and Immigration Policy Attitudes in the Iowa Caucuses: "Trying to Out-Tancredo Tancredo"'. *Political Behavior* 33(3): 433–54.

Konczal, L., and L. Varga. 2012. 'Structural Violence and Compassionate Compatriots: Immigrant Health Care in South Florida'. *Ethnic and Racial Studies* 35(1): 88–103.

Ku, L. 2009. 'Health Insurance Coverage and Medical Expenditures of Immigrants and Native-born Citizens in the United States'. *American Journal of Public Health* 99: 1322–28.

Kullgren, J.T. 2003. 'Restrictions on Undocumented Immigrants' Access to Health Services: The Public Health Implications of Welfare Reform'. *American Journal of Public Health* 93(10): 1630–33.

Lakoff, G. 2006. *Thinking Points: Communicating our American Values and Vision*. New York: Macmillan.

Lauby, F. 2016. 'Leaving the "Perfect DREAMer" Behind? Narratives and Mobilization in Immigration Reform'. *Social Movement Studies* 15(4): 374–87.

Lukes, M. 2015. *Latino Immigrant Youth and Interrupted Schooling: Dropouts, Dreamers and Alternative Pathways to College*. Bristol: Multilingual Matters.

Mangan, D. 2014. 'Health-Care Maze Remains for Undocumented Immigrants'. CNBC. Retrieved 25 November 2014 from http://www.cnbc.com/id/102212898.

Marotti, A. 2015. 'Task Force Urges State Health Exchange for Undocumented Immigrants'. Retrieved 8 January 2015 from http://www.chicagobusiness.com/article/20150108/NEWS03/150109914/task-force-urges-state-health-exchange-for-undocumented-immigrants.

Marrow, H.B., and T.D. Joseph. 2015. 'Excluded and Frozen Out: Unauthorised Immigrants' (Non) Access to Care after US Health Care Reform'. *Journal of Ethnic and Migration Studies* 41(14): 2253–73.

McConnell, E.D. 2011. 'An "Incredible Number of Latinos and Asians": Media Representations of Racial and Ethnic Population Change in Atlanta, Georgia'. *Latino Studies* 9(2–3): 177–97.

McGuire, S., and M.K. Canales. 2010. 'Of Migrants and Metaphors: Disrupting Discourses to Welcome the Stranger'. *Advances in Nursing Science* 33(2): 126–42.

McKay, F.H., S.L. Thomas and R. Warwick Blood. 2011. 'Any One of These Boat People Could be a Terrorist for All We Know!' Media Representations and Public Perceptions of "Boat People" Arrivals in Australia'. *Journalism* 12(5): 607–26.

Menjívar, C., and L. Abrego. 2012. 'Legal Violence: Immigration Law and the Lives of Central American Immigrants'. *American Journal of Sociology* 117(5): 1380–1421.

Menjívar, C., and D. Kanstroom (eds). 2013. *Constructing Immigrant 'Illegality': Critiques, Experiences and Responses*. Cambridge: Cambridge University Press.

Nandi, A., S. Loue and S. Galea. 2009. 'Expanding the Universe of Universal Coverage: The Population Health Argument for Increasing Coverage for Immigrants'. *Journal of Immigrant and Minority Health* 11(6): 433–36.

Negrón-Gonzales, G. 2014. 'Undocumented, Unafraid and Unapologetic: Re-Articulatory Practices and Migrant Youth "Illegality"'. *Latino Studies* 12(2): 259–78.

New America Media. 2013. 'DACA Recipients Surprised to Learn They Qualify for Health Care'. Retrieved on 14 December 2014 from http://newamericamedia.org/2013/09/daca-recipients-surprised-to-learn-they-qualify-for-health-care.php.

Newton, L. 2009. *Illegal, Alien, or Immigrant: The Politics of Immigration Reform*. New York City: New York University Press.

Nicholls, W.J. 2013. *The DREAMers: How the Undocumented Youth Movement Transformed the Immigrant Rights Debate*. Stanford, CA: Stanford University Press.

O'Brien, G.V. 2003. 'Indigestible Food, Conquering Hordes, and Waste Materials: Metaphors of Immigrants and the Early Immigration Restriction Debate in the United States'. *Metaphor and Symbol* 18(1): 33–47.

Ommundsen, R., et al. 2014. 'Framing Unauthorized Immigrants: The Effects of Labels on Evaluations'. *Psychological Reports* 114(2): 461–78.

Ortega, A.N., et al. 2007. 'Health Care Access, Use of Services, and Experiences among Undocumented Mexicans and Other Latinos'. *Archives of Internal Medicine* 167(21): 2354–60.

Park, L.S.H. 2011. *Entitled to Nothing: The Struggle for Immigrant Health Care in the Age of Welfare Reform*. New York: NYU Press.

Patler, C., and J.A. Cabrera. 2015. 'From Undocumented to DACAmented: Impacts of the Deferred Action for Childhood Arrivals (DACA) Program'. Institute for Research on Labor and Employment.

Pear, R. 2012. 'Limits Placed on Immigrants in Health Law'. *New York Times (Money & Policy)*. Retrieved 17 September 2012 from http://www.nytimes.com/2012/09/18/health/policy/limits-placed-on-immigrants-in-health-care-law.html.

Portes, A., P. Fernández-Kelly and D. Light. 2012. 'Life on the Edge: Immigrants Confront the American Health System'. *Ethnic and Racial Studies* 35(1): 3–22.

Public Law 111-152. 2010. 'Health Care and Education Reconciliation Act of 2010'. Washington, DC: US Government Printing Office. Retrieved on 20 August 2020 from http://www.gpo.gov/fdsys/pkg/PLAW-111publ152/content-detail.html.

Robert Wood Johnson Foundation. 2009. 'Cost Savings and Cost-Effectiveness of Clinical Preventive Care'. Policy Brief, No. 18.

Rodriguez, C.Y., and J. Hurtado. 2014. 'States Work around Obamacare to Help Undocumented Immigrants'. Retieved 9 April 2014 from http://www.cnn.com/2014/04/09/us/obamacare-undocumented-immigrants/index.html.

Rousseau, C., et al. 2008. 'Health Care Access for Refugees and Immigrants with Precarious Status: Public Health and Human Right Challenges'. *Canadian Journal of Public Health* 99(4): 290–92.

Ruiz-Casares, M., et al. 2010. 'Right and Access to Healthcare for Undocumented Children: Addressing the Gap between International Conventions and Disparate Implementations in North America and Europe'. *Social Science & Medicine* 70(2): 329–36.

Ryan, C., K.M. Carragee and W. Meinhofer. 2001. 'Theory into Practice: Framing, the News Media, and Collective Action'. *Journal of Broadcasting & Electronic Media* 45: 175–82.

Sanchez, G.R., et al. 2011. 'Explaining Public Support (or Lack Thereof) for Extending Health Coverage to Undocumented Immigrants'. *Journal of Health Care for the Poor and Underserved* 22: 683–99.

Schrecker, T., et al. 2010. 'Advancing Health Equity in the Global Marketplace: How Human Rights Can Help'. *Social Science & Medicine* 71(8): 1520–26.

Shear, M.D., and V. Yee. 2017. '"Dreamers" to Stay in U.S. for Now, but Long-Term Fate is Unclear'. *New York Times (Politics)*, 16 June. Retrieved on 20 August 2020 from https://www.nytimes.com/2017/06/16/us/politics/trump-will-allow-dreamers-to-stay-in-us-reversing-campaign-promise.html.

Sohoni, D., and J. Bickham Mendez. 2014. 'Defining Immigrant Newcomers in New Destinations: Symbolic Boundaries in Williamsburg, Virginia'. *Ethnic and Racial Studies* 37(3): 496–516.

Sommers, B.D. 2013. 'Stuck between Health and Immigration Reform: Care for Undocumented Immigrants'. *New England Journal of Medicine* 369: 593–95.

Spencer, S. 2016. 'Postcode Lottery for Europe's Undocumented Children: Unravelling an Uneven Geography of Entitlements in the European Union'. *American Behavioral Scientist* 60(13): 1613–28.

Stimpson, J.P., F.A. Wilson and S. Dejun. 2013. 'Unauthorised Immigrants Spend Less Than Other Immigrants and US Natives on Health Care'. *Health Affairs* 32(7): 1313–18.

Suárez-Orozco, C., et al. 2011. 'Growing Up in the Shadows: The Developmental Implications of Unauthorised Status'. *Harvard Educational Review* 81(3): 438–73.

Sundaram, V. 2013. 'DACA Recipients Surprised to Learn They Qualify for Health Care'. New America Media. Retrieved 21 September 2013 from http://newamericamedia.org/2013/09/daca-recipients-surprised-to-learn-they-qualify-for-health-care.php.

Tam, R. 2014. 'What's Holding Undocumented Immigrants Back from Seeking Health Care?' PBS-Newshour. Retrieved on 20 August 2020 from http://www.pbs.org/newshour/updates/whats-holding-undocumented-immigrants-back.

Teutsch, S. 2006. 'Cost-Effectiveness of Prevention'. Retrieved 13 July 2006 from Medscape. http://www.medscape.com/viewarticle/540199.

Thorbjørnsrud, K. 2015. 'Framing Irregular Immigration in Western Media'. *American Behavioral Scientist* 59(7): 771–82.

Vanthuyne, K., et al. 2013. 'Health Workers' Perceptions of Access to Care for Children and Pregnant Women with Precarious Immigration Status: Health as a Right or a Privilege?' *Social Science & Medicine* 93: 78–85.

Viladrich, A. 2012. 'Beyond Welfare Reform: Reframing Undocumented Immigrants' Entitlement to Health Care in the United States. A Critical Review'. *Social Science & Medicine* 74: 822–29.

———. 2019. '"*We Cannot Let Them Die*": Framing Compassion towards the Health Needs of Unauthorized Immigrants in the United States (U.S.)', *Qualitative Health Research* 29: 1447–1460.

Viladrich, A., and M. Percal. 2016. 'Creating the Model Immigrant: U.S. Media Framing and the Dreamers'. Immigration Studies Working Group Report, Queens College, City University of New York.

Washington Post. 2009. 'Let Illegal Immigrants Buy into Health Plans'. Retrieved 26 December 2009 from http://www.washingtonpost.com/wp-dyn/content/article/2009/12/25/AR2009122501753.html.

Willen, S.S. 2012. 'How is Health-Related "Deservingness" Reckoned? Perspectives from Unauthorised Im/migrants in Tel Aviv'. *Social Science & Medicine* 74(6): 812–21.

Willen, S.S., J. Mulligan and H. Castañeda. 2011. 'Take a Stand Commentary: How Can Medical Anthropologists Contribute to Contemporary Conversations on "Illegal" Im/migration and Health?' *Medical Anthropology Quarterly* 25(3): 331–56.

Willen, S.S., et al. 2017. 'Syndemic Vulnerability and the Right to Health'. *The Lancet* 389(10072): 964–77.

Wodak, R., and B. Busch. 2004. 'Approaches to Media Texts', in J. Downing et al. (eds), *The SAGE Handbook of Media Studies*. Thousand Oaks, CA: SAGE, pp. 105–23.

Wong, T.K. 2017. 'National DACA Study: Center for American Progress'. Retrieved on 20 August 2020 from https://cdn.americanprogress.org/content/uploads/2017/11/02125251/2017_DACA_study_economic_report_updated.pdf.

World Health Organization (WHO). 2003. 'International Migration, Health and Human Rights'. Geneva.

Yoo, G.J. 2001. 'Constructing Deservingness: Federal Welfare Reform, Supplemental Security Income, and Elderly Immigrants'. *Journal of Aging and Social Policy* 134: 17–34.

Yukich, G. 2013. 'Constructing the Model Immigrant: Movement Strategy and Immigrant Deservingness in the New Sanctuary Movement'. *Social Problems* 60(3): 302–20.

Zimmerman, A. 2012. 'Documenting Dreams: New Media, Undocumented Youth and the Immigrant Rights Movement'. A Case Study Report Working Annenberg School For Communication and Journalism, University of Southern California.

2

Constructing the Undeserving Citizen

The Embodied Consequences of Immigration Enforcement in the US South

Nolan Kline

Introduction

On 30 January 2018, President Donald Trump delivered his first State of the Union Address and made multiple references to undocumented immigrants. He argued that undocumented immigration was to blame for illegal drugs circulating in the country, gang violence, lack of employment for low-wage workers, and murder in some communities. In linking undocumented immigration and murder, specifically, the president focused on Latinx (a gender-neutral way to refer to Latino/a) immigrants, referencing a gang known to have members from Latin America. It is no surprise that the president, who has insisted on constructing a full-length wall between the United States and Mexico and at one point argued that Mexican immigrants entering the US were rapists and criminals, would repeatedly suggest that undocumented immigrants from Latin America were dangerous criminals during his address to the nation. Political rhetoric conflating undocumented Latinx immigration and criminality not only fuels xenophobia and racism, but such rhetoric also contributes to existing notions of undocumented immigrants' so-called 'undeservingness' to social services and entitlements.

In the United States, undocumented immigrants face numerous social vulnerabilities due to their immigration status. These vulnerabilities directly impact immigrants' health because of the market-based medical system in which most residents access health services through employer-provided health insurance. Unemployed indigent US citizens who meet certain economic eligibility criteria are eligible for Medicaid, the nation's safety net health programme, and uninsured older adults are eligible for Medicare, a programme designed specifically for the elderly. Undocumented immigrants, however, face great difficulties in accessing health services as they do not typically receive private health insurance from their employers, and they are ineligible for state-funded health services such as Medicaid and Medicare because of their documentation status. More than just being excluded from services, however, undocumented immigrants are also considered 'undeserving' of public benefits because of their immigration status (Berk et al. 2000; Goldman, Smith, and Sood 2005, 2006; Carrasco-Garrido et al. 2007; Derose, Escarce and Lurie 2007; Bauer et al. 2010; Galarneau 2011; Viladrich 2012). Combined, legal exclusions and moral conceptualizations of undeservingness create a layered form of vulnerability for undocumented immigrants living in the United States.

Adding to the existing layered vulnerability, immigration enforcement efforts, such as laws that use local police officers as de facto immigration agents, have proliferated across the states (Gordon and Raja 2012). These laws grant local police officers the authority to stop and arrest anyone suspected of being undocumented, effectively turning everyday public spaces like roadways, parks, markets, shopping malls and places of worship into possible sites of detection, translating into an amplified risk of deportation (Coleman 2012; Menjívar 2014; Stuesse and Coleman 2014). These localized immigration enforcement regimes further merge with federal efforts to be 'tough on immigration', demonstrated in recent years by Donald Trump's executive orders restricting entry to some immigrants and refugees from predominately Muslim countries.

As numerous scholars have described, undocumented immigrants' undeservingness is based on myriad social, political and economic factors (Horton 2004; Yoo 2008; Castañeda 2009, 2010; Goldade and Okuyemi 2011; Larchanché 2012; Marrow 2012; Viladrich 2012; Willen 2012a). In this chapter, I examine how immigration enforcement policies can perpetuate notions of undocumented immigrants as undeserving citizens. Drawing from ethnographic fieldwork in Atlanta, Georgia, I show how immigration statutes and their resultant impacts constitute a process of citizenship-making through instilling fear in undocumented Latinx immigrants (Kline 2017, 2019a). Such efforts reinforce notions of undocumented immigrants as racially 'other' and criminally deviant, and can contribute to internalized notions of undeservingness to rights and entitlements. As I argue, not only do borders move geographically inwards as a result of increasingly localized immigrant policing regimes, but the border can further become embodied and transform into a somatic technology.

Deservingness and Citizenship Theories

Medical anthropologists who study immigration have used the analytic of 'deservingness' to examine undocumented immigrants' experiences of living in societies where they are routinely denied entitlements. As anthropologist Sarah Willen argues, deservingness is a way to morally assert a sense of belonging, and it captures judgements about groups of people that are distinct from legal conceptualizations of rights and entitlements (Willen 2012a, 2012b). In referring to undocumented immigrants as rapists, murderers, sources of drug crime, and by perpetuating a well-worn trope about immigrants 'stealing' jobs, Donald Trump, for example, casts judgements about immigrants not belonging in the United States by using (in part) moral frames about crime. Moreover, as Willen argues, deservingness assessments are always relational and conditional, hinging on a comparison of self to other, and weighing considerations of 'presumed or actual characteristics – intrinsic or extrinsic, mutable or immutable – regardless of the salience of such characteristics to the issue in question' (Willen 2012a: 814). Immigration status is one such characteristic upon which deservingness judgements are made, and as several medical anthropologists have demonstrated, immigration status and deservingness assessments have shaped political discourse and action, particularly regarding undocumented immigrants' deservingness to health services (Chock 1991; Guetzkow 2010; Castañeda 2012; Marrow 2012; Viladrich 2012; Willen 2012a; Yarris and Castañeda 2014). Furthermore, deservingness assessments can result in specific ways of living in the world, such as fearing everyday spaces, living with fear and anxiety, and, in some cases, developing somatic responses to the risk of apprehension (Willen 2007; Kline 2017). For example, as Willen has shown, migrants fearing deportation in Israel may move through public spaces constantly assessing their safety and security, and moving their heads in multiple directions to assess the possibility of police presence (Willen 2007). In addition to changing how undocumented immigrants might navigate public spaces, deservingness assessments often play out in health care institutions (Horton 2004; Goldade 2009; Abadía-Barrero 2016), especially for undocumented immigrants, who are typically ineligible for public entitlement programmes.

In the United States, public perceptions about undocumented immigrants as being undeserving of health and social services stems from conflated notions of racial otherness and criminal deviance (De Genova 2004; Sheikh 2004; Hiemstra 2010). The country has a long history of excluding undocumented immigrants from health and social services based on racial categories (Fairchild 2004), and most recently, political discourse about undocumented immigrants' alleged criminality has served as a way to contribute to justifications for excluding immigrants from a host of social entitlements. Political discourses about immigrants as criminal alien others fit into a broader scheme of ways in which the US criminal justice and legal system has changed over time to govern immigrants through crime – or, as Inda and Dowling explain, to use crime and punishment as a way to control immigrant populations (Inda and Dowling 2013). Governing immigrants through crime is best demonstrated by the proliferation of multiple, overlapping immigration enforcement regimes that comprise state and federal laws and local police activity (Kline 2017). These laws demonstrate ways in which policymakers use policy to construct immigrants as 'undeserving' citizens (Kline 2019b).

Citizenship as analytical construct refers to how populations struggle for political, social or economic recognition and considers sets of rights, entitlements and obligations (Ong 1996; Isin and Turner 2002; Janoski and Gran 2002; Lister 2002; Miller 2002a, 2002b; Heath, Rapp and Taussig 2004; Petryna 2004; Rose and Novas 2005; Ecks 2005; Luibhéid 2005; Holston 2008; Nguyen 2008; Horton 2014). Rather than a synonym for national belonging, citizenship is instead a way to examine power dynamics and forms of resistance to assert demands. For example, in her work on the aftermath of the Chernobyl disaster in Ukraine, anthropologist Adriana Petryna describes biological citizenship as the way in which those affected by the disaster claim group membership in an effort to make demands upon the state, seeking recognition and social welfare programmes in the face of lost employment and diminishing state protections (Petryna 2002, 2004). By employing the body and its harmed status as a way of asserting group membership, Petryna argues that those affected by Chernobyl used their injured status to demand public accountability, compensation, medical care and political power (Petryna 2002: 7). In other words, the injured used their bodies to demand rights and, by extension, they exercised a citizenship claim.

In this chapter, I use citizenship theories to consider power relationships at work, and how they impact undocumented immigrants. Borrowing from Nikolas Rose and Carlos Novas, I discuss immigration policies as 'citizenship projects', or, the way in which 'authorities [think] about (some) individuals as potential citizens [or non-citizens], and the ways they [try] to act upon them' (Rose and Novas 2005: 339). As I have argued elsewhere,[1] considering immigration policies as citizenship projects allows for examining how such policies can contribute to perpetuating notions of undocumented immigrants' 'undeservingness' to health care (Kline 2019b), particularly in a place like Atlanta, Georgia, where overlapping immigration enforcement regimes have embodied consequences.

Immigration Laws in Atlanta

Atlanta is the ninth largest metropolitan area in the United States and is the economic hub for Georgia, a largely rural state, and the US South as a whole. Georgia, like much of the US South, has a large agricultural economy, and Latinx immigration to Georgia had historically been associated with agricultural work (Walcott and Murphy 2006). Immigration to the state's urban centre, Atlanta, rose during the 1970s and 1980s due to growth in the poultry, textile and construction industries (Winders 2005; Yarbrough 2010). Throughout the 1990s, Atlanta experienced significant economic growth driven by the construction, finance, transportation and utility industries (Odem 2008). Furthermore, Mexican immigration to Atlanta, in particular, accelerated before the 1996 Olympics (Bess 2008; Associated Press 2010; Grillo 2010; Olsson 2014), when a construction labour shortage aroused concerns that major construction projects may not be completed in time for the Olympic games. To ensure construction deadlines were met, state officials met with the Mexican Consul to request assistance with bringing labourers from Mexico to work in Atlanta. After the 1996 Olympic games, Latinx immigration to Atlanta continued in order to meet labour demands for Atlanta's housing boom. Between 2000 and 2010, Atlanta's Latinx population grew by more than 100 per cent, and recent estimates suggest that more than 588,000 Hispanic or Latinx identifying people live in the Atlanta area (Pew Research Center 2016). Documentation status is not accounted in official estimates of the Latinx population, but the overall number of undocumented immigrants in Atlanta is estimated to be a quarter of a million people (Passel and Cohn 2017). At the time of the economic downturn and housing bubble burst, a series of strict immigration laws began passing the Georgia legislature, which some legislators explained as a form of economic scapegoating of immigrants for Georgia's failing economy (Kline 2019a). These laws included preventing undocumented immigrants from obtaining a Georgia driver's licence, and banning undocumented students from attending some of the state's colleges and universities. In 2011, Georgia, following states like Arizona, passed the 'Illegal Immigration Reform and Enforcement Act', or House Bill (HB) 87.

In many ways, HB 87 did nothing more than reassert federal laws. Federal statutes prohibit undocumented immigrants from receiving publicly funded benefits, and HB 87 restating such prohibitions sent a symbolic message to immigrants that they were still unwelcome (see, for example, Calavita 1996). In addition to restating existing forms of social and health service exclusions, HB 87 further required immigrants to carry proof of their legal status at all times, and authorized local law enforcement to request proof of legal status from anyone suspected of being undocumented. When HB 87 passed, it also criminalized any form of assistance to undocumented immigrants, including transporting an undocumented person in a personal vehicle or providing any kind of non-emergency health service using public funds. For example, if undocumented patients reported to a state-funded medical centre, such as Grady Memorial Hospital, and sought care for a condition that was not life-threatening, the law made it a crime for a health provider to treat the patient. Although a federal court overruled the specific provisions about *assisting* undocumented immigrants, the rest of the law remained intact, including officers' authority to request proof of immigration status from anyone suspected of being undocumented. Despite being overturned by the court, the passage of such a draconian law signalled attempts to control undocumented immigrants, so much so that the law extended beyond immigrants to encompass all persons who could potentially assist undocumented immigrants, including health providers.

Compounding problems created by state laws like HB 87 are two federal statutes: Secure Communities and Section 287(g) of the Immigration and Nationality Act. Secure Communities is a federal fingerprint-matching programme that automatically sends an arrestee's fingerprints to national databases to assess their immigration status. If no authorized status is found, the Immigration and Customs Enforcement (ICE) agency may detain the person, and ultimately start the deportation process. The Obama administration eventually ended the Secure Communities programme, but Donald

Trump, almost immediately after taking office, reinstated it. Similarly, the 287(g) programme also serves to police immigrant populations: through 287(g), local law enforcement enter agreements with ICE and are given the authority to enforce federal immigration laws. These two federal laws, and HB 87, point to a localized form of immigration enforcement that often takes the form of roadblocks or checkpoints where police officers stop motorists and ask for their driver's licences.

Roadblocks and checkpoints are routinely organized outside of predominately Latinx apartment complexes and neighbourhoods. Although the checkpoints are ostensibly safety checks where police attempt to control driving under the influence of alcohol and ensure compliance with safety belt laws, undocumented immigrants I met in Atlanta reported that police would only stop vehicles with Latinx-looking drivers as they approached checkpoints. Georgia's driver's licence laws, HB 87, Secure Communities, 287(g), and local police practices all demonstrate how a routine traffic stop can potentially result in the deportation process for undocumented immigrants. Accordingly, many undocumented Latinx immigrants I met in Atlanta following HB 87's passage, reported a fear of encountering police (Kline 2017), leading them to avoid driving and leaving their homes, even in situations of medical need.

Methodology

To examine the impacts of immigrant policing in Atlanta, I spent one year working closely with an immigrant rights organization, the Georgia Latinx Alliance for Human Rights (GLAHR). GLAHR works to assert immigrants' rights to social services and deservingness to all sets of rights and entitlements enjoyed by US citizens. In addition to aligning myself with GLAHR and participating in all GLAHR events during my time in the field, I also conducted semi-structured interviews with undocumented immigrants connected to GLAHR. Interviewees had lived in Atlanta for varying amounts of time: some interviewees grew up in Atlanta, having moved there with their parents when they were children. Others had been in Atlanta multiple decades, and others had lived in the area for close to five years. They worked in the construction industry, cleaned rooms in the high-rise hotels that played prominent roles in the city, served food at a variety of restaurants, staffed small businesses, and were overall a part of the economic fabric of one of the nation's largest economies. In addition to interviewing immigrants, I also interviewed health providers who see undocumented immigrant patients, staff from health-related non-governmental organizations, non-clinical hospital staff, state agency workers, state legislators, and non-health-related activist organization leaders. Further, I logged hundreds of hours of participant observation experiences at GLAHR, inside the Georgia Capitol, at hospitals, and at other sites where I began to trace the impacts of immigrant policing.

As part of the ethnography on policing, I adopted activist methodologies where a researcher makes a political commitment and develops relationships of reciprocity and mutual accountability (Pulido 2008). As Shannon Speed argues, activist anthropology puts researchers and participants in dialogue with each other to work towards a shared political goal (Speed 2008: 71). In adopting an activist methodology, I worked with GLAHR to advance local immigrant rights efforts, and I routinely assisted GLAHR with organizing marches, rallies and draft press releases about immigration-related issues. My activist methodology afforded me access to GLAHR members, collectively called *GLAHRiadores*, a reference to the Spanish word for 'gladiators', and allowed me to participate first-hand in Georgia's immigrant rights movement. Through this participation, I ultimately examined how immigration enforcement regimes reinforce undocumented immigrants' undeservingness to health services and can result in embodied forms of governance.

Fear, Trauma and Health

As I have described elsewhere (Kline 2017, 2019a), immigrant policing efforts in Atlanta operate through fear, and force immigrant families to make strategic decisions about their potential exposure to police in order to reduce their risk of being deported. Limiting police exposure can inform some immigrants' health behaviours and willingness to seek health services. For example, one woman, Marisa,[2] reflected on how she avoided seeking care and explained that feeling sick, such having symptoms of a cold or even influenza, was not a sufficient reason to leave her home: 'It's just not safe to drive, not even if I'm sick. What would I do if they stopped me? Who would take care of my children?' She and another participant, Ariana, also explained the toll that this fear took on them. As Ariana explained, 'I feel traumatized. All these laws make me feel like I have post-traumatic stress or something. That's what it feels like – trauma. Every day I leave the house but I'm not sure I'll return. It's horrible to live with this constant fear'. Post-traumatic stress disorder (PTSD) is a mental and emotional condition that can occur after a severe injury or shock. Symptoms can include flashbacks to traumatic events, difficulty sleeping, nightmares, and social withdrawal (Breslau 2004). Although PTSD problematically advances a Western biomedical understanding of socially driven phenomena (Breslau 2004; Kienzler 2008), for the immigrants I met in Atlanta, the term summarized how immigrant policing was resulting in physiological and emotional distress.

Like Ariana, other immigrants explained that they felt an acute sense of fear and trauma living in Atlanta, and compared those feelings to their home country: 'I feel like I live in a war zone', one participant said. 'It's never safe and you have to always be on the lookout. In Mexico, you run the risk of getting kidnapped or killed; here, you run the risk of getting stopped and deported. I'm not safe here, and I'm not safe there – there's nowhere safe for me'. Feelings of fear and trauma linked to immigration enforcement policies ultimately shaped how some undocumented immigrants decided to seek health services. As one interviewee explained to me: 'Atlanta's not like Chicago or New York, you have to take a car to get everywhere... We won't leave the house unless it's to go to work, even if someone's sick and needs medicine – we just won't risk it because there might be police'.

In addition to impacting undocumented immigrants' willingness to seek health services, immigration laws and police practices in Atlanta also altered some undocumented immigrants' health behaviours, such as engaging in daily exercise (Kline 2018). One woman I interviewed explained that increased police presence in her neighbourhood discouraged her from taking daily walks for exercise:[3] 'I have arthritis and I'm trying to stay healthy,' she explained, 'so I try to go for walks every day. If the police start following me around all the time, I won't be able to go out anymore. How will I exercise?' Fearing police apprehension, this woman ultimately ceased her daily exercise routine. Accounts of immigrants changing their health-related behaviours and feeling as if they have post-traumatic stress underscore the embodied consequences of immigration enforcement. The threat of deportation results in internalized anxieties and changed behaviours, and may ultimately lead to internalized feelings of undeservingness to social services.

Living in a 'Borrowed Country'

During interviews with immigrants, I often discussed racism and xenophobia as policy contexts informing immigrant-policing initiatives. In one conversation, however, the interviewee, Renata, rationalized harsh US immigration policies by claiming a sense of "not belonging here." I met her through a GLAHRiador, who mentioned that Renata would be willing to speak to me about immigration enforcement but that she would not leave her house because her husband had been arrested and she feared that she too might be apprehended by police. Renata had moved to Atlanta in 2000 from Mexico City. She was born in Guatemala, and she moved to Mexico and then the United States, hoping to earn a living wage. When we met, her husband was being detained and had received a deportation order, and so she worried about how she would care for her three children on her own. With assistance from her church, Renata was able to continue supporting her children and paying her rent, but she was unsure of how long she could sustain this way of living. Further, she explained that in some ways she felt she lived in someone else's country, or a *país ajeno*: 'I understand why the police are around all the time and why we can't get Medicaid or health insurance; we're living in a country that doesn't belong to us; this isn't our country'. This particular sentiment, though not one that occurred frequently in interviews, underscored how immigration enforcement policies can result in embodied forms of undeservingness.

Alarmingly, such sentiments dismiss the many ways in which immigrants like Renata establish firm roots in the United States, and make myriad meaningful social and economic contributions. While fear may be an embodied and emotive response to immigrant policing, feeling that a country 'does not belong to you' underscores how immigrant policing regimes assert undocumented immigrants' undeservingness to social services, and how being framed as an undeserving citizen can shape immigrants' perspectives. Ironically, undocumented immigrants make significant contributions to the public social service programmes they are excluded from, as anthropologist Sarah Horton has shown (Horton 2016). Employers are prohibited from hiring undocumented labourers, but some undocumented immigrants will borrow authorized employee's papers to gain employment, and as Horton argues, some employers may actively encourage such a practice to maximize the amount of contributions made to the personal social security accounts – the US's federal retirement programme. By borrowing an authorized employee's papers to gain employment, some undocumented immigrants thus directly benefit others by paying into a fund they never draw from. Instead, the person whose papers they borrow will receive a financial benefit by having someone else's wages contributing to their own social security account.

Health providers also commented on notions of undeservingness stemming from immigration enforcement laws. One provider, Sharon, explained that some US citizens viewed undocumented immigrants as undeserving of any form of health care, as other anthropologists have shown, and she saw this directly play out in her work. Sharon is a nurse who works in the state's genetic testing facility. She screens newborn children's blood for a variety of diseases, and often contacts hospital officials to coordinate the tests. In her work, she has encountered hostility towards immigrants from hospital officials across the state. When we met and talked about the numerous health-related impacts of immigrant policing efforts, she expressed shock that hospital officials would balk at important testing needed to determine potentially fatal but easily treatable conditions for children they assumed to be undocumented. Sharon noted that some US citizens conflate Latinx identity with 'illegality', and that hospital employees with whom she communicates are sometimes guilty of this type of conflation: 'There is an automatic assumption that these folks are "illegal". I think there is this notion that we don't have to give them the same care'.

Sharon described an example of when she encountered this type of rationale from an employee at a hospital in rural Georgia, near some of the state's large agricultural fields where undocumented migrant farmworkers provide cheap labour: 'I had to give a kid a blood draw across the state for what could be a lethal disorder but very treatable, it's called MCAD, and it's the kind of disorder where mostly the central treatment is avoiding fasting'. MCAD, or 'Medium-chain acyl-CoA dehydrogenase deficiency', is a disease where the body cannot break down fats properly, and it can result in sudden death. The fatal outcome can be avoided, however, if individuals with MCAD avoid fasting, making it an important condition to screen for and notify patients about. 'So this kid had very concerning results,' Sharon continued, 'and the paediatrician is on the phone with me saying, "I'm trying to get this kid tested and everyone is refusing him", and I'm like "okay, let me see what I can do for you", but everyone is telling me no'. Frustrated with the challenges the paediatrician experienced, Sharon took things into her own hands. 'So I call the birth hospital and say you ultimately "own" [responsibility for] this child to some extent, so just draw some blood on this kid'.

The staff member at the hospital where the child was born did not find her argument persuasive, however. '[The hospital staff then said] "Well this family is Spanish-speaking, I'm sure they are illegal, I'm sure they don't have insurance, so who is going to pay for this?" And I'm like "this is a $150 test"'.

The hospital official Sharon spoke with refused to treat a patient because they felt the patients' family would not pay and so was not willing to shoulder the $150 cost of the test because of assumptions about the family's immigration status. 'There are 500 things wrong with that statement', Sharon said. 'But let's come down to money if that's what's important to you. It's a $150 test, so what seems better to you? Maybe you are out $150 or this kid *dies*'. The cost of life and death were so striking to Sharon that she eventually found a way to pay for the test. 'So ultimately I had to say, if you send it to [my facility's] genetics lab, I can make sure it is paid for out of newborn screening funds.' Sharon's office has a small fund to cover tests for children whose parents do not have insurance coverage so that the office can cover emergency testing. Despite Sharon's assumption of the cost of the test, the hospital staff person remained dissatisfied. '[They said to me], "Well who is going to pay to get there?" And I said, "Here is our FedEx number [Sharon growled, retelling the conversation], put it on this [shipping] account". And the child was born here. And I said, "This child was born into a hospital here, so he is an American citizen and I bet he qualifies for Medicaid"'. In the United States, children's health insurance is typically covered through private plans obtained from their parents' employers or through Medicaid. Only US citizens and lawful permanent residents meeting specific residency requirements are eligible for Medicaid, but all children born in the country are granted US citizenship, thus making newborns eligible for Medicaid. The rural hospital staff member could probably have found a way to pay for the newborn's test if she had made the effort to enrol the child in Medicaid. Instead, the hospital official required Sharon to pay for the test, and for the postage to send the blood to her office, for a test that would determine whether the child had a life-threatening disease.

There is no way to determine the citizenship status of the child Sharon advocated for, but as other medical anthropologists have shown, even if they qualify for Medicaid, children of undocumented parents may not receive care because of confusion about their eligibility, fear of being reported to immigration officials, or – as this exprerience showed – racism from medical officials (Baumeister and Hearst 1999; Ku and Matani 2001; Kullgren 2003; Huang, Stella and

Ledsky 2006; Castañeda and Melo 2014). Clinical racism, like the type Sharon described, is a way of articulating some immigrants' undeservingness to social services because of their immigration status. Conflated notions of 'illegality', criminality and deservingness result in providers like the one Sharon described freely discriminating against some immigrant patients because they assume their reasons for migration are rooted in individual choice and an assumption to 'want' to break the law (Yarris and Castañeda 2014). Medical providers, however, may be able to resist these types of discourses of 'choice' that perpetuate notions of undeservingness to health services.

For example, one provider, a Dr Taylor,[4] explained that the patients he treats, regardless of their immigration status, did not 'choose' to be sick: 'For example, a mother with a little baby who's six months old, and he has a 103°F degree fever and she doesn't want to go to the doctor, but she decides that she'll come and see me because her baby has a 103-degree fever and she appears at my doorstep. Well that little child doesn't have any control over his situation. He didn't ask to be where he is right now, he didn't ask to be sick'. Accordingly, Dr Taylor explained that he would treat patients regardless of citizenship status because it was the morally and ethically responsible action. While Dr Taylor does not challenge the broader discourse of individual responsibility that is informed by neoliberal economic ideals and shapes the market-based medical care system in the United States, his perspective is nevertheless able to challenge the assumptions of criminality and deviance that shape the perspectives of some officials, like those that Sharon communicated with.

Embodied Sentiments and a Call to Action

Following Rose and Novas's understanding of 'citizenship projects' as ways in which policymakers think about and act upon certain populations, immigrant policing regimes underscore how policymakers design initiatives to complicate immigrants' daily lives in order to encourage them to 'self-deport'. Findings from this chapter show how citizen projects can be internalized and can perpetuate anti-immigrant sentiments. Renata's assertion that 'we live in a borrowed country' underscores how harsh immigrant policing efforts can result in some undocumented immigrants internalizing sentiments of not belonging and being undeserving of social services. Similarly, immigrant-policing regimes reinforce racist views about immigrants as criminal others, as the situation Sharon described indicates. Health providers may be able to counter rhetoric that suggests immigrants are inherently criminally deviant because of how they chose to enter the United States, as Dr Taylor's comments suggest, but in the aggregate, findings reported here underscore the need for US immigration policy change. Comprehensive immigration reform, access to driver's licences, and ending immigrant-policing regimes that promote racial profiling are among the first policy changes needed. Such changes would face large political obstacles, however, as demonstrated by elected officials like Donald Trump perpetuating political rhetoric that reinforces racist and xenophobic views about immigrants that directly inform ideas about them being underserving to social services.

Anthropologist Anahi Viladrich (2012) has demonstrated how some policies may lead to internalized feelings of undeservingness among undocumented immigrants, and findings in this chapter also point to how immigration enforcement efforts continue to promote internalized undeservingness. Operating primarily through producing fear, immigration enforcement regimes can be understood as citizenship projects that shape undocumented immigrants' health-related experiences. Stories of undocumented immigrants being fearful to seek health care services or leave their homes at certain times of the day demonstrate how immigration enforcement policies may ultimately create embodied feelings of undeservingness.

Immigration policies that serve as citizen projects demand specific kinds of resistance techniques. These efforts can include ongoing political mobilization to assert rights and entitlements, and organizations like GLAHR are currently engaging in such actions. These efforts include 'know your rights' campaigns, popular education events, impact litigation, and other techniques designed to combat immigrant policing and to assert immigrants' rights. Overall, GLAHR and other similar immigrant rights organizations aim to achieve a pathway to citizenship for all undocumented immigrants in the United States, and a more stable way of life that would include access to institutions of higher education and living without constant fear of deportation. Additionally, resistance efforts may require not only challenges to immigration enforcement laws, but may also need to engage in efforts to reverse the consequences of persistent feelings of fear and trauma that may have resulted in embodied understandings of undeservingness to social services.

To reverse internalized notions of undeservingness, immigrant rights advocates, organizations and researchers can actively assert undocumented immigrants' deservingness of social entitlements based on broad notions of human rights. Doing so may avoid perpetuating problematic forms of making deservingness assessments contingent upon factors such as having US-born children or engaging in certain types of labour, which can reproduce heteronormative or economically contingent forms of expressing social belonging.

Nolan Kline is an assistant professor of anthropology and the co-coordinator of the global health programme at Rollins College in Florida. His primary research areas include immigrant policing, Latinx im/migrant health, and health policy. Much of his research is informed by theories of biopolitics, citizenship, critical race theory, and the political economy of health. His book, *Pathogenic Policing: Immigration Enforcement and Health in the US South*, was published in 2019 and traces the health-related consequences of immigration legislation and police practices in Atlanta, Georgia. As an applied, medical anthropologist, his work intersects with public health, policy and activism.

Notes

1. This chapter draws on findings that are reported elsewhere. Specifically, parts of this chapter focus on deservingness projects and citizenship projects that have appeared in Kline 2019b. Similarly, I have discussed fear, trauma, and immigration regimes in Kline 2017 and Kline 2019a.
2. All names are pseudonyms to protect individuals' identities. Experiences from Marisa and Ariana appear in Kline 2017, 2018 and 2019a.
3. This participant's experiences also appeared in Kline 2017, 2018 and 2019a.
4. Dr Taylor's experiences appear in Kline 2019a.

References

Abadía-Barrero, C.E. 2016. 'Neoliberal Justice and the Transformation of the Moral: The Privatization of the Right to Health Care in Colombia'. *Medical Anthropology Quarterly* 30(1): 62–79.

Associated Press. 2010. 'Southeast Sees Big Influx of Illegal Immigrants'. *NBC News*.

Bauer, H.M., et al. 2010. 'Barriers to Health Care for Abused Latina and Asian Immigrant Women'. *Journal of Health Care for the Poor and Underserved* 11(1): 33–44.

Baumeister, L., and N. Hearst. 1999. 'Why Children's Health is Threatened by Federal Immigration Policies'. *Western Journal of Medicine* 171: 58–61.

Berk, M.L., et al. 2000. 'Health Care Use among Undocumented Latino Immigrants: Is Free Health Care the Main Reason Why Latinos Come to the United States? A Unique Look at the Facts'. *Health Affairs* 19(4): 51–64.

Bess, M.K. 2008. 'Across Imagined Boundaries: Understanding Mexican Migration to Georgia in a Transnational and Historical Context'. MA thesis, Georgia Southern University.

Breslau, J. 2004. 'Cultures of Trauma: Anthropological Views of Posttraumatic Stress Disorder in International Health'. *Culture, Medicine, and Psychiatry* 28(2): 113–26.

Calavita, K. 1996. 'The New Politics of Immigration: Balanced-Budget Conservatism and the Symbolism of Proposition 187'. *Social Problems* 43: 284.

Carrasco-Garrido, P., et al. 2007. 'Health Profiles, Lifestyles and Use of Health Resources by the Immigrant Population Resident in Spain'. *The European Journal of Public Health* 17(5): 503.

Castañeda, H. 2009. 'Illegality as Risk Factor: A Survey of Unauthorized Migrant Patients in a Berlin Clinic'. *Social Science & Medicine* 68(8): 1552–60.

———. 2010. 'Im/migration and Health: Conceptual, Methodological, and Theoretical Propositions for Applied Anthropology'. *NAPA Bulletin* 34(1): 6–27.

———. 2012. 'Over-Foreignization, or Unused Potential? A Critical Review of Migrant Health in Germany and Responses toward Unauthorized Migration'. *Social Science & Medicine* 74: 830–38.

Castañeda, H., and M.A. Melo. 2014. 'Health Care Access for Latino Mixed-Status Families: Barriers, Strategies, and Implications for Reform'. *American Behavioral Scientist* 58(14): 1891–1909.

Chock, P.P. 1991. 'Illegal Aliens and Opportunity: Myth-Making in Congressional Testimony'. *American Ethnologist* 18(2): 279–94.

Coleman, M. 2012. 'The Local Migration State: The Site-Specific Devolution of Immigration Enforcement in the US South'. *Law & Policy* 34(2): 159–90.

De Genova, N. 2004. 'The Legal Production of Mexican/Migrant Illegality'. *Latino Studies* 2(2): 160–85.

Derose, K.P., J.J. Escarce and N. Lurie. 2007. 'Immigrants and Health Care: Sources of Vulnerability'. *Health Affairs* 26(5): 1258–68.

Ecks, D.S. 2005. 'Pharmaceutical Citizenship: Antidepressant Marketing and the Promise of Demarginalization in India'. *Anthropology & Medicine* 12(3): 239–54.

Fairchild, A.L. 2004. 'Policies of Inclusion: Immigrants, Disease, Dependency, and American Immigration Policy at the Dawn and Dusk of the 20th Century'. *American Journal of Public Health* 94(4): 528–39.

Galarneau, C. 2011. 'Still Missing: Undocumented Immigrants in Health Care Reform'. *Journal of Health Care for the Poor and Underserved* 22(2): 422–28.

Goldade, K. 2009. 'Health Is Hard Here' or 'Health for All?'. *Medical Anthropology Quarterly* 23(4): 483–503.
Goldade, K., and K.S. Okuyemi. 2011. 'Deservingness to State Health Services for South–South Migrants: A Preliminary Study of Costa Rican Providers' Views'. *Social Science & Medicine* 74(6): 882–86.
Goldman, D.P., J.P. Smith and N. Sood. 2005. 'Legal Status and Health Insurance among Immigrants'. *Health Affairs* 24(6): 1640.
———. 2006. 'Immigrants and the Cost of Medical Care'. *Health Affairs* 25(6): 1700.
Gordon, I., and T. Raja. 2012. '164 Anti-Immigration Laws Passed Since 2010? A MoJo Analysis', *Mother Jones, Politics*, March/April Issue. Retrieved on 11 June 2020 from https://www.motherjones.com/politics/2012/03/anti-immigration-law-database/.
Grillo, J. 2010. 'The Immigration Dilemma', *Georgia Trend*, December. Retrieved on 11 June 2020 from https://www.georgiatrend.com/2010/12/01/the-immigration-dilemma/.
Guetzkow, J. 2010. 'Beyond Deservingness: Congressional Discourse on Poverty, 1964–1996'. *The Annals of the American Academy of Political and Social Science* 629(1): 173–97.
Heath, D., R. Rapp and K.S. Taussig. 2004. 'Genetic Citizenship', in D. Nugent and J. Vincent (eds), *A Companion to the Anthropology of Politics*. Malden, MA: Blackwell, pp. 152–67.
Hiemstra, N. 2010. 'Immigrant "Illegality" as Neoliberal Governmentality in Leadville, Colorado'. *Antipode* 42(1): 74–102.
Holston, J. 2008. *Insurgent Citizenship: Disjunctions of Democracy and Modernity in Brazil*. Princeton, NJ: Princeton University Press.
Horton, S. 2004. 'Different Subjects: The Health Care System's Participation in the Differential Construction of the Cultural Citizenship of Cuban Refugees and Mexican Immigrants'. *Medical Anthropology Quarterly* 18(4): 472–89.
———. 2014. 'Debating Medical Citizenship: Policies Shaping Undocumented Immigrants' Learned Avoidance of the U.S. Health Care System', in L.A. Lorentzen, *Hidden Lives and Human Rights in the United States: Understanding Tragedies of Undocumented Immigration*. Oxford: Praeger, pp. 297–320.
———. 2016. *They Leave Their Kidneys in the Fields: Illness, Injury, and Illegality among US Farmworkers*. Los Angeles: University of California Press.
Huang, Z.J., M.Y. Stella and R. Ledsky. 2006. 'Health Status and Health Service Access and Use among Children in US Immigrant Families'. *Journal Information* 96(4): 634–40.
Inda, J.X., and J.A. Dowling. 2013. 'Introduction: Governing Migrant Illegality', in J.X. Inda and J.A. Dowling (eds), *Governing Immigration through Crime: A Reader*. Stanford, CA: Stanford University Press, pp. 1–34.

Isin, E.F., and B.S. Turner. 2002. 'Citizenship Studies: An Introduction', in E.F. Isin and B.S. Turner (eds), *Handbook of Citizenship Studies*. London: Sage, pp. 1–10.

Janoski, T., and B. Gran. 2002. 'Political Citizenship: Foundations of Rights', in E.F. Isin and B.S. Turner (eds), *Handbook of Citizenship Studies*. London: Sage, pp. 13–50.

Kienzler, H. 2008. 'Debating War-Trauma and Post-Traumatic Stress Disorder (PTSD) in an Interdisciplinary Arena'. *Social Science & Medicine* 67(2): 218–27.

Kline, N. 2017. 'Pathogenic Policy: Immigrant Policing, Fear, and Parallel Medical Systems in the US South'. *Medical Anthropology* 36(4): 396–410.

———. 2018. '"It's Too Risky to Leave the House": Immigrant Policing and Health-Related Mobility', in Cecilia Vindrola, Anne Pfister and Ginger Johnson (eds), *Healthcare in Motion: Immobilities in Health Service Delivery and Access*. New York: Berghahn Books, pp. 35–52.

———. 2019a. *Pathogenic Policing: Immigration Enforcement and Health in the US South*. New Brunswick, NJ: Rutgers University Press.

———. 2019b. 'When Deservingness Policies Converge: US Immigration Enforcement, Health Reform and Patient Dumping'. *Anthropology & Medicine* 26(3): 280–95.

Ku, L., and S. Matani. 2001. 'Left Out: Immigrants' Access to Health Care and Insurance'. *Health Affairs* 20(1): 247–56.

Kullgren, J.T. 2003. 'Restrictions on Undocumented Immigrants' Access to Health Services: The Public Health Implications of Welfare Reform'. *American Journal of Public Health* 93(10): 1630–33.

Larchanché, S. 2012. 'Intangible Obstacles: Health Implications of Stigmatization, Structural Violence, and Fear among Undocumented Immigrants in France'. *Social Science & Medicine* 74(6): 858–63.

Lister, R. 2002. 'Sexual Citizenship', in E.F. Isin and B.S. Turner (eds), *Handbook of Citizenship Studies*. London: Sage, pp. 191–208.

Luibhéid, E. 2005. *Queer Migrations: Sexuality, US Citizenship, and Border Crossings*. Minneapolis: University Of Minnesota Press.

Marrow, H.B. 2012. 'Deserving to a Point: Unauthorized Immigrants in San Francisco's Universal Access Healthcare Model'. *Social Science & Medicine* 74(6): 846–54.

Menjívar, C. 2014. 'The "Poli-Migra" Multilayered Legislation, Enforcement Practices, and Can We Learn About and From Today's Approaches'. *American Behavioral Scientist* 58(13): 1–15.

Miller, T.A. 2002a. 'Citizenship and Severity: Recent Immigration Reforms and the New Penology'. *Georgetown Immigration Law Journal* 17: 611–66.

———. 2002b. 'Cultural Citizenship', in E.F. Isin and B.S. Turner (eds), *Handbook of Citizenship Studies*. London: Sage, pp. 231–43.

Nguyen, V.K. 2008. 'Antiretroviral Globalism, Biopolitics, and Therapeutic Citizenship', in A. Ong and S.J. Collier (eds), *Global Assemblages:*

Technology, Politics, and Ethics as Anthropological Problems. Oxford: Blackwell, pp. 124–44.
Odem, M. 2008. 'Unsettled in the Suburbs: Latino Immigration and Ethnic Diversity in Metro Atlanta', in S.W. Hardwick, A. Singer and C.B. Brettell (eds), *Twenty-First Century Gateways: Immigrant Incorporation in Suburban America*. Washington, DC: Brookings Institution Press, pp. 105–36.
Olsson, T.C. 2014. 'Latino Immigration', in *New Georgia Encyclopedia*. Retrieved 1 February 2017 from https://www.georgiaencyclopedia.org/articles/history-archaeology/latino-immigration.
Ong, A. 1996. 'Cultural Citizenship as Subject-Making: Immigrants Negotiate Racial and Cultural Boundaries in the United States'. *Current Anthropology* 37(5): 737–62.
Passel, J.S., and D.V. Cohn. 2017. '20 Metro Areas are Home to Six-in-Ten Unauthorized Immigrants in US'. Pew Research Center. Retrieved 1 February 2017 from http://www.pewresearch.org/fact-tank/2017/02/09/us-metro-areas-unauthorized-immigrants/.
Petryna, A. 2002. *Life Exposed: Biological Citizens after Chernobyl*. Princeton, NJ: Princeton University Press.
———. 2004a. 'Biological Citizenship: The Science and Politics of Chernobyl-Exposed Populations'. *Osiris* 19: 250–65.
Pew Research Center. 2016. 'Hispanic Population and Origin in Select U.S. Metropolitan Areas, 2014'. Retrieved 1 February 2017 from http://www.pewhispanic.org/interactives/hispanic-population-in-select-u-s-metropolitan-areas/.
Pulido, L. 2008. 'FAQs: Frequently (Un)Asked Questions about Being a Scholar Activist', in C.R. Hale (ed.), *Engaging Contradictions: Theory, Politics, and Methods of Activist Scholarship*. Berkeley: University of California Press, pp. 341–65.
Rose, N., and C. Novas. 2005. 'Biological Citizenship', in S.J. Collier and A. Ong (eds), *Global Assemblages: Technology, Politics and Ethics as Anthropological Problems*. Oxford: Blackwell Publishing, pp. 439–63.
Sheikh, I. 2004. 'Racializing, Criminalizing, and Silencing 9/11', in D.C. Brotherton and P. Kretsedemas (eds), *Keeping Out the Other: A Critical Introduction to Immigraiton Enforcement Today*. New York: Columbia University Press, pp. 9–16.
Speed, S. 2008. 'Forged in Dialogue: Toward a Critically Engaged Activist Research', in C.R. Hale (ed.), *Engaging Contradictions: Theory, Politics, and Methods of Activist Scholarship*. Berkeley: University of California Press, pp. 213–36.
Stuesse, A., and M. Coleman. 2014. 'Automobility, Immobility, Altermobility: Surviving and Resisting the Intensification of Immigrant Policing'. *City & Society* 26(1): 105–26.
Viladrich, A. 2012. 'Beyond Welfare Reform: Reframing Undocumented Immigrants' Entitlement to Health Care in the United States. A Critical Review'. *Social Science & Medicine* 74(6): 822–29.

Walcott, S.M., and A. Murphy. 2006. 'Latino Communities in Atlanta: Segmented Assimilation under Construction', in H.A. Smith and O.J. Furuseth (eds), *Latinos in the New South: Transformation of Place.* London: Routledge, pp. 153–66.

Willen, S.S. 2007. 'Toward a Critical Phenomenology of "Illegality": State Power, Criminalization, and Objectivity among Undocumented Migrant Workers in Tel Aviv, Israel'. *International Migration* 45(3): 8–38.

———. 2012a. 'How is Health-Related "Deservingness" Reckoned? Perspectives from Unauthorized Im/migrants in Tel Aviv'. *Social Science & Medicine* 74(6): 812–21.

———. 2012b. 'Migration, "Illegality", and Health: Mapping Embodied Vulnerability and Debating Health-Related Deservingness'. *Social Science & Medicine* 74(6): 805–11.

Winders, J. 2005. 'Changing Politics of Race and Region: Latino Migration to the US South'. *Progress in Human Geography* 29(6): 683–99.

Yarbrough, R.A. 2010. 'Becoming "Hispanic" in the "New South": Central American Immigrants' Racialization Experiences in Atlanta, GA, USA'. *GeoJournal* 75(3): 249–60.

Yarris, K., and H. Castañeda. 2014. 'Special Issue Discourses of Displacement and Deservingness: Interrogating Distinctions between "Economic" and "Forced" Migration'. *International Migration* 53(3): 644–69.

Yoo, G.J. 2008. 'Immigrants and Welfare: Policy Constructions of Deservingness'. *Journal of Immigrant & Refugee Studies* 6(4): 490–507.

3

Structural Violence, Tuberculosis and Health-Care Processes

Bolivian Immigrants in Buenos Aires and São Paulo

Alejandro Goldberg, Cássio Silveira, Tatiane Barbosa and Denise Martin

Introduction

This chapter presents some results of a comparative ethnographic study conducted during 2015–16 in Buenos Aires (Argentina) and São Paulo (Brazil). The research proposed a regional comparative perspective focusing on adult Bolivian immigrants of both sexes who work and/or reside, often with their families, in clothes sweatshops in the centre of São Paulo and in south-west Buenos Aires. Our investigation also studied the public health centres that were located close to the sweatshops in each city.

This multi-sited ethnography took place in the work–home environment, in the health services, and among immigrant organizations and groups. The fieldwork combined participant observation, in-depth interviews and the analysis of narratives. The methodology applied to our research made it possible to find out and describe certain health issues related to specific risk situations found in the lives, work and accommodation of these immigrants during their integration process after arrival at their destination, and detect why and in what context these situations arise. The analysis focuses on the sphere of public health in both cities. We explored ways in which these immigrants experience their illness and how they describe, interpret and explain it, and act in relation to it, tracking the analysis in their therapeutic itineraries.

The central aim of this chapter is to describe the contexts of social vulnerability (Grimberg 2008; Goldberg 2014) of Bolivian immigrants in Buenos Aires and São Paulo in terms of their lives, work and accommodation, identifying the main associated illnesses and focal points of social suffering, with an emphasis on tuberculosis (TB), as well as health-care access in relation to these aspects.

Structural violence is defined as violence caused by the economic and social structure that generates violent and discriminatory social inequalities (Fassin 2007). In the words of Philippe Bourgois, the concept is referred to as 'the economic and political organization of society that imposes conditions of physical and/or emotional suffering, from high levels of morbidity and mortality to poverty and abusive, precarious work conditions' (Bourgois 2010: 12–13). In the field of health, we have reviewed a number of medical anthropological studies that apply the concept to different case studies of infectious diseases, including TB (Farmer 2001, 2004a; Jung Ho 2004; Alsan et al. 2011), the same with the categories of social suffering (Das et al. 2001) and trauma (Fassin and Rechtman 2009). The proposed focus includes the analysis of different forms of violence, experiences of suffering, and the social, political and economic inequalities that characterize the societies of our study. In fact, some of the Bolivian immigrants we met were recruited in Bolivia through local agents in an organized network of human traffickers (Goldberg 2014, 2016).

When the immigrants reach their destinations, they are subjected to labour exploitation under servitude conditions – in many cases similar to slavery conditions – in textile sweatshops that frequently make clothes for major brand export companies. The immigrants' lack of documents and the fact that they are seldom allowed to leave the sweatshop are a violation of their right to health care, as well as all other rights. Taking into consideration an analysis of health inequalities, we focused on diseases suffered by this group of immigrants that are linked to their working and living conditions in Buenos Aires and São Paulo, where there is a growing incidence of TB.

The general working hypothesis for our research was that the increased incidence of TB among Bolivian immigrants in Buenos Aires and São Paulo mainly arose as a complex result of migratory processes. These processes are associated with the local and international requirements of the textile industry in the current phase of neoliberal capitalist globalization, which leads to precarious ways of life, work and accommodation in a context of social vulnerability and situations that put the health of these immigrant workers at risk.

Comparative social science case studies in the problematic field of migratory processes and health are very important but scarce (Goldberg, Martin and Silveira 2015.) They should offer a phenomenological perspective of the approach to the disease, understood as an experience that 'affects a body in the world' (Good 2003: 245), that occurs at a certain time in history, society, politics and geography, in a life experience context and in a specific social world. Using the theoretical and methodological tools provided by medical anthropology, by means of a dialectic relational approach coordinating micro–macro analyses, it is thus feasible to accept the existence of an environment that causes disease, in which specific illnesses such as TB develop, including the leading role played by ideological, political and sociocultural factors in that environment. These factors range from different types of violence – overwork, overcrowding and deficient nutrition – to the difficulties that immigrant workers in sweatshops face in accessing health care.

The structural violence exerted by capitalism coercively penetrates the lives of people in certain subordinate social groups. This violence includes the highly precarious working and living conditions in textile factories, and different types of limitations to accessing the health system to treat TB and other illnesses. The situation of violence makes the population more vulnerable, limiting their view of their world and their capacity for action. Under this perspective, suffering becomes a political matter that emerges from an unequal relationship between the person and the social order, appearing through the ways in which that unease penetrates the individual experience and is expressed through bodily paradigms (Quaranta 2006.) The capitalist system has a specific way of 'sickening bodies' through marks that are expressed in them, embodied (Csordas 1994) as a manifestation of labour deterioration and exhaustion caused by certain social relations. The body is at once a social product and the product of those relations (Taussig 1992), just as suffering is the sociocultural form of pain, and as such, it is distributed differentially depending on the social class, imposing the representation that subordinate sectors of society are accustomed to tolerating it (Otegui Pascual 2009.) This is reflected in the approach to our comparative study case, in which the differential sharing out of suffering hides behind a certain stereotyping through which 'specific collectives, in correlation with the place they occupy in structural and macrosocial processes, are exposed in a significantly unequal way to processes of morbidity and mortality, and to facing facts of suffering' (ibid.: 152) such as suffering from TB. Consequently, we should note that the complex nature of the socio-sanitary situation cannot be approached exclusively through numerical data, and that economic, political, ideological and sociocultural aspects that cannot be reduced to numerical data are necessary to detect and treat diseases with a high incidence rate among this specific population, such as TB (Goldberg 2014; Goldberg, Martin and Silveira 2015).

Bolivian Immigration in Buenos Aires and São Paulo

Buenos Aires and São Paulo are two of the most ethnically diverse cities in South America. They have some aspects in common that enable a comparative approach: a strong presence of mostly European but also Asian immigrants who arrived between the late nineteenth and early twentieth century, and managed to ascend socially, followed by the incorporation of internal migrants from the northern regions of Argentina and Brazil respectively; societies stratified socially and racially; differential concentrations of income per capita compared to other cities in the region; economic centralization; and industrial development, including clothing manufacture. With this in mind, we set out from the assumption that refers to the model of a 'global city' (Sassen 1999; García Canclini 1999) as a territorial urban space of unequal socio-economic, ideological, cultural, religious, political, nutritional and health relationships resulting from neoliberal globalization processes consolidated around the world over the past thirty years.

Since the late nineteenth century, the phenomenon of international and domestic migration has been an important factor in the urban life of both Buenos Aires and São Paulo. The cultural diversity that immigrants have brought to these cities, together with the sheer number of immigrants, has traditionally been viewed in harmonic terms as a 'community', both in official discourse and within society in general, referring to mostly European but also Asian immigrants, who settled in there cities during that period. However, this did not happen completely homogeneously or without conflict. The way these immigrants integrated socially and joined the workforce shows the structural process of upward social mobility experienced in both cities, in a sociopolitical context in favour of immigration. Over time, some of the descendants of those immigrants have been able to attain positions of power in local societies with a high degree of acceptance. They have also been able to interact on certain levels with the upper classes of these societies and have become part of the national 'white' elite.

Unlike these transatlantic migratory processes, which were of a 'definitive' nature and took place in connection with population growth policies and the specific requirements of the local employment markets, international migration today occurs increasingly as a response to 'temporary' demand for workers and the displacement of peoples expelled from their communities and/or countries due to environmental factors, wars and other consequences of the global neoliberal hegemony. Within the current migratory system of South America, since the 1980s Brazil and Argentina have become countries that attract and receive immigrants from countries along their borders, especially Bolivia, Paraguay and Peru. More recently, immigrants and refugees from Africa, along with people from Southern Asia, have formed part of the immigrant groups in transit in the Southern Cone, thereby altering the routes that had previously headed for the United States and Europe (Goldberg and Silveira 2013).

Domestic and international labour migration into both cities has taken place in a different context to the earlier 'European' migratory flows. The emphasis is no longer on integration but instead there is a tendency towards the exclusion of these 'dark-skinned' immigrants (black and indigenous, non-European), with notable situations of racism and discrimination, labour exploitation, segregation and precarious residency and accommodation situations, as well as difficulties in accessing public social services such as health care. Official figures show that Bolivians in São Paulo and in Buenos Aires represent the second largest foreign grouping in these cities, after the Portuguese and Paraguayans repectively; at the same time, it should be noted that these two cities alone contain half of the foreign populations of Brazil and Argentina. But it is not only in quantitative terms that this immigrant group is particularly relevant. From the perspective of a sociocultural analysis of the racialization process, Bolivians are one of the most stigmatized immigrant groups (according to Goffman 1980) in both societies in terms of 'negative visibility'. In fact, Bolivian immigrants are an especially vulnerable social group, subject to a racialization process based on twofold stigmatization: firstly because of their phenotypic features ('indians'), and secondly because of their lower class in the structure of their host societies ('poor') (Goldberg 2010; Goldberg and Silveira 2013).

Furthermore, the concept of racialization of labour can be used in transnational environments (Bonacich and Wilson 2008.) Following this, it is possible to provide a specific comparative example in a contemporary regional context to illustrate the concept. Like the invasion of the American continent and the extractive colonial world system created by Europe from that moment (Indo-African slave labour in the colonies), we can consider the racialization process of global labour with the current conditions of new colonial globalization that has created a racialized world labour system where racialization is applied to subordinate and disproportionately exploited groups. Among them, our comparative case studies represent a local/regional example of the racialization of global migrant labour exploitation in the clothing industry by transnational capital that has arisen or is sustained by globalization.

In this sense, although a proportion of Bolivian immigrants currently form part of the sociocultural groups that make up the subordinate sectors of these two cities, it is worth clarifying that we do not in any way intend our analytical model to disregard the significance of attraction processes such as 'siren calls' or the bright lights of the city, or indeed any of the pull factors that major urban centres exert on domestic (from rural areas) and international migratory flows, mainly in terms of access to consumerism, the search for employment, education and health care for children, access to social services, improved social status, the oft-coveted 'progress' and the 'dream' of well-being for the family. Once at their new big city destination, however, immigrants come across a far more difficult and undesirable situation: inequality, stigmatization and discrimination processes, social-labour-residential instability, dietary changes and other sociocultural conflicts. To a greater or lesser extent, this situation has a negative impact on their health. This has been the case for some Bolivian immigrants arriving in Buenos Aires and São Paulo since the 1980s, with the dream, the goal and the specific urge to help their families back home or to pay off debts. They find themselves in a new context and with a very different outlook to what they had probably first imagined: alone, in a huge unknown city, with little or no money, not knowing what to do, where to go, where to find work or where to live. This is similar to the experiences of the subjects of our comparative study, with the difference being that most of our subjects were fraudulently or dishonestly recruited at their point of origin by friends or family members, and transferred directly to clothes sweatshops in São Paulo and Buenos Aires. This reflects the link between migration and human trafficking for the purposes of exploiting their labour under conditions similar to slavery, working in a sector where brutal exploitation is mostly ignored in the public sphere (Goldberg 2016).

The above is a specific manifestation of the structural violence committed by global capitalism against certain subordinate social groups – a violence that is hidden by different domestic, international and transnational social and political stakeholders, who take advantage of the needs of these people and the situations in which their rights are being violated. We refer to certain domestic and foreign multinational clothing companies in the manufacturing sectors of both cities, some of which outsource work to sweatshops, many of them even run by Bolivians who started off working there themselves.[1] Thus, the brands manufacture illegally with minuscule labour costs, with the complicity and the protection of impunity offered by an influential part of the local and national political and judicial structures of both societies (Goldberg 2014).

The dominant clothing companies, however, have retained control over design, marketing, image, patterns and tailoring, while they outsource garment-making, ironing and finishing to factories and facilitators; these, in turn, subcontract to home workers or to other factories. The factory owners, distributors and wholesalers take 80 per cent of the sector's entire earnings (Lieutier 2010; Coutinho 2015). Given this context, the workers accept their exploitation, hoping to open their own sweatshop sometime in the future.

Tania, a female immigrant born in Oruro, Bolivia, who emigrated to São Paulo in 1994, told us about her experience:

> I wasn't looking for work, but she [the woman she knew in Bolivia who had brought her to São Paulo] lived here, and had left Bolivia, and my father met the woman who said she needed people to work in Brazil in exchange for payment of $500 a month. I came, and when I arrived that was not the case. It was a factory and there were lots of Bolivians living right there. I left Bolivia and she told me she'd pay me in Brazil, but she didn't. Several of us got angry and we escaped from there ... We were locked up, they didn't let us out and they locked away our papers. We went to put the rubbish out and escaped from there.

Tania said she used to work from 4 A.M. in that factory, almost without a break ('for a bite to eat'). At the time she was just fifteen and had travelled with her father's authorization.

Rosa, a female immigrant from La Paz, Bolivia, worked in a sweatshop in Buenos Aires and is currently a member of a textile cooperative in Buenos Aires.

> When the situation in Bolivia was bad in 2004, we couldn't find work. So I made the decision to come here to Argentina, so that I could work; we were listening to the radio and there was an announcement that dressmakers were needed. There was a person who brought people here, [so] I went to that woman's house. We were in such a bad way that we didn't even have anything to eat in Bolivia. She had lots of contacts along the journey. For example, we didn't need to show our passports in person, she already had people who showed them, we didn't carry out luggage across the

border either, she had people who [were] allowed it to cross. We arrived here and were picked up by her husband in his car; he came to collect us and took us to the house where she had two workshops, one upstairs and one downstairs, and the people that she had brought to set up the downstairs workshop, she brought ten people to work. We all came together in what we call the 'fleets', or groups of travellers. Our journey was broken up into sections, but nobody bothered us with anything because she had already sorted everything out, she had contacts and we were asked for nothing. When we arrived here, she put us to work. We made jackets for top brands, but we didn't know that the brands were that big. They paid us per garment and we worked from seven in the morning until one or two in the morning. We had one hour for lunch, for tea; as soon as you finished your tea you had to go [back] to work. We lived there, he had mostly couples there, they had very basic rooms and he gave us a basic room where there were also machines. We were locked up, we weren't allowed out.

Like in other organizational systems of capitalist society, Domínguez (2010) argues that it is feasible to see how the textile industry grows based on relationships of power, domination/subordination and negotiation between players, corporate sectors and agents who form part of both the group of immigrants and the receiving society, who impose, maintain and establish their hegemony. Similarly, Rivera Cusicanqui explains the situation described in the case of Buenos Aires as:

Subordination, exploitation; a workforce that is paying for their migratory right of passage; in the first step they receive what is known as 'differed reciprocity' – it is deferred in time and acts as a cycle of return: a person was exploited and it is now his turn to exploit. It seems colonialist in a very cruel way, but this rule is not colonial. In any case, [it] is a class relationship, because the exploited are not considered savages. They are considered apprentices but not savages. The workshop dynamic functions due to an organized promise of progress, a type of deferred calculation: today I'm a dressmaker, but in the future I could have my own workshop. It can't be a permanent condition of servitude. This is why it is not slavery. There are very clear manumission rules. And a progressive manumission process. Once you pass the first step you gain a certain right to something else; from there you move on to a second step and you can consider yourself independent and [can] interact on an equal footing with your former exploiter. People do not work in workshops due to simple resignation; there is a secret pride that motivates them and gives the sacrifice a sense of purpose. (Colectivo Situaciones-Colectivo Simbiosis Cultural 2011: 22–24)

As we shall see, this sacrifice involves situations of social suffering for these migrant workers, with a severe impact on their health.

Processes of TB Health Care for Bolivian Immigrants Working and Living in Sweatshops in Buenos Aires and São Paulo

From a general sociocultural epidemiological perspective, cities of this scale and with these characteristics frequently bring with them illnesses of different types, depending on variables such as lifestyle, social class, nationality, ethnicity, gender, occupation and income, among other factors (WHO 2010.) When we focus on the subordinate sector of the urban societies of Buenos Aires and São Paulo, we find that certain sociocultural groups (indigenous migrants in poor neighbourhoods, inhabitants of slums, homeless people, intravenous drug users, immigrants, refugees, etc.) continue to suffer from contagious illnesses related to the socially vulnerable contexts of their precarious life-work-accommodation (Goldberg 2014).

In 2010, in the countries within the sub-region of Latin America and the Caribbean, 80 per cent of the population lived in large cities

> characterized by a growth of population pockets in slums, with major infrastructure deficits and high levels of poverty. ... Slums ... are identified as being settled in areas vulnerable to landslides, floods and environmental contamination; problems in the quality of housing and overcrowding; insufficient access to drinking water, basic sewers and health services; violence that leads to behaviour disorders; alcohol and drug abuse, etc. It is in these environments that the *Mycobacterium tuberculosis* finds the best chances of developing and being transmitted. This is why it is common for the rate of TB in large cities to be higher than the national average of countries. (OPS 2011: 7)

Furthermore, migrant workers are exposed to chronic diseases (cardiovascular disease, diabetes, etc.) resulting from sedentary lifestyles and urban stress, in addition to poor, unhealthy and deficient nutrition and marginal access to health services. Consequently, epidemiological profiles are related to the aforementioned sociocultural inequalities, to the violation of rights, the lack of public resources and social services, and at the same time the complex and diverse social and ethnic composition of these societies.

Illness as a result of sweatshop living and working conditions is frequent and recurring among these Bolivian immigrant workers – particularly the women, who are the majority and often live there with their children. They work in rooms that are crowded, cluttered and unventilated. The air is contaminated with particles of cloth, thread, dust and fluff produced by the machines. These circumstances and the number of hours they work (twelve to nineteen) cause serious posture, breathing and eyesight problems. For pregnant women, the intensity of the work, exacerbated by dietary deficiencies, leads to life-threatening risks for mother and baby, including chronic anaemia and a lowering of defences that can lead to diseases such as TB. In addition to the TB risk factors – pollution, overcrowding, fatigue, dietary deficiencies, and different types of violence – the vulnerable Bolivian workers also develop anxiety and depression as a result of migrating to this new environment.

We contend that in Buenos Aires and São Paulo, the socio-structural processes in these cities affect, impact and even determine the biological dimensions of TB among these subjects and how they get health care for it. Migrants' rights, including the right to free public health care, are guaranteed by the constitutions and migration laws in force in the respective countries, but these are often violated in the ways described above (Goldberg 2014; Goldberg, Silveira and Martin 2016).

One of the challenges of our proposed methodology, within the framework of comparative research, was cross-referencing epidemiological statistics and ethnographic data processed during the course of the fieldwork. TB is still one of the infectious diseases linked to poverty, and is one of the major causes of death in the world, being the second largest cause of death among such diseases, after AIDS (WHO 2016). However, this is a reflection not only of the enormous political, economic, social and epidemiological differences persisting globally between central and peripheral countries, but also of inequalities that can be identified on a national, regional or local level. The latest official data reports 23.6 cases of TB per 100,000 people in Argentina. Buenos Aires and its metropolitan area together accounted for over half of the total number of cases – of which half were found in Bolivians. Similarly, if the city is analysed as a unit, it appears that neighbourhoods in south-west Buenos Aires, where most of clothes sweatshops are, have the highest incidence rates of this disease (MINSAL 2012). The incidence rate in Brazil is even higher, with 36 cases of TB per 100,000 people (MS 2014). In the centre of the city of São Paulo, where the largest number of Bolivian immigrants live, Bolivians account for 58 per cent of all cases (Martínez et al. 2012).

Just as Goldberg (2010, 2014) indicated in previous works an increase over the past ten years in the rates of pulmonary TB among Bolivian immigrants living and working in sweatshops in Buenos Aires, so Porto Scaff Pinto showed an increase in the number of cases of this disease among South American immigrants[2] in São Paulo:

The number of South American immigrants suffering from TB increased from 2.7% in 2006 to 4.6% in 2013. Some 1,916 new cases of TB among South American immigrants in São Paulo were reported in the period between 2006 and 2013, accounting for 4.2% of the total cases of TB in the municipality. As described above, the incidence rate of TB in São Paulo suggests a downward trend. The number of TB cases among South American immigrants increased [from] 2006 [to] 2011 from 155 to 361 cases respectively. (Porto Scaff Pinto 2015: 40–47)

According to the epidemiological data presented, it is this author's hypothesis, consistent with our work and in common with aspects detected in the context of south-west Buenos Aires, that the incidence rate of TB among these immigrants 'could be related to living conditions in sewing workshops … which … mainly undermine the respiratory system. … Descriptions of sweatshops demonstrate that they are a highly favourable context for becoming infected with TB' (Porto Scaff Pinto 2015: 81–82). In both of the comparative cases of this study, TB treatment abandonment rates are higher among immigrants when compared to 'natives', standing at 13.3 per cent in São Paulo and 19.2 per cent in Buenos Aires (Goldberg 2010; Porto Scaff Pinto 2015). A recurring factor among the reasons for abandonment is the six months of treatment that patients have to undergo, in many cases with a clear intolerance to the medication. One of the main problems with treating and monitoring TB in Bolivian patients is the permanent mobility of their migratory processes, as well as their way of life-work-accommodation, which in some cases resembles slavery conditions in textile sweatshops. In these cases, as we were able to corroborate from some of the interviews, workers are often not authorized by the sweatshop owners to see a doctor or to collect the appropriate medication from the health centre to continue the treatment.

Paula, a Bolivian nurse interviewed as part of the fieldwork done at the Barra Funda Basic Health Unit in the centre of São Paulo, believed that Bolivian textile immigrants from the workshops who experienced some of the symptoms related to the development of TB, only go to see a doctor

> when they have a cough that doesn't go away, or when they start to cough up blood. The treatment ends up being hindered due to discomfort caused by the medication and the days that the worker has to take off work to take the medication. Some workshop managers are sympathetic, but others are not, and some abandon the treatment because of this. Those who continued with the treatment were very satisfied and were able to complete it.

Furthermore, our field investigations found in both Buenos Aires and São Paulo some health centres make delated TB treatment. With the exception of numerous highlighted cases where these immigrants go directly to the emergency services when the disease is in an advanced stage (and are immediately hospitalized), there is insufficient and/or distorted information among public health-care workers in both cities about Bolivian immigrant patients, often based on prejudice. Indeed, some of the subjects interviewed as part of our research complained about the poor treatment they received from doctors and nurses in some centres.

From the large number of cases highlighted in our comparative study of subjects who had suffered or are suffering from TB, that of María is a prime example, as it shows the group of complex socio-sanitary and sociocultural dimensions that interact when it comes to analysing the migratory problem in question. Another female immigrant from La Paz, Bolivia, she arrived in São Paulo in 2010 with her husband to work and save money, 'which is why we all come, right?', working and living in a textile sweatshop belonging to a Bolivian owner for a time in order to eventually be able to 'leave' and set up their own clothing production at home. Beyond this 'expected' path followed by María and her husband, this woman's path has a particular feature that is in turn linked to her experience of suffering from TB (it should be emphasized that she was undergoing treatment for the illness at the time of the interview). At some point during migration or at the destination, María converted to evangelism and was recruited to attract worshippers among São Paulo's Bolivian immigrant community. It was because of this that she contracted TB during one of her evangelical visits to a sweatshop,[3] when she had already set up her own production and was sewing garments with her husband. She had no prior knowledge of the disease when she was infected from contact with a Bolivian immigrant textile worker at the sweatshop, because she was in the first months of pregnancy and undernourished: 'I went to preach the word of God and at one of the workshops there was a fellow Bolivian who had that illness, but I didn't know what he had, [and only] found out afterwards when I was being treated'. Among the symptoms experienced by María, respiratory problems (fatigue and difficulty breathing) were particularly prominent. When she was no longer able to continue with her work routine and started coughing up blood, she decided to visit a health centre where they analysed her sputum. Four days later the centre called to confirm that the tests were positive and that she had TB. What they did not tell her at the time, and as she only discovered after receiving the X-ray and blood test results, was that she had caught multi-drug-resistant tuberculosis (MDR-TB),[4] so her treatment, which was continuing at the time of interview, involved taking TB drugs every day. These were second-line drugs, which are more expensive, scarce and have more side effects. In her case, because she was pregnant, she experienced twice the side effects:

> I caught one that was already resistant, that was not common, and because of this I am now taking medication, eleven pills plus an injection every day. The drugs made me feel bad, they were a lot for me, particularly as I'm expecting… Lots of vomiting, I took the drugs and vomited, I didn't eat well, I just vomited and vomited and lost strength, and when I took the drugs they left me feeling numb; I wasn't able to do anything with a numb body, I couldn't even work. It was as painful as giving birth, the baby must have been feeling something because my pain was so bad. I told the doctors: 'The drugs are killing me!'

María's narrative shows a time sequence referring to the adverse effects of the drugs that she took in the past – 'they made me feel bad' – and a change in the present – 'but they have now started to change me, and now, as I'm Christian, I pray when I take the drugs and they don't make me feel so bad'. When asked whether she prayed when she took the drugs so that they would make her better, or so they would not make her feel bad, María replied: 'So they don't make me feel bad'.

This use of evangelical prayer, in this case, to ensure that the eleven pills that María took each day as part of the pharmacological treatment to cure the MDR-TB did not cause side effects ('so they don't make me feel bad'), was discussed by Ramírez Hita (2005) in her analysis of medical models and transactions present in the framework of healthcare pluralism in the city of Potosí, Bolivia. In her detailed description of Bolivia's Quechua population's process of affiliation to Pentecostal evangelism, the author shows how these subjects increasingly go to the Lord first when they are suffering from any disease, before going to the doctor or to the traditional Andean medicine healer-specialist.

It should be noted that evangelicalism is against the practice of Andean religion and medicine, not only because it is competition for 'customers', but because of a conflict over knowledge and practices shown in the rejection of all things related to the worship of gods and spirits in Andean cosmology, which it considers to be 'the devil's work' and 'against God's commandments'. Very much like the case of Afro-Brazilian Candomblé in Brazil, where Andean religion's believers see souls, the evangelist sees demons:

> Traditional medicine and all that is related to ancestral forms of healing –
> a repertoire that includes prayers to saints, some type of divination or
> contact with souls – is considered 'witchcraft'. And all kinds of 'witch-
> craft' or folk medicine [from the Spanish invasion of America onwards]
> is considered by the church to be satanic, and hence [is] strongly per-
> secuted. It is believed that the only one who can heal, prophesize or
> perform miracles is the Holy Ghost. (Ramírez Hita 2005: 153–54)

Therefore, to turn to Andean medicine healer-therapists is to turn to sorcerers – that is, it is to connect with Satan. In this context, Andean medicine specialists lose influence, prestige and power within the community in favour of the new therapists: pastors. As part of this same process, the image of these healer-therapists becomes negative, to the point of becoming stigmatized.

On an individual-family-domestic level there is a substantial change in self-care knowledge and practices (Menéndez 1983) favouring religious beliefs as a therapy, thus creating a system of 'self-care through prayer' (Ramírez Hita 2005: 136). Where a health problem has not been resolved through self-care through prayer, the patient will go directly to the evangelical pastor for a 'healing' and then, at the same time, to the doctor, ignoring completely the Quechua medicine specialist. Ramírez Hita argues that evangelicalism, especially Pentecostalism, has an extensive health discourse. The core of its doctrine is based on the healing of body and soul:

> One of the cornerstones of this church is that its worshippers join funda-
> mentally because they [have] witnessed some kind of healing or curing in
> themselves or a family member. The process of health/illness/care takes
> on special characteristics in the realm of this doctrine. Messages are sent
> to prevent, diagnose and heal the worshipper's ailments, illness and suf-
> fering in religious ceremonies that tend to be held three times a week.
> (Ramírez Hita 2005: 141)

In this sense, evangelical religion coexists in a more compatible, coordinated way, and fundamentally in a less conflictive way, with Western scientific medicine.[5]

As she is suffering from a case of MDR-TB, María has to go to a hospital in the city's Consolação neighbourhood to collect her drugs and to do the relevant tests ('this hospital is only for those who have tuberculosis'). The interviewee stated that at first she was 'forced' to take the drugs in the presence of staff at the health centre who saw her every day, as 'they do not trust me and they say that I don't follow the treatment properly'. This was during the first few months of treatment, as she currently only takes the drugs 'on Saturdays and Sundays'. This is in line with the direct observation treatment applied in TB control programmes all over the world as part of protocols established for cases of MDR-TB, because if the disease were to become an epidemic it could take many lives and resources (which is what really interests state health authorities). Thus, all patients are instructed to take the drugs under the supervision of health personnel for the six months of treatment. If the patient refuses to do so, the health-care protocol requires hospitalization and isolation in quarantine.

Similarly, María said that when she started to feel better (according to her, because she prayed when taking the drugs) she asked her health-care physician about the possibility of suspending treatment. The doctor's reaction, probably due to the aspects that we mentioned above, was seemingly unexpected. María retold events as follows:

> I said to the doctor, 'I'm going to quit, I'm not going to continue, why should I carry on making myself feel bad, there had been a day when I'd stopped taking it'. And she said, 'No, there's no way you can stop this, you have to take it for six months... If you're going to stop, I'm going to have you deported to Bolivia. I'm going to call the Immigration Services right now'. Things got ugly there. I told her it'd be better for me, [as] I didn't have the strength to work. And I started to cry right there. I said, 'I can't look after my son, I can't cook, I can't do anything, and you don't understand me'. Then she got very aggressive. 'Then I'm going to have you deported,' she said, 'because you can't be here. You're killing more people, you're going to kill more people', she told me, as if I was a murderer.

María was finally convinced of the need to complete the six months of treatment, to allow her to return to Bolivia in the near future with her two children, and her third when it was born. The final question that we asked her during the interview was: Why do you think that some people catch TB here, like the person that you said infected you? Her answer simply and clearly summarizes, in her own words, the socio-epidemiological situation that our research is covering:

> Because sometimes we forget to look after our health. I think that it's caused by the environment. We close ourselves in; sometimes we say... there aren't many windows, the sun doesn't get in, maybe [we] also live in a damp place. I think that's it: [we] live in a place where there is no ventilation, no rest, you just work. I didn't know that Bolivians caught this disease here. I thought that I was the first person like that, but when I went to the hospital I saw that there were many.

This situation, recounted here by one of its sufferers, was verified empirically in fieldwork over two years at an infectious diseases hospital in Buenos Aires (Goldberg 2010). This research showed an increase in the hospitalization of Bolivian patients of both sexes who worked and lived in the clothes sweatshops in the south-west of the city. In the opinion of one of the community health agents[6] interviewed in São Paulo, 'if socio-occupational conditions improve, health conditions improve'.

Final Considerations

Global health can be defined as the field that studies the effects of globalization on human health (Missoni and Pacileo 2006). In this research we have looked into some of the consequences, in terms of illness/ailments/diseases/afflictions of different types, with especial focus on TB, suffered by subjects belonging to a specific subordinate sociocultural group in the cities of Buenos Aires and São Paulo, part of a particular migratory process that results in precarious forms of life-work-accommodation, in some cases involving contexts of social vulnerability similar to slavery. Thus, the structural violence that goes hand in hand with neoliberal capitalist globalization processes, and the many other forms of violence that this breeds in the day-to-day lives of the subjects, has a differential impact on their health, based on the context of inequalities in these two cities, which in turn reproduces and deepens these processes.

In the case of São Paulo, a large number of Bolivian immigrants do not go to health centres for treatment for their illnesses due to ignorance, fear or linguistic barriers, but mainly because they have to continue working, as otherwise they will not be paid for the clothes they produce. They frequently self-medicate or use traditional Andean (Aymara-Quechua) naturist medicine, but this is never as recurrent as in Bolivia. As we have shown in one of the cases recorded, health-care processes among Bolivian clothes manufacturing workers in São Paulo are influenced by the widespread presence of neo-Pentecostal evangelical churches. In Buenos Aires, meanwhile, the illegal/clandestine nature of most manufacturing-dwelling units where Bolivian textile workers live and work means it is normally impossible for external people such as doctors to enter the factory, or for workers to be allowed out to see a doctor.

Furthermore, data gathered from fieldwork shows that TB is an illness that is barely known in Bolivia, and so interview subjects generally associated it with their way of living and working in the clothes sweatshops, and frequently with a cold or pneumonia. This, in turn, partly explains the fact that when workers start to experience symptoms of the illness they continue working 'as normal' for as long as they can (because if they do not work, they do not get paid), which in turn increases the risk of infection in the enclosed space of the factory. Likewise, because they are not allowed to leave the factory to see a doctor, it is frequently the case that TB sufferers are only taken for emergency hospital treatment – either by the owner of the sweatshop or a workmate – when the advanced symptoms of the illness (extreme weakness, sputum with blood) prevent them from working. The situation described here is one of the real obstacles in access to health care for these immigrant workers, which exceeds the formal framework of rights that are 'guaranteed' and enshrined in Argentine and Brazilian legislation. This dimension of analysis allows us to show the influence of sociocultural determiners in the health problems of these groups, fundamentally in relation to infectious diseases like TB. In parallel, a large number of these workers are unaware of their right to free public health care. At the same time, the treatment is difficult because of discomfort and side effects from the medication, as well as the inconvenience of having to get it from a health centre. Here we see the importance of the work in on-site health mediation, promotion, prevention and care carried out by community health agents in São Paulo, while the situation is even worse in Buenos Aires as such a figure does not exist in the public health system there.

Finally, as well as the structural violence existent in these countries, one would be wary of the recent implementation of neoliberal policies in the two countries, which will intensify the deepening of processes of social inequality, unemployment, poverty and instability in the lives of large social groups (some of which actively organize, fight and put up resistance). This will have a greater impact among subordinate groups and lead to further exploitation, which could lead to another crisis such as the one that occurred in Argentina at the beginning of this century. Within this framework, new laws on flexible working conditions (passed in Brazil in 2017 and likely to become law in Argentina over the course of 2019), and the hidden processes of privatization of the public health sector that are occurring in both countries, means there is a scenario for workers that could lead to even more precarious socio-occupational situations, and even more obstacles in accessing health care. In other words, situations may arise in future that are potentially worse than those we have examined in this chapter in the life-work-accommodation of Bolivian immigrants in clothes sweatshops in São Paulo and Buenos Aires. If so, they will inevitably have a negative impact on the already poor health of immigrant and native workers and their families.

Acknowledgements

We wish to thank the Centro de Saúde Escola Barra Funda 'Dr Alexandre Vranjac', particularly the 'Estratégia de Saúde da Família' team, for their support in carrying out the fieldwork. We are also grateful for the funding provided by the Centro de Estudos Augusto Leopoldo Ayrosa Galvão (CEALAG, Departamento de Saúde Coletiva da Faculdade de Ciências Médicas da Santa Casa de São Paulo).

Alejandro Goldberg is a social anthropologist at the University of Buenos Aires-CONICET. He has a Masters in medical anthropology and a PhD in social and cultural anthropology, specialized in medical anthropology and international health, from the University of Rovira and Virgili in Catalonia. The title of his PhD thesis was '"To Be an Immigrant Is Not an Illness": Immigration, Life and Working Conditions in Spain. The Health/Illness/Care Process of Senegalese Immigrants in Barcelona'. He does ethnographical research in social anthropology, medical anthropology and international migrations. He has lectured at graduate and postgraduate levels in different universities of Europe and Latin America.

Cássio Silveira is a Brazilian sociologist. He is professor at the Medical School of Santa Casa de São Paulo (FCMSCSP), in the postgraduate programme in public health, and at the Federal University of São Paulo (UNIFESP) in the Department of Preventive Medicine. He has experience in the field of sociology, acting mainly in the following themes: sociology of health, health system and transnational migration processes and health.

Tatiane Barbosa is a Brazilian nurse working in public health at Santos City Hall. She earned her doctorate in collective health from the graduate programme in public health at the Catholic University of Santos (UNISANTOS). She is a specialist in health education for preceptors of the Unified Health System (SUS) at the Instituto Sírio-Libanês de Ensino e Pesquisa and the Universidade Federal de São Paulo (UNIFESP).

Denise Martin is a Brazilian anthropologist. She is a professor at the Catholic University of Santos (Unisantos), in the postgraduate programme in public health, and at the Federal University of São Paulo (UNIFESP) in the Department of Preventive Medicine. She coordinates the Cátedra Sergio Vieira de Mello-Unisantos/UNHCR (UN agency for refugees). She is publisher of the Journal Interface – Comunicação, Saúde, Educação. She has experience in the field of anthropology, with an emphasis on health anthropology, acting mainly in the following themes: interface between anthropology and health, mental health, transnational migration processes and health.

Notes

1. As part of the transnational, relational approach used, we were able to corroborate that the mechanism of transnational exploitation, and exploitation within the Bolivian community, is one of many features shared by cases in Buenos Aires and São Paulo (Goldberg and Silveira 2013.) In simple terms, this complex mechanism is based on the idea that those who have been there longest, have acquired papers and have been exploited previously are hired to recruit, bring in and exploit recently arrived compatriots in more vulnerable conditions. So it is that a proportion of male Bolivian immigrants who start to work in the sweatshops see it as a transitory phase that entails regularizing their migratory situation, buying a sewing machine, setting up their own factory and then exploiting other workers who are in a situation of greater vulnerability (i.e. in the phase they themselves were in when they started out).
2. Although the study in question does not limit its analysis to the specific group of Bolivian immigrants, since official epidemiological statistics in Brazil were not disaggregated by nationality until 2016, it was deduced that most of those South American immigrants indicated by the author were, and continue to be, of Bolivian nationality, as they make up the highest percentage of existing immigrants in the municipality of São Paulo (Silveira et al. 2009).
3. Particularly in the case of São Paulo, there was evidently a strong presence of evangelical neo-Pentecostal churches among the local Bolivian community. It is common for evangelizers, a large number of whom are women, to make visits on the ground to sweatshops in the city centre, whose owners and workers are Bolivian.
4. MDR-TB can be caused by repeated abandonment of the treatment over time, or more frequently by the patient catching the disease from a strain of multi-resistant bacillus, which is especially resistant to two of the first-line medications (isoniazid and rifampicin). However, the infection may become even more resistant, as extremely drug-resistant tuberculosis

(XDR-TB) develops, which is resistant to these two medications, to fluoroquinolones and to any of the second-line injectable antibiotics.
5. The Evangelical Church respects and accepts biomedicine because it is recognized in the Bible. It identifies doctors as legitimate representatives of this medical care system, but at the same time considers that science can make mistakes and sometimes gets it wrong (they are, of course, right in this respect). This grey area left by science is where the 'spiritual' field comes into play, not only through the invocation of the 'Lord' and the intervention of his representative, the pastor, as an agent effective in rectifying the action of the 'devil' and his 'forces of evil'; but also as a 'guide' or 'rector' of medical practice. They may turn to the doctor because it is not a sin, but they are not allowed to depend on doctors or medicine. So it is that doctors and their powers are represented as intermediaries between the patient and divine power. We might say that they put the doctors in the hands of God, and God in the hands of the doctors.
6. The Program Community Health Workers is an integral part of the Family Health Strategy in the context of Brazil's primary health-care system. These are organized into teams of multidisciplinary composition, including at least a family doctor and a community public health nurse, a nursing assistant and four to six community agents of health care. The work was developed from 'micro-territories', defined as areas with the registration and monitoring of a number of families for each team (between 600 and 1,000 families), with a maximum of 4,500 people registered. Each community agent of health care accompanies a maximum of either 150 families or 450 individual people (Goldberg and Silveira 2013: 8).

References

Alsan, M., et al. 2011. 'Poverty, Global Health and Infectious Disease: Lessons from Haiti and Rwanda'. *Infectious Disease Clinics of North America* 3(25): 611–22.

Bonacich, S., and J. Wilson. 2008. 'The Racialization of Global Labour'. *American Behavioral Scientist* 52(3): 342–55.

Bourgois, P. 2010. *En busca de respeto: vendiendo crack en Harlem*. Buenos Aires: Siglo XXI.

Colectivo Situaciones-Colectivo Simbiosis Cultural. 2011. *De chuequistas y overlockas: Una discusión en torno a los talleres textiles*. Buenos Aires: Editorial Retazos.

Coutinho, B. 2015. 'Imigração laboural e a produção de vestuário na cidade de São Paulo: entre a informalidade e a expectativa de mobilidade social ascendente'. *Cadernos OBMigra* 1(3): 79–98.

Csordas, T. 1994. *Embodiment and Experience*. Cambridge: Cambridge University Press.

Das, V., et al. (eds). 2001. *Remaking the World: Violence, Social Suffering and Recovery*. Berkeley: University of California Press.

Domínguez, C. 2010. 'Procesos de identificación y diferenciación en familias y jóvenes bolivianos del AMBA'. BA thesis in Social Anthropology, Universidad de Buenos Aires.

Farmer, P. 2001. *Infections and Inequalities: The Modern Plagues* (Updated with a new preface). Berkeley: University of California Press.

———. 2004a. 'An Anthropology of Structural Violence'. *Current Anthropology* 45(3): 305–25.

———. 2004b. *Pathologies of Power: Health, Human Rights, and the New War on the Poor* (Updated with a new preface). Berkeley: University of California Press.

Fassin, D. 2007. *When Bodies Remember: Experiences and Politics of AIDS in South Africa*. Berkeley: University of California Press.

Fassin, D., and R. Rechtman. 2009. *The Empire of Trauma: An Inquiry into the Condition of Victimhood*. Princeton, NJ: Princeton University Press.

García Canclini, N. 1999. *La globalización imaginada*. Buenos Aires: Paidós.

Goffman, E. 1980. *Estigma: La identidad deteriorada*. Buenos Aires: Amorrortu.

Goldberg, A. 2010. 'Análisis de la relevancia de los factores socioculturales en el proceso asistencial de pacientes con tuberculosis, usuarios del Instituto Vaccarezza-Hospital Muñiz: Un abordaje etnográfico desde la Antropología Médica'. *Revista Argentina de Salud Pública* 1(5): 13–21.

———. 2014. 'Contextos de vulnerabilidad social y situaciones de riesgo para la salud: tuberculosis en inmigrantes bolivianos que trabajan y viven en talleres textiles clandestinos de Buenos Aires'. *Cuadernos de Antropología Social* 39: 91–114.

———. 2016. 'La parte invisibilizada de la migración transnacional boliviana hacia Argentina'. *Andamios* 13(32): 357–78.

Goldberg, A., D. Martin and C. Silveira. 2015. 'Editorial: Por um campo específico de estudos sobre processos migratórios e de saúde na Saúde Coletiva'. *Interface: comunicação, saúde, educação* 19(53): 229–32.

Goldberg, A., and C. Silveira. 2013. 'Desigualdad social, condiciones de acceso a la salud pública y procesos de atención en inmigrantes bolivianos de Buenos Aires y São Paulo: una indagación comparativa'. *Saúde e Sociedade* 22(2): 283–97.

Goldberg, A., C. Silveira and D. Martin. 2016. 'Tuberculosis en inmigrantes bolivianos de São Paulo y de Buenos Aires: un abordaje sociosanitario-etnográfico-comparativo'. VIII 'Santiago Wallace' Conference on Research in Social Anthropology, Buenos Aires, 27–29 July.

Good, B. 2003. *Medicina, racionalidad y experiencia: Una perspectiva antropológica*. Barcelona: Bellaterra.

Grimberg, M. 2008. 'Contextos de vulnerabilidad social al Vih-Sida en América Latina: Desigualdad social y violencias cotidianas en jóvenes de sectores subalternos'. *Thule* 20/21: 31–54.

Jung Ho, M. 2004. 'Sociocultural Aspects of Tuberculosis: A Literature Review and a Case Study of Immigrant Tuberculosis'. *Social Science & Medicine* 4(59): 753–62.

Lieutier, A. 2010. *Esclavos: Los trabajadores costureros de la ciudad de Buenos Aires*. Buenos Aires: Retórica Ediciones.

Martínez, V., et al. 2012. 'Equity in Health: Tuberculosis in the Bolivian Immigrant Community of São Paulo, Brazil'. *Tropical Medicine & International Health* 17: 1417–24.

Menéndez, E. 1983. 'Modelo médico hegemónico, modelo alternativo subordinado, modelo de autoatención, caracteres estructurales', in E. Menéndez (ed.), *Hacia una práctica médica alternativa: hegemonía y autoatención (gestión) en salud*. Mexico City: Cuadernos de la Casa Chata, pp. 1–20.

Ministerio de Salud de la Nación (MINSAL). 2012. 'La salud en Argentina en 2011'. Buenos Aires.

Ministério da Saúde do Brasil (MS). 2014. 'Programa Nacional de Controle da Tuberculose'. Brasilia.

Missoni, E., and G. Pacileo. 2006. 'Le politiche delle Organizzazioni Internazionali e gli obiettivi di sviluppo del Millennio', in *A caro prezzo: Le diseguaglianze nella salute*. 2nd Report from the Italian Observatory on Global Health. Pisa: Edizioni ETS, pp. 150–63.

Organización Panamericana de la Salud (OPS). 2011. 'Situación de Salud en las Américas: Indicadores Básicos'. Washington, DC.

Otegui Pascual, R. 2009. 'El sufrimiento: la forma sociocultural del dolor', in M. Grimberg (ed.), *Experiencias y narrativas de padecimientos cotidianos: Miradas antropológicas sobre la salud, la enfermedad y el dolor crónico*. Buenos Aires: Antropofagia, pp. 147–66.

Porto Scaff Pinto, P. 2015. 'Análise espacial e espaço-temporal dos casos de tuberculose em imigrantes sulamericanos no município de São Paulo entre 2006 e 2013'. Master's thesis in Public Health, Faculty of Medical Sciences, Santa Casa de São Paulo.

Quaranta, I. 2006. *Corpo, Potere, Malattia: Antropologia e Aids nei Grassfields del Camerun*. Rome: Meltemi Editore.

Ramírez Hita, S. 2005. *Donde el viento llega cansado: Sistemas y prácticas de salud en la ciudad de Potosí*. La Paz: Cooperazione Italiana.

Sassen, S. 1999. *La ciudad global*. Buenos Aires: Eudeba.

Silveira, C., et al. 2009. 'Projeto inclusão social urbana: nós do centro. Metodologia de pesquisa e de ação para inclusão social de grupos em situação de vulnerabilidade no centro da cidade de São Paulo'. São Paulo: Arnaldo Vieira de Carvalho Foundation, Faculty of Medical Sciences, Santa Casa de São Paulo.

Taussig, M. 1992. *Un gigante en convulsiones: el mundo humano como sistema nervioso en emergencia permanente*. Barcelona: Gedisa.

World Health Organization (WHO). 2010. 'Hidden Cities: Unmasking and Overcoming Health Inequities in Urban Settings'. Geneva.

———. 2016. 'Global Tuberculosis Report 2015'. Geneva.

4

Women, Migration and Health

An Inquiry into Gender-Based Violence and the Limits of Maternity Care Services in Southern Europe's Borderlands

Chiara Quagliariello

Introduction

The arrival of increasing numbers of pregnant women is one of the topics at the core of the political and media debate on migration across the Mediterranean. There are two opposing discussions on this theme, and on migration by sea more generally. The first is the humanitarian discourse, according to which pregnant women are to be seen as individuals who, more than other categories of migrants, deserve to be saved and received in Europe. This population is described as one that is particularly in need of help, given their physical condition. In humanitarian arguments, the representation of pregnant migrants is therefore one of particularly vulnerable subjects to whom relief and assistance must be provided. This rhetoric is reinforced, sometimes explicitly and at other times indirectly, by the representations in the media. Some examples are the iconographic images of the refugee with a newborn in her arms (Pinelli 2017), the sensationalist images of the refugee rescued at sea in an advanced state of pregnancy, and the refugee who gave birth on the military ship intended for border control of the Mediterranean. These scenes refer to imaginations and feelings related to the themes of pity and compassion (Fassin 2007). The resulting representation is not only one of people who need help, but also of people who are harmless and would not be dangerous for the host countries, unlike the representations of many of the male migrants, especially if they are Muslims (Friese 2017).

In the security argument, by contrast, pregnant migrants are resilient individuals who deliberately use their physical condition to receive more help from the countries in which they are received. From this perspective, these women take advantage of their state of pregnancy to enjoy greater benefits in terms of health care, but also politically and socially. Being pregnant is expected to facilitate the procedures required for accessing a residence permit for humanitarian reasons and, subsequently, citizenship. The choice to come and give birth in Europe – as affirmed by the proponents of this second argument – would go hand in hand with a strategic attempt to benefit from a privileged path, both in material and legal terms, in the country in which they are welcomed. If pregnancy reduces the chance of women being included in policies of returning migrants, it then represents a burden on the welfare system of host countries (Bridges 2011) and a threat to the body of the nation (Weiss 2002). Although these arguments occupy a large space in the political and media debates in Europe, where invasion rhetoric counters that of respect for human rights, knowledge about the experiences (and destinies) of pregnant women who arrive in Europe by sea remains limited.

Italy, because of its central position in the Mediterranean, plays a leading role in welcoming and managing people who leave the African continent and travel to Europe by sea. Together with this geographical factor, Italy's role has been enhanced by the increasingly restrictive migration policies in other Southern Europe borderlands, such as Spain[1] in the west and Greece[2] in the east, and by the coordinated search and rescue at sea programmes directed by the international Frontex agency. The fact that Italy is the main Mediterranean country through which it has been possible to enter Europe[3] in recent years has led to an increase in migrant arrivals. According to data provided by the International Organization for Migration (IOM), more than 181,000 people arrived in Italy in 2016, which is 18 per cent more than the number of arrivals recorded in 2015 (IOM 2016). Women made up 13 per cent of arrivals in 2016, an increase of 6 per cent compared to the number of female arrivals registered in Italy in 2015 (ibid.). If the feminization of migratory flows is a widely documented phenomenon in the socio-anthropological literature (Andall 2000; Anthias and Lazarinis 2000; Salazar and Parreñas 2001; Salih 2003; Ehrenreich and Hochschild 2004), the experiences of women travelling illegally across the Mediterranean to apply for asylum in Europe remain largely unexplored (Freedman 2016; Grotti et al. 2017). The origin of the pregnancies these women experience – such as the fact that in most cases these are unwanted pregnancies – has been particularly neglected.

The experiences of migrants who arrived in Italy while pregnant are the main subject of the research I carried out on the island of Lampedusa and in the city of Palermo, Sicily.[4] Lampedusa, located about 200 km from Sicily, to which it belongs on an administrative level, represents the southernmost Italian territory in the Mediterranean. Its close proximity to the coast of North Africa (just 180 km of sea separate the island from Tunisia) makes this island of about 6,000 inhabitants a place that historically has frequently been traversed by migrations from the African continent to Europe (Cuttitta 2015). This chapter focuses on migrant women of Nigerian origin who arrived in Lampedusa in 2016 and were later transferred to Palermo. The choice to concentrate my analysis on this group of migrants had two main motivations. The first was statistical, as Nigerians are the most numerous of those involved in the landings. According to the IOM data (2016), they represent 21 per cent of all arrivals registered in Italy in 2016. Nearly a third of this population is made up of women (11,009 women out of 37,500 people who arrived in 2016). There were 3,040 arrivals of unaccompanied minors, 80 per cent of whom were female. The trends are the same in Lampedusa itself, where, among the migrants arriving by sea in 2016, the Nigerian population represented the largest group (1,878 people out of 11,089 arrivals). Again, nearly a third of the total were women (558 women out of 1,878 people). Unaccompanied minors, 70 per cent of them female, correspond to 166 people in 2016. The choice to reflect on the experiences of Nigerian migrants is also linked to a theoretical reason. The interweaving of gender-based violence and forms of discrimination linked to the skin colour – such as the fact that they are black women – emerges emblematically in the experiences of this population.

This chapter, which is based on the stories of Nigerian women and girls who disembarked in Lampedusa in 2016, aims to highlight the limits of the maternity care system, and the Italian reception system more generally, offered to migrants. As will be seen, the living conditions Nigerian women experienced in Italy clash with the principles defended by the humanitarian discourse. More specifically, the idea that there exists a humanitarian hierarchy among the different categories of migrants according to the level of vulnerability associated with gender variables (Mai 2014) is contrasted with the reality of the reception system, where the fact of being a woman does not represent an element that guarantees greater attention in terms of assistance. At the same time, the fact of becoming a mother does not facilitate a woman's access to citizenship, nor even a recognition of their status as a refugee, as supported by the rhetoric of security.

The reference to intersectionality theories (Crenshaw 1991; Anthias and Yuval-Davis 1992) will allow reflection on violence related to gender and skin colour factors, but also on stereotypes – especially with regard to prostitution issues – connected to Nigerian-origin migrant women. The first part of the chapter is dedicated to the social profiles of the Nigerians I encountered in Lampedusa and Palermo, and to an analysis of the violence these women suffered during the migratory journey. In the second part of the chapter, I analyse the difficulties women encountered in accessing voluntary termination of pregnancy (VTP) services,[5] and the impact of living conditions in Italian reception system on their health. I argue that the structural violence and the discrimination that pregnant African women are subjected to continue after their arrival in Europe. Institutional violence connected to reproductive health laws and the functioning of the reception system overlap the physical and physiological trauma that women undergo during migration.

Methodology

The analyses I propose are based on research I carried out on the island of Lampedusa and in the city of Palermo, Sicily, between July 2016 and March 2017. The study was realized through qualitative methods, such as participant observation in the physical and institutional spaces migrant women pass through, from their arrival in Lampedusa until their transfer to the hospital wards and the Extraordinary Reception Centres (CAS) in Palermo.[6] More particularly, participant observations were conducted in the following places: Lampedusa harbour, where migrant women arrive after the search and rescue operations in the Mediterranean Sea; Lampedusa maternity service; two maternity services in Palermo and one CAS in Palermo where migrant women live while they wait for news about their residency permit request on humanitarian grounds. In each of these places, participant observations focused on the interactions between migrant women and personnel who give them, at different levels, assistance during and after pregnancy. The personnel involved in the study were, in particular, six gynaecologists working at the maternity services in Lampedusa and Palermo, two social workers, two psychologists and three ordinary employees working at the CAS analysed in Palermo. The research was also based on semi-structured interviews. Twenty interviews were conducted with Nigerian women and girls; the migrants interviewed were aged between 18 and 34. Six interviews were carried out with health professionals: two with the gynaecologists from the maternity service in Lampedusa, and four with the gynaecologists from the maternity services in Palermo. Finally, the gathering of statistical data in the maternity services made it possible to examine the main health needs of Nigerian migrants who arrived in southern Italy between 2015 and 2016. A description of research objectives and the collection of consent from of the institutional actors preceded the observation activities and the interviews with migrant women. Interviews with Nigerian migrants were carried out in English; those with health professionals were in Italian and have been later translated into English. In order to respect the anonymity of the people who participated in the research, the names that appear in the chapter are pseudonyms.

Gender-Based Violence in Migration from Nigeria to Europe

According to data published by the Italian immigration office[7] and the European Border and Coast Guard Agency (Frontex), Nigerian migrants who arrived in Lampedusa in 2016 had two social profiles. A first group, which corresponds to about 60 per cent of female migrants who disembarked on the island, was made up of young girls aged between 16 and 20. In most cases, these girls were pushed by third parties to leave Nigeria; 90 per cent of these girls came from the rural areas of Edo State or from the capital of this region, Benin City. The childhood of these young Nigerian women was characterized by extreme poverty and limited access to education. Most of them had attended only elementary school (Onyejekwe Chizene 2005). Some of them had been 'sold' by their families to women (the so-called *madams* in Yoruba language) or to men (the so-called *oga* in Yoruba language) responsible for introducing them into the prostitution market in Europe. Others had been kidnapped against the will of their families. Most stated they had undergone a voodoo ritual – the so-called *juju* in Yoruba language – through which they were considered to have committed themselves to an economic agreement with the madam before leaving Nigeria (Singleton 1990; Frank 1995; Guillemaut 2008; Taliani 2012). Many pointed out that they had been cheated by these figures because of lies about the work that awaited them in Europe. Most were only informed after their departure from Nigeria about the real work to be done and the ways in which the contracted debt (an amount often exceeding 25,000 euros) would be repaid:

> To push me to leave, the lady with whom I travelled from Nigeria told me that she would find me a job as a waitress in Italy. After we crossed the border, she explained to me what I would really do. At that point it was impossible for me to escape. I tried to rebel but it ended badly: the lady beat me and left me without food for two days. (Blessing, 18 years old)

Several studies (Lavaud-Legendre 2003; Akor 2011; Taliani 2012; Osezua 2016) highlight how the trafficking of human beings for sexual purposes is not a new phenomenon among Nigerian girls coming from Edo State. However, the characteristics of this phenomenon seem to be evolving. The girls who enter the forced prostitution market are increasingly younger and less educated, and thus more easily induced to leave by the local networks engaged in this traffic (Lavaud-Legendre and Peyroux 2014; IOM 2017). At the same time, the travel conditions to Europe have also changed. The possibility of accessing Italy by land or air travel has become increasingly difficult in recent years. Therefore, unlike in the 1990s and 2000s, when girls involved in the forced prostitution market mainly travelled via air links, today their journeys take place through provisional boats also used by other African migrants. One of the aims of undertaking the journey by sea is to make this traffic less visible. Furthermore, although it is longer and more dangerous for young Nigerians, using boats is cheaper for those interested in making money from this traffic.

The other group of Nigerian migrants is composed of women who decide on their own to leave Nigeria. These women usually have a higher level of education (middle school or higher education) and are older (aged between 22 and 34) than the first group. Even the region of origin is different. In most cases, these women come from the central areas of the country, such as the Abuja and Nassarawa regions, or from the northern part of the country, such as the Kano region. Some of them have chosen to leave, sometimes even leaving their children in Nigeria, after having experienced several episodes of domestic violence from their husbands or other men in their family. Others have chosen to avoid forced marriages with men who can be over twenty years older than themselves. In other cases, it is the economic crisis that Nigeria has been experiencing in recent years that has encouraged women to leave the country, together with their husbands:

> Until a few years ago, people from other African countries were looking for work in Nigeria. Things have changed in recent years, our currency has collapsed, and many people have been fired. With the economic crisis, poverty has increased and the level of security has decreased. This is why many of us decide to leave. (Jennifer, 27 years old)

The scenario that Jennifer's testimony describes is confirmed by sociological studies that underscore how the economic recession that Nigeria has experienced, starting from the collapse in oil prices in 2014, explains the increasing migratory flows to Europe (Adepoju 2017). As mentioned, along with the local economic trends, other problems – related especially to the issue of gender violence – push women to leave. In these cases, it is possible to consider the migratory choice as a biographical rupture, or a social revolution, that women have made towards their partners and/or their families. In some cases, there is a risk of sexual violence from armed militias, forcing women to flee. This problem has mainly emerged in the case of women from the northern areas of the country, which, in the last few years, have endured armed conflicts between the Nigerian state and the Boko Haram terrorist group.

Stratification of Gender-Based Violence during the Migratory Journey

Although Nigerian migrants have different geographic origins, social profiles and family histories, most of them are exposed to the same forms of violence during their migratory journey. Osas, 24 years old, from the Nassarawa region, underlines how the risk of facing violence during the migratory journey is linked to three main elements – being a woman, being black and being Catholic:

> The first problem is that many men take advantage of women during migration. Another important problem is that in Libya, as elsewhere in North Africa, blacks are considered to be 'animals' and [are] treated like slaves. If an Arab man has to hurt a woman, he will choose a black woman and not an Arab one, especially if the black woman does not wear a veil or is not a Muslim.

The risk of suffering physical violence is therefore primarily linked to gender identity. The relationships of domination experienced by Nigerian women, however, also link to other elements, such as skin colour and ethnic-religious factors. The exposure to the risk of physical violence characterizes all stages of the migratory journey towards Europe, which requires the crossing of two land borders – that between Nigeria and Niger, and that between Niger and Libya – and one maritime border, the central Mediterranean. The men that women deal with during their journey have different roles and statuses. Among these men we find their fellow countrymen, other migrants of sub-Saharan origin, smugglers and cross-border traffickers, police officers, members of armed militias in Libya and police forces who run prisons in Libya. The greater the positions of power that the men hold, the more significant are the risks of exposure to physical violence for the women.

For young Nigerian girls destined to enter the forced prostitution market, the migratory journey lasts two or three weeks. Generally, the young women are not involved in the planning of different stages of their travel. This is organized by the madams or other figures (such as the so-called bodyguards, or *boga* in Yoruba language) that the girls travel with from Nigeria to Libya. Once they reach this country, the young women are entrusted to local militias that control all departures by sea. The cost of the Mediterranean crossing is paid in advance by the madam and is added to the economic debt contracted before leaving Nigeria. The stories of the interviewees demonstrate that, despite the agreements between the people travelling with them to Libya and those waiting for them in Italy, access to the last leg of the journey to Europe is not always immediate. The length of the stay in Libya depends on many factors, such as the need to avoid the checks against illegal departures carried out by the Libyan coastguard, the wait for favourable weather conditions for the sea voyage, and the tendency of local militias to ask the Nigerian girls for sexual services in exchange for access to the sea. As a result, for some of the interviewed girls, the stay in Libya lasted several weeks or months, during which they were forced to prostitute themselves for the Libyan militias.

Migration to Europe is often longer and more complicated for Nigerian migrants who organize their journey independently. Bilateral agreements between sub-Saharan African countries, including Nigeria, and the European Union hinder the possibility for migrants to obtain a visa to leave their countries (Huysmans 2000). The externalization process of European border controls through increasingly restrictive visa policies means that the only way to leave is by illegally crossing different African states (Fassin 2011; Menjívar 2014). The journey from Nigeria to Italy lasts, on average, between seven and eight months. Some women travel with their partners or other family members, but others face the migratory journey alone. In this last case, many of the women I interviewed stressed the need to seek the protection of a male figure from the first stage of their journey, in order to escape the risk of sexual violence in Niger. Female dependence on a male figure, often a compatriot, continues throughout the crossing of the Sahara Desert, before the arrival in Libya. This protection by male migrants encountered while travelling helps women to escape physical violence from traffickers in border areas (Ticktin 2008). The lack of autonomy is described as a source of suffering for migrant women who, although having sufficient financial resources of their own, are in need of male support in order to advance on their journey. Killings and other forms of abuse that migrants travelling alone in the Sahara Desert are victims of reduce any possibility of choice. The situation usually worsens for women once they arrive in Libya. Women describe the detention centres administered by the Libyan police, as well as the buildings where they live as prisoners after being captured by local militias, as a real hell. Couples who travelled together are often separated, as are any couples formed during the migration journey:

> When we arrived in Libya, the military asked us to form two lines: men on one side, women on the other. My husband, with whom I had left Nigeria, did not want to leave me. He was afraid that the soldiers would take the women and men to different sites and we would never find each other again. When one of the soldiers noticed that he was holding me close to him, he shot him. My husband began to tremble, and he died under my eyes. I remember it perfectly. At that moment I understood that the only way to survive in Libya was to obey the armed men. (Favour, 26 years old)

The loss of the protection of their own partners, or of one of other migrants met while travelling, increases the risk of sexual violence for women. A report published by Amnesty International (2016) highlights how sub-Saharan migrants are systematically exposed to this risk in Libya. The data are confirmed by the experiences of many of the women I interviewed, who were victims of multiple episodes of sexual violence by the Libyan police and Libyan local militias. The result of these trends is an increase in the number of migrants who get pregnant: 'Pregnancy is part of the price you pay to get to

Europe' (Joy, 29). Migrants' unplanned pregnancies can be described, then, as an emblematic example of embodying borders processing. For numerous migrants I interviewed, pregnancy opened the access to a Mediterranean crossing: 'When you're pregnant, you have more chances [that the] military replace you with another woman, and they let you leave' (Victory, 26).

Data from the local immigration office and from Frontex show that among the 558 female Nigerian migrants who arrived on Lampedusa in 2016, fewer than 200 had left Libya with their own partners or travelling companions. Among these, more than 150 said they did not know where their partners were or whether they were still alive. Of these 558 Nigerian women who arrived in Lampedusa, 79 were pregnant (or 14 per cent), and within this group, 80 per cent stated that they did not know the identity of the child's father.

Health Needs and Access to VTP

Most of the migrants I met define their pregnancy as an unwanted experience. Although the difficult travel conditions and deprivations to which they had been subjected in Libya had had an impact on their health – hypothermia, dehydration, wounds and burns on the body are some examples – the main health need that women expressed after their arrival in Lampedusa was the immediate termination of a pregnancy. As evidenced by the statistical data I collected in 2016 at the Lampedusa maternity service, 166 migrants underwent a medical examination. Among these, 79 came from Nigeria; more than half of these (43) requested an abortion. In most cases, women openly declared to medical personnel that they had been victims of sexual violence. Being pregnant is generally associated with the violence suffered in Libya, and not with any unprotected sexual relationship during previous stages of the journey. This fact highlights the extent to which the physical abuse that occurs on Libyan territory inflicts major trauma on women's lives. During their consultations with gynaecologists, migrants often defined their pregnancy as a source of distress that added to the physical and psychological maltreatment experienced during migration.

Women's non-verbal language also expresses a refusal of their physical condition. The impossibility of accessing any hospital in Libya means that the ultrasound examination performed in Lampedusa usually constituted the first diagnostic test women had undergone since the beginning of their pregnancy. Nevertheless, in almost every medical consultation I attended, women preferred not to see the foetus's silhouette: the prevalent behaviour was to look in the opposite direction of the screen connected to the ultrasound device. In the event that gynaecologists discover some clinical problems, women ask for their pregnancy to be interrupted. If, on the contrary, the medical information on foetus health is positive, the patients remain silent, asking no questions. The arrival of a child that women consider a 'stranger' sometimes leads to a feeling of shame. During her medical consultation, Rita, 25 years old, said: 'I often wonder what colour the child's skin will be after all that happened in Libya'. For her part, Precious, 27 years old, described the possibility of ending her pregnancy as 'the beginning of a new life in Europe'.

Despite their determination, access to voluntary termination of pregnancy (VTP) is not always possible for Nigerian migrants. Italian law (Law 194/1978) allowing legal abortion states that the request for VTP must be communicated to gynaecologists before the end of the third month of pregnancy. Therefore, a request for abortion is only possible for migrants who arrive in Italy before this limit. In other cases, gynaecologists automatically exclude the possibility of migrants accessing VTP. The opportunity provided by the law to ask for a therapeutic abortion after the third month of pregnancy – this procedure is intended for cases where serious health problems have arisen for the foetus, or where pregnancy is unsustainable for the mother from a psychological point of view – is rarely taken into account by Italian medical staff. Furthermore, an additional obstacle is the lack of a hospital equipped to carry out this pharmacological and/or surgical intervention in Lampedusa: the island's maternity service offers only medical consultations. Hospitals where VTP can be accessed are located in Sicily, for example in Palermo.[8] Although the impossibility of *in loco* access to VTP services expresses the unequal condition migrants and local women from Lampedusa experience compared to Italian patients, the migrants' situation is even more complex because they are not free to leave the island. In this way, bureaucratic procedures, which are necessary for arranging their transfers to Sicily, may also endanger the possibility of undertaking VTP for migrant women who arrive in Lampedusa with a pregnancy of under three months:

> Every time I fill out a medical certificate to migrant people for pregnancy termination, I ask myself: can this certificate really help the patient? Because of the time required for organizing transfers to Sicily, many women lose their right to terminate their pregnancy. It is absurd that no exception is

made for these patients who cannot move independently, do not know Italian law and have undergone horrible experiences. As gynaecologists, we cannot do anything for them. Sometimes we try to pressure for their transfer, but the state machine does not always listen to the doctors. (Cristina, gynaecologist working at the Lampedusa maternity service since 2015)

The administrative system, which is responsible for migrants' transfers to Sicily, therefore limits the autonomy of patients to the point of indirectly hindering the right of women to end their pregnancies. The subordination of this right to the time the Italian state requires for migrant relocation in Sicily can be described as institutional violence against pregnant migrant women. As Cristina's testimony highlights, the influence of doctors' opinions on the Italian state's 'management system' is limited. Medical emergencies – those patients who cannot wait for collective transfers to Sicily and so are transported by medical helicopter – are the only exception to the trends described so far. In 2016, five Nigerian patients were transported by helicopter to Sicily as they faced the risk of having a miscarriage resulting from the difficult travel conditions across the Mediterranean Sea. By contrast, over 90 per cent of Nigerian migrants who asked for VTP were included in the collective transfers organized by Italian state, because this kind of health need is not considered to be a medical emergency.[9]

The Life of Migrant Women in Italy

The structures where migrant women reside after their arrival in Lampedusa are the Extraordinary Reception Centres (CAS) that were created by the Italian state in 2015 in order to cope with the increasing migratory flows across the Mediterranean.[10] These centres are located in all Italian regions, including Sicily.[11] Although these structures all have the same purpose, such as the reception of migrants during their asylum request assessments by the Italian courts, they can host a variable number of individuals (from 10 to 300) and they are managed by very different societies and organizations, both for-profit organizations (e.g. former owners of hotels) and non-profit organizations (e.g. cooperatives, non-governmental organizations). Furthermore, although these structures are understood as temporary places of residence, they accommodate 78 per cent of migrants and asylum seekers.[12] The increasing arrivals in recent years have made the Italian reception system overcrowded, with a consequent augmentation of the time needed for the evaluation of individual dossiers.

Thus, migrants who should only stay a few days on Lampedusa – the reception centre sited on the island is solely intended for registration and the initial reception[13]– are transferred after several weeks to the CAS in Sicily, where they remain for many months, if not more than a year, until their asylum request has been analysed by Italian courts. For pregnant migrants, their stay in these structures lasts the whole period of pregnancy, up to the first months after childbirth. Although people involved in the humanitarian sector (Agier 2008) describe this category of migrant as a population particularly in need of assistance and care, these principles do not coincide with better treatment women enjoy in the CAS I examined in Sicily. The diet of pregnant women, who receive the same food that is offered to the rest of 35 migrants residing in this centre, is emblematic in this regard: 'We eat pasta every day. Even if doctors tell us we have to eat other things, [yet] they still give us pasta' (Mary, 26). A woman's life inside the migration centre can be described as a 'suspended life', where the days pass in the same way: 'All that we do here is eat and sleep. We spend [all] our days doing nothing than this' (Miracol, 24). The reduction of daily life to a simple alternation of physiological needs (eating and sleeping) recalls the bio-political concept of the 'naked life' introduced by Giorgio Agamben (1998). This concept used to describe the situation of Jews in concentration camps, and that of displaced people in refugee camps, where we can witness a reduction of people's lives to biological existence (*Zoé*), without preserving any social or human life dimension (*Bios*), applies well to the time migrant women spend within the CAS investigated in Sicily.

These forms of daily life are not without consequences for women's health. Physical isolation and social exclusion – this structure, like most of the CAS in Italy, is located far from the city centre – are at the origin of pathologies that women undergo within the Italian reception system. The most common symptoms are headaches, gastritis, gestational diabetes, dermatitis, allergies, infections and forms of depression. These pathologies can be described as 'produced' by the living conditions these women face in the Italian reception system. In parallel, the physical transformation of women's physique during pregnancy works as an 'embodied memory' of the violence suffered in Libya, often leading to other forms of suffering. Symptoms of discomfort increase after particular events, such as the impossibility of accessing legal abortion, or the choice to abandon the child after its birth. Although Italian law provides for the presence of a psychologist in all reception centres, only a few have psychologists who speak English. Linguistic and cultural mediation services are also guaranteed in only some of these centres. These services, for example, were absent in the centre I investigated in Sicily, as in many of the CAS located in southern Italy, where migrants' reception has become a 'business' for the organizations that manage the structures where they live. The main result of these deficiencies within a system that has been created to provide assistance to migrants is that women's exchanges with psychologists able to support them during times of difficulty rarely take place. Despite the presence of other people from Nigeria, the prevailing sensation found among the women I interviewed was one of solitude.

Another phenomenon to be underlined is that the reception centre employees – often men – sometimes treat lightly the symptoms of malaise that migrants manifest. Expressions such as 'Is it really that bad?' or 'Is all this drama really necessary?' demonstrate an inclination to underestimate the suffering the women show, to the point of questioning the credibility of their stories. In the same way, comments such as 'I wonder why women from Nigeria are always pregnant?' show how sexist and racist prejudices can contaminate the employees who are engaged in the daily care of migrant women (Ribeiro Corossacz 2013). In some cases, the fact that about 30 per cent of the foreigners who practise prostitution in Italy are from Nigeria leads to a prejudiced belief in an 'innate correlation' between Nigerian nationality and a marked female sexuality.[14] The idea of a greater predisposition to prostitution among Nigerian women translates, likewise, into a frequent recourse to vulgar and aggressive language that is absent in interactions with other groups of migrants.

The need to reflect on the quality of care offered to migrant women also emerges from other situations observed during the research. Although the segmentation of health professionals (such as gynaecologists, medical ultra-sonographers, midwives) is typical of pregnancy care paths in Italy, the fragmentation of medical personnel involved in maternal and child health care appears particularly significant in the case of pregnant migrant women. Among the healthcare professionals whom women encounter during their pregnancy we find: general practitioners who carry out medical consultations at CAS; gynaecologists and midwives whom women meet at the clinics where they undergo ultrasound examinations; and gynaecologists and midwives in the hospitals where the women give birth. The physical distance between the CAS, the diagnostic centres and the hospitals often reduces the number of meetings between pregnant women and medical staff. Likewise, the transfer of clinical information from one place to another, and between different health professionals, increases the risk of medical errors, but also the risk of a loss of women's health dossiers. Finally, as in the case of psychologists, communication with doctors and midwives collides with the major problem of linguistic and cultural barriers; this is an obstacle that usually limits the transmission of information on medical interventions – sometimes invasive – to be made during childbirth (see Ana Cristina Vargas in this volume). According to the theories of Paul Farmer (2004), these tendencies can be described as examples of the structural violence suffered by migrants within the maternity services and the reception system in Italy.

Legal Itineraries: The Stain of 'Nigerian-ness'

Nigerian nationality constitutes a discriminating factor within the legislative system used (not only) in Italy to regulate the entry of foreign citizens. According to international conventions on the right to asylum, such as European Directive 36/2011, the possibility for migrants to be recognized as refugees depends largely on their nationality (Schuster 2011). Nigeria, like most countries in sub-Saharan Africa, is not included among the countries that are officially considered areas 'at risk' for the local population.[15] The only exceptions are the victims of the Boko Haram terrorist group in the north-eastern areas of Nigeria. This population corresponds to a minority within the sample studied, and more generally among the Nigerian population who have arrived in Italy in recent years. In most cases, the legal category applied to Nigerian women and men is that of 'economic migrant' – a category not entitled to access the right to asylum (Lavaud-Legendre and Peyroux 2014). Gender-based violence suffered by migrants, like the status of mothers, does not contribute to promoting the recognition of women as legitimate individuals for entering the category of asylum seekers.

For 90 per cent of the women who choose to leave Nigeria to escape domestic violence or to look for a better future in Europe, the time spent in the CAS and the observance of administrative procedures required for the construction of a personal dossier to be analysed by Italian courts does not lead to the desired result. As has emerged from the study conducted in Sicily, asylum applications are usually rejected. For migrants – who often become mothers in the meantime – there are two remaining possibilities: to return home, as Italian law states;[16] or to remain in Italy as undocumented migrants – individuals without documents authorizing them to stay in Europe. The willingness to continue the migration project generally leads women to choose the latter situation. The undocumented condition, however, will expose them to new forms of violence. The main risk, which affects many

Nigerian women who live without legal documentation in Italy, is entering the prostitution market – a situation that, although produced by the migratory laws, contributes to feeding negative stereotypes towards this group of migrants (Jaksic 2016).

According to the Italian legal system, Nigerian women and girls who are suspected of being involved in human trafficking for sexual purposes are not automatically included in the category of refugees (Law 24/2014). The request from the judges for a detailed analysis of the elements that emerge from their stories forces these women to provide concrete evidence of their status as 'victims' – the only way by which they will be able to attain the status of refugees later on (Taliani 2011; Andrijasevic and Mai 2016).[17] The protection programmes the Italian state offers to these women and girls during the time needed by the judges correspond to the fact that they are hosted in centres especially devoted to victims of the sexual market. The protection guaranteed in these structures where women and girls often live for a long time (from eight months to one year) only partially distances them from the risk of being intercepted by the forced prostitution networks. On the one hand, the number of these structures is limited, and does not allow accommodation for the growing number of Nigerian migrants considered to be potential victims of human trafficking. According to the IOM (2017) analyses, these represented about 80 per cent of women and girls who arrived in Italy in 2016 – a number equal to 8,277 people (versus 3,380 in 2015). Furthermore, the checks carried out by Italian police authorities in the areas adjacent to these spaces remain limited. Escapes and kidnappings by madams of young Nigerians girls are a widespread phenomenon, not only in Palermo and Sicily but throughout Italy. Many migrants practise forced prostitution while residing in the centres designed to combat this phenomenon. In Sicily, as in other regions of Italy, the use of clandestine abortion is increasing among Nigerian women. This practice, generally imposed by the madams on the girls involved in the forced prostitution market, has also emerged from stories told by other Nigerian migrants.

Conclusions

The analyses presented in this chapter show how the main element that characterizes the experiences of Nigerian women and girls who come to Europe while pregnant is a continuum of violence (Kelly 1987; Scheper-Hughes and Bourgois 2003; Krause 2015) before, during and after the migratory journey. The physical and psychological abuses suffered during the journey represent a first layer of often indelible suffering. The violence of the laws encountered in the countries where migrants are received reinforces these negative experiences. The restrictions imposed by Italian law on access to legal abortion are an example of institutional violence against people who are trying to prevent an unwanted physical condition, reminding them of the traumas suffered during migration. Furthermore, the fact that, among the criteria that determine the verdicts of Italian courts with regard to requests for protection, nationality of origin has a greater influence than individual stories and migratory experiences, is representative of the violence exercised through laws and migration policies. Like restrictions on access to legal abortion, this form of institutional violence amplifies the negative experiences women suffer on their journey to Europe.

The research carried out in Lampedusa and Sicily shows how these trends have an impact on women's health, with a consequent result of a progressive deterioration of physical and psychological well-being, and a strengthening of the level of social fragility (Bourgois 2001). Isolation and a lack of autonomy within the reception system are causes of suffering for the migrants, as well as of undocumented status that often forces them to move into the prostitution market. The cumulative nature of the physical, psychological, structural and institutional violence experienced by Nigerian migrants can be described, in conclusion, as a phenomenon in which gender-based relationships are intertwined with elements related to skin colour and native nationality; all these elements seem to work, separately and together, as discriminating factors against this female population. Thus, the representation of pregnant migrants as people who may strategically use their physical condition to more easily access residency permits and citizenship, as well as the recognition of human rights that should be guaranteed by the reception system, appear to be totally misleading, to the point of becoming another source of violence against this category of migrant.

Chiara Quagliariello is currently working as Marie Skłodowska-Curie postdoctoral fellow at the Ecole des Hautes Etudes en Sciences Sociales in Paris and the City University of New York within the Global Individual Fellowship 'Racialization in Reproduction: Maternal Health Crisis among Black Women in Europe and the US.' She has had study and research experiences at the Fundamental Rights Laboratory in Turin, the European University Institute in Florence, University College London and the Max Planck Institute of Social Anthropology. She has a long experience in field research in Italy, France and Senegal. Her research interests include medical anthropology, particularly childbirth models; reproductive rights; social and health inequalities; gender, class and ethnicity; intercultural medicine; and medical challenges in migrant patients' health care.

Notes

1. This border, corresponding to the Spanish enclaves of Ceuta and Melilla on the northern coast of Morocco, was closed in 2010 following agreements signed by Spain, Morocco and Algeria.
2. This border was closed on March 2016, following the EU–Turkey agreements.
3. The analyses refer to a period prior to the agreement drawn up between Italy and Libya in the summer of 2017. Since then, arrivals in Italy by sea have strongly declined.
4. The research was conducted as part of the ERC Starting Grant project, EU Border Care, titled 'Intimate Encounters in EU Borderlands: Migrant Maternity, Sovereignty and the Politics of Care on Europe's Periphery', directed by Vanessa Elisa Grotti at the European University Institute near Florence, Italy. The research was organized into two phases: seven months of research in Lampedusa and a month of research in Palermo.
5. Law no. 194/1978 regulates access to legal abortion in Italy. The high number of gynaecologists who oppose this procedure for reasons linked to conscientious objection, however, makes this right not always applicable.
6. The Italian reception system is organized on three levels. The first level includes the First Aid and Reception Centres (CPSA or *hotspot*), where migrants are hosted when they arrive in Italy. There are five of these centres in Italy, one of which is located in Lampedusa. The second level includes the Extraordinary Reception Centres (CAS) and the First Reception Centres (CPA), where migrants are hosted after their transfer from the CPSA. The third level includes the Reception Centres for Asylum Seekers (CARA) and the Protection System for Asylum Seekers and Refugees (SPRAR). To this set of structures are added the Centres of Identification and Expulsion (CIE), where migrants who have not obtained a residence permit live while waiting to be returned to their native countries. Representatives of the prefectures, the main police institutions in Italy, manage all these structures. In the case of migrants who are received at the CPSA of Lampedusa, their stay in the CAS in Sicily usually represents an intermediate step before being transferred to similar structures located in other regions of Italy. In the case of pregnant women, police institutions seek to prolong women's stay in the CAS located in Sicily in order to avoid multiple transfers on Italian territory during preg-

nancy and/or immediately after delivery. This is how it was possible for me to follow in Palermo the life trajectories and the care assistance offered to pregnant women whom I had previously met in Lampedusa.

7. This office, belonging to the Italian police and present in all municipalities and cities of Italy, deals with the registration of migrants who are residents or in transit through the national territory. In the case of Lampedusa, this office records all migrants landing on the island via search and rescue operations conducted in the Mediterranean by the Italian coastguard and the Frontex European police border control programme.
8. In this regard, it is necessary to remember the general difficulty to access legal abortion in Sicilian hospitals, where gynaecologists who are conscientious objectors represent 87.6% of the total.
9. The same applies for local women from Lampedusa. In the case of a medical emergency, these women are transferred to Sicily via medical helicopter. In other cases, the journey needed to access hospital services located in Sicily, including VTP services, are at their own expense (although Sicily reimburses 10% of these health expenses).
10. These structures were introduced in 2015 (Legislative Decree 142/2015, article 11).
11. See Note 6.
12. These data come from the document published in January 2017 by the Parliamentary Enquiry Commission on Migrants' Reception, Identification and Expulsion, as well as on the Conditions of Detention of Migrants and on the Public Resources Involved. See https://immigrazione.it/docs/2017/data-statistical-23-January-2017.pdf, last accessed 8 August 2020.
13. See Note 6.
14. About 100,000 women were involved in prostitution in Italy in 2016: of these, 55% were foreigners, 30% of whom came from Nigeria (Dossier Statistico Immigrazione 2016).
15. In 2016, there were 123,482 applications for asylum in Italy (this figure corresponds to about 10,000 applications a month, up 47% compared to 2015); 61% of requests were unsuccessful. The rejection therefore involved two-thirds of applications, or more than 55,000 people. With regard to people from Nigeria, there were 26,934 requests in 2016 (this corresponds to one-fifth of all applications received in Italy, and shows an increase of 48% compared to 2015); 71% of these requests had a negative outcome. The same trend emerges in the case of other migrants of sub-Saharan origin (for example, 73% of applications from Senegalese migrants had a negative outcome). In contrast, most of asylum applications coming from people who arrived from Syria, Afghanistan, Somalia and Eritrea were successful (for example, 92% of Syrian applications and 75% of Somali and Eritrean applications were accepted). See http://www.ismu.org/2018/02/richiedenti-asilo-record-nel-2017/, last accessed 7 August 2020.

16. According to Italian law (DL 89/2011), migrants who have not obtained a residence permit must return at their own expense to their home country. In the case of Nigeria, Italy has signed an agreement with this country to promote the return policy. This agreement, which is in contrast to the international principles of free movement of persons, encounters various obstacles in its application because of the high costs. To date, the repatriation of Nigerian migrants does not take place systematically, and is mainly only applied to males.
17. In recent years, there have been some jurisprudential developments. The decision that the court of Salerno made in February 2017 to accord, in the first instance, refugee status to two Nigerian girls who were considered potential victims of sexual exploitation is an example.

References

Adepoju, A. 2017. 'Nigeria: Leaving Africa's Giant', in G. Carbone (ed.), *Out of Africa: Why People Migrate*. Milan: ISPI, pp. 119–40.

Agamben, G. 1998. *Homo Sacer: Sovereign Power and Bare Life*. Stanford, CA: Stanford University Press.

Agier, M. 2008. *Gérer les indésirables: Des camps de réfugiés au gouvernement humanitaire*. Paris: Flammario.

Akor, L. 2011. 'Trafficking of Women in Nigeria: Causes, Consequences and The Way Forward'. *International Journal of Sociology and Social Policy* 2: 89–110.

Amnesty International. 2016. 'Refugees and Migrants Fleeing Sexual Violence, Abuse and Exploitation in Libya'. Retrieved 15 December 2017 from https://www.amnesty.org/en/latest/news/2016/07/refugees-and-migrants-fleeing-sexual-violence-abuse-and-exploitation-in-libya/.

Andall, J. 2000. *Gender, Migration and Domestic Service: The Politics of Black Women in Italy*. London: Routledge.

Andrijasevic, R., and N. Mai. 2016. 'Editorial: Trafficking in Representations: Understanding the Recurring Appeal of Victimhood and Slavery in Neoliberal Times'. *Anti-Trafficking Review* 7: 1–10.

Anthias, F., and G. Lazarinis. 2000. *Gender and Migration in Southern Europe: Women on the Move*. Oxford and New York: Berg.

Anthias, F., and N. Yuval-Davis. 1992. *Racialized Boundaries: Race, Nation, Gender, Colour, Class and the Anti-Racist Struggle*. London: Routledge.

Bourgois, P. 2001. 'The Power of Violence in War and Peace: Post-Cold War Lessons from El Salvador'. *Ethnography* 2(1): 5–34.

Brigdes, K. 2011. *Reproducing Race: An Ethnography of Pregnancy as a Site of Racialization*. Berkeley: University of California Press.

Crenshaw, K.W. 1991. 'Mapping the Margins: Intersectionality, Identity Politics, and Violence against Women of Color'. *Stanford Law Review* 43(4): 1241–99.

Cuttitta, P. 2015. 'La frontiérisation de Lampedusa: Comment se construit une frontière'. *L'Espace politique* 1(25).
Dossier Statistico Immigrazione. 2016. Rome: IDOS.
Ehrenreich, B., and A.R. Hochschild. 2004. *Global Women: Nannies, Maids, and Sex Workers in the New Economy*. New York: Henry Holt and Company.
Farmer, P. 2004. 'An Anthropology of Structural Violence'. *Current Anthropology* 45(3): 305–25.
Fassin, D. 2007. 'Humanitarianism as a Politics of Life'. *Public Culture* 19(3): 499–520.
———. 2011. 'Policing Borders, Producing Boundaries: The Governmentality of Immigration in Dark Times'. *Annual Review of Anthropology* 40: 213–26.
Frank, B. 1995. 'Permitted and Prohibited Wealth: Commodity-Possessing Spirits, Economic Morals, and the Goddess Mami Wata in West Africa'. *Ethnology* 34: 331–46.
Freedman, J. 2016. 'Sexual and Gender-Based Violence against Refugee Women: A Hidden Aspect of the Refugee Crisis'. *Reproductive Health Matters* 24(47): 18–26.
Friese, H. 2017. 'Representations of Gendered Mobility and the Tragic Border Regime in the Mediterranean'. *Journal of Balkan and Near Eastern Studies* 19(5): 541–556.
Grotti, V., et al. 2017. 'Pregnant Crossings: A Political Economy of Care on Europe's External Borders', in S. Shekhawat and D. Aurobinda (eds), *Women and Borders: Refugees, Migrants and Communities*. London: I.B. Tauris, pp. 63–85.
Guillemaut, F. 2008. 'Sex, Juju and Migrations: An Anthropological Look at the Migratory Processes of African Women in France'. *Recherches sociologiques et anthropologiques* 39(1): 11–26.
Huysmans, J. 2000. 'The European Union and the Securitization of Migration'. *Journal of Common Market Studies* 38(5): 751–77.
International Organization for Migration (IOM). 2016. 'Mediterranean Migrant Arrivals in 2016'. Retrieved 14 August 2020 from https://www.iom.int/news/mediterranean-migrant-arrivals-top-363348-2016-deaths-sea-5079.
———. 2017. 'La tratta di esseri umani attraverso la rotta del Mediterraneo Centrale: dati, storie e informazioni raccolte dall'Organizzazione Internazionale per le migrazioni'. Retrieved 10 August 2020 from http://www.italy.iom.int/it/notizie/rapporto-oim-sempre-pi%C3%B9-giovani-e-sempre-pi%C3%B9-vulnerabili-le-potenziali–vittime–di–tratta.
Jaksic, M. 2016. *La traite des êtres humains en France: De la victime idéale à la victime coupable*. Paris: Editions CNRS.
Kelly, L. 1987. 'The Continuum of Sexual Violence, Women', in J. Hanmer and M. Maynard (eds), *Violence and Social Control*. New York: Springer, pp. 46–60.

Krause, U. 2015. 'A Continuum of Violence? Linking Sexual and Gender-Based Violence during Conflict, Flight, and Encampment'. *Refugee Survey Quarterly* 34(4): 1–19.

Lavaud-Legendre, B. 2003. *Prostitution nigériane: Entre rêves de migration et réalité de la traite.* Paris: Karthala.

Lavaud-Legendre, B., and O. Peyroux. 2014. 'Mineures nigérianes et originaires des Balkans en situation de traite en France: Regards pluridisciplinaires sur les processus d'asservissement et les échecs de la protection'. *Revue européenne des migrations internationals* 30(1): 105–30.

Mai, N. 2014. 'Between Embodied Cosmopolitism and Sexual Humanitarianism: The Fractal Mobilities and Subjectivities of Migrants Working in the Sex Industry', in V. Baby-Collins and L. Anteby (eds), *Borders, Mobilities and Migrations: Perspectives from the Mediterranean in the 21st Century.* Brussels: Peter Lang, pp. 175–92.

Menjívar, C. 2014. 'Immigration Law beyond Borders: Externalizing and Internalizing Border Controls in an Era of Securitization'. *Annual Review of Law and Social Science* 10: 353–69.

Onyejekwe Chizene, J. 2005. 'Influences of Global Human Trafficking Issues on Nigeria: A Gender Perspective'. *Journal of International Women's Studies* 7(1): 141–51.

Osezua, C.O. 2016. 'Gender Issues in Human Trafficking in Edo State, Nigeria'. *African Sociological Review* 20(1): 36–66.

Pinelli, B. 2017. 'Borders, Politics and Subjects: Introductory Notes on Refugee Research in Europe'. *Etnografia e Ricerca Qualitativa* 1: 5–24.

Ribeiro Corossacz, V. 2013. 'L'intersezione di razzismo e sessismo: Strumenti teorici per un'analisi della violenza maschile contro le donne nel discorso pubblico sulle migrazioni'. *Antropologia* 15: 109–29.

Salazar Parreñas, R. 2001. *Servants of Globalization: Women, Migration and Domestic Work.* Stanford, CA: Stanford University Press.

Salih, R. 2003. *Gender in Transnationalism: Home, Longing and Belonging among Moroccan Migrant Women.* London: Routledge.

Scheper-Hughes, N., and P. Bourgois. 2003. 'Introduction: Making Sense of Violence', in N. Scheper-Hughes and P. Bourgois (eds), *Violence in War and Peace: An Anthology.* Malden, MA: Blackwell Publishing, pp. 1–31.

Schuster, L. 2011. 'Turning Refugees into "Illegal Migrants": Afghan Asylum Seekers in Europe'. *Ethnic and Racial Studies* 34(8): 1392–1407.

Singleton, M. 1990. 'Which Christians? What Witches? A Survey in South-West Nigeria'. *Psychopathologie Africaine* XXIII(1): 61–76.

Taliani, S. 2011. 'A Credible Past and a Shameless Body: History, Violence and Repetition in the Lives of Asylum Seekers Women in Italy'. *Societés politiques comparées* 32: 1–36.

———. 2012. 'Coercion, Fetish and Suffering in the Daily Lives of Young Nigerian Women in Italy'. *Africa* 82(4): 579–608.

Ticktin, M. 2008. 'Sexual Violence as the Language of Border Control'. *Signs: Journal of Women in Culture and Society* 33(4): 863–89.

Weiss, M. 2002. 'The Body of the Nation: Terrorism and the Embodiment of Nationalism in Contemporary Israel'. *Anthropological Quarterly* 75(1): 37–62.

Part II

From the Individual to the Community

5

Roma and the Right to Health

A Transnational Approach to Structural Vulnerability

Pietro Cingolani

Introduction

In this chapter I analyse the relationship between the right to health, structural vulnerability and forms of transnational mobility. As already highlighted in the Introduction to the present volume, disease is not exclusively a biomedical issue but is also a product of the sociopolitical conditions in which people live (Nguyen and Peschard 2003). Quesada, Hart and Bourgeois use the concept of structural vulnerability to explain the health conditions of undocumented migrants in the United States. As these authors point out, 'structural vulnerability focuses on how a host of mutually reinforcing insults (ranging from the economic and political to the cultural and psychodynamic) that dispose individuals and communities towards ill health are embodied' (Quesada, Hart and Bourgeois 2011: 4). Individuals living in situations of exploitation and social devaluation internalize these conditions and modify their behaviour, action and self-perception. This literature helps to problematize the concept of agency: individuals never act in complete freedom but are conditioned by external forces that also define their perception of the most appropriate and adequate responses to the problems that they experience, including in the context of their own health. The concept of vulnerability thus highlights social inequalities and invites an elaboration of responses in both the social and the political spheres.

The transnational perspective has made an important contribution to migration and mobility studies. This perspective highlights how migrants maintain emotional, social, economic and cultural ties between their countries of departure and their countries of arrival (Levitt and Glick Schiller 2004). These links are also important when migrants seek answers to their own health concerns (Bell et al. 2015; Villa-Torres et al. 2017).

Within the transnational perspective, there has been for some time a tendency to underestimate the power of differences between various types of migrants; transnationalism has been described as a form of emancipation and a new cosmopolitan identity (Canzler, Kaufmann and Kesserling 2008). In response to these viewpoints, mobility scholars have increased their attention to the different positions of actors; they have analysed how power dynamics intersect with mobilities in 'differentiated politics of mobility' (Cresswell 2010: 552). As Hannam, Sheller and Urry (2006: 11) explain, 'analysing mobilities thus involves examining many consequences for different peoples and places, located in what we might call the fast and slow lanes of social life'.

Often, therefore, in order to explain transnational mobility in the health sector, social inequalities have been given little weight, and forms of mobility for health reasons have not been viewed in relation to aspects of structural violence. For example, cross-border health care and medical tourism research has focused on studying the health trajectories of people who choose to use therapeutic systems in multiple countries because they have many economic and social resources (Mainil 2012).

As I explain more fully below, travelling to seek treatment solutions can also be the answer to strong social exclusion in the immigration context; at the same time, one can fully fulfil one's health rights while remaining immobile. An example is patients who have the economic wherewithal to order expensive drugs from online pharmacies and have them delivered directly to where they live. If the theme of inequality is central, the constraints, causes and effects of mobility in relation to health can be better observed (Cingolani and Ferrero 2015).

The Roma are an interesting case for studying the relationship between structural vulnerability, mobility and health. In this chapter I attempt to understand how the conditions of life of Romanian Roma in Italy and in Romania produce various forms of transnational mobility. In the first part, the reader is introduced to the characteristics of the Roma population, with particular reference to the living conditions within the camps. Next, I discuss the conditions for accessing health-care services in both Italy and Romania, and I present the specific context in which the research was carried out, analysing the complex relationship between Roma patients and health-care workers. In the last part of the chapter, through four illustrative stories, I present different forms of transnationalism that individuals have adopted in response to situations of marginality and illness.

Roma and Health Conditions in Italy: A General Overview

Delimiting any subject of a study implies, from the very definition of the subject, certain epistemological presuppositions. The relationship between the Roma and health care is indeed complex, starting with the definition of the two terms.

The first point to clarify is which social group is being referred to. The term Roma is often used in an undifferentiated way in public discourse, by workers and also in health surveys. The populations to whom this term refers in fact constitute a 'galaxy of minorities' (Dell'Agnese and Vitale 2007); in other words, they are communities that do not have a single history, a strongly homogeneous culture, or a single language or religion. One of the few traits shared by the members is the differential treatment they receive from the outside.

This group, described in a homogeneous way, has often been ascribed specific characteristics differentiating it from the majority population. One of these characteristics is nomadism. In Italy, since the 1980s, the use of the term 'nomad' has spread in the administrative arena – this term has been deemed politically correct because it was believed to reflect a common cultural trait. However, nomadism was a feature of the past and, by the 1980s, could be ascribed to the behaviour of only a very small percentage of these populations – according to some authors less than 20 per cent (Vitale 2010).

Out of respect for the presumed nomadism, Italian public institutions built specific residential structures: the nomad camps. These originated as resting areas for groups of mobile people, and one of the main objectives was to 're-educate' their inhabitants; that is, to bring them closer to the practices and organizational forms of local populations, for example by enrolling their children in school.

In the nomad camps, Roma were often treated not as individuals but were turned into a nameless mass by the bureaucracy. Residency in the camps was regulated through complex bureaucratic rules aimed at the systematic control of the people present, through frequent requests for renewal of residence permits and continuous checks by local police.

In addition to official camps in Italy, many spontaneous settlements appeared over the years, often near formal camps. These camps were frequently inhabited by Roma families who had been expelled from the regular camps or by those not recognized or officially catered to by the social services of the cities. The relationship between formal and informal camps is not clear-cut because public authorities in fact implemented interventions and checks of various kinds in many of the spontaneous settlements.

The city authorities ascribed social labels to the occupants of the camps according to their needs: sometimes they were considered deviant, sometimes as poor and needy people who had to be looked after. There were families who, until their arrival in Italy, had always lived in homes but had agreed to settle in the rest areas and to 'revert to gypsy' (Piasere 2004) in response to the logic of the non-Roma and to access the few resources intended for them. The Roma populations residing in the camps were therefore understood according to a differential treatment; they adopted emergency, assistance and reception solutions, always based on the principle of social control and on the idea of guaranteeing public security.[1] The camps are the product of a dominant discourse that defined the Roma as nomadic and uninterested in integrating into society. The camps then ended up determining relations between the Roma and the external society. The dimension of separation generated by them has in fact limited the opportunities for equal interaction between Roma and non-Roma, and has meant that non-Roma have become accustomed to thinking of Roma as radically other.

The differential logic on which the construction of the camps was based can be found in many interventions in other areas as well, such as in the working, educational and even health sectors, and has had a profound effect on people's quality of life. In the equipped rest areas of many Italian cities, hygienic conditions have proven to be critical; the occupants live in conditions of permanent psychological precariousness, and often develop conflictual relations with the residents of the districts, who accuse them of being responsible for the degradation of their neighbourhoods. Life in the camps has also had consequences for the schooling of children and for the employment of adults, as well as for legal status.

Another point to clarify is whether there are specific health conditions affecting the Roma. These populations have been the subject, over time, of studies that have generated a static vision of reality. As highlighted by Alunni (2015), if we analyse studies on the health aspects of the Roma, many are about hereditary health issues (Trevisan 2004); qualitative studies that combine an analysis of health conditions with a sociopolitical analysis are much rarer. Some authors (Monasta et al. 2012), starting with an analysis of the literature produced on the topic of Roma and health in Italy, conclude that many studies have serious limitations because of the categories used to interpret the results. The precarious health conditions of the Roma are often traced to a presumed nomadism and not to the difficulty of accessing basic services. Many studies have emphasized the low compliance with vaccination campaigns, without pointing out that these data must be connected to the lack of services in the different areas in which these populations reside. There is also a tendency on the part of the authors to generalize, without taking into account the extreme territorial variations linked to the migration background, the specific characteristics of the groups, or the way local opportunities are structured. Several studies were also conducted on very small portions of the population, making generalization difficult. Epidemiological investigations conducted in Italy refer only to populations living in conditions of severe housing precariousness, and not to the entire Roma population.[2]

From these investigations, supplemented by more qualitative contributions deriving from experiences of social intervention, scholars have come to define the health profile of the target population, identifying a series of recurrent elements: high birth rates, low life expectancy at birth, and a high rate of diseases among both adults and children. They also emphasize that the most common diseases among adults are cardiovascular, osteoarticular, respiratory, metabolic and gastro-enteric; depression and migraines are also prevalent. Among minors it is evident that respiratory diseases, gastro-intestinal infections, dental infections and infectious diseases are widespread (Ricordy, Motta and Geraci 2014).

As already mentioned, several authors have pointed out that health interventions present a differentialist approach confirming the exceptional conditions in which Roma are forced to live (European Commission 2014; ERRC 2006). Alunni (2017), for example, presents the experience of mobile medical units in the camps of Rome, and demonstrates how these interventions, characterized by a humanitarian rhetoric, fit into a state surveillance policy that actually keeps Roma away from enjoying the full rights of citizenship and health. Similar considerations are presented by Nacu (2011) when she analyses the intervention by volunteer doctors in the shanty towns around Paris. Romanian Roma living in these slums in France are deliberately left in legal limbo by the institutions, and the only contact they have with the health-care system is through the mediation of volunteer workers. Many of these conditions I have likewise found in the experiences of the Roma population that I have studied.

Romanian Roma in the City of Turin

The information presented in this chapter is the result of ethnographic research among Roma Romanians conducted in the city of Turin and in the Romanian departure territories between 2012 and 2014.[3] In Turin, Roma coming from Romania are only part of the whole Roma population present. Piedmontese Sinti with Italian citizenship were present in the urban area before them. They were followed, from the mid-1960s, by Roma groups from Eastern Europe, especially from Bosnia, Serbia, Croatia, Kosovo, Macedonia and Montenegro. These populations increased following the Balkan wars of the 1990s, when many of them arrived in Italy as asylum seekers.

Romanian Roma arrived in the city at the end of the 1990s and increased significantly after 2007, when Romania joined the European Union, which lowered travel costs. Estimates of the Roma population in Turin are highly inaccurate, because they are the result of censuses conducted at different times in the regular camps, the spontaneous settlements, public housing and private accommodation. At the time I conducted my research, there was a total of just over three thousand Roma in Turin, of which about fifteen hundred were Romanians; the majority resided in spontaneous settlements.[4]

Most of the interviews and observations were made in what was the largest spontaneous camp in the city, the Lungo Stura camp. This camp no longer exists because at the end of 2015 it was closed. It was succeeded by an impressive relocation project for the inhabitants, lasting about two years, in which some people moved to rented apartments in Turin, some moved to other Italian cities, and some returned to Romania thanks to financial help provided by the project; the majority, however, just moved to other spontaneous camps within the city.[5]

The Romanian Roma present in the camp had come mostly from Western Romania, from the historic region of Banat; a smaller group had come from Eastern Romania, from the historical region of Moldova. Romanian Roma families are divided according to many criteria. They are distinguished, for example, by their belonging to subgroups (*natsia* in the Romani language) based on professional characteristics, even if they have often lost the memory of the origins of these denominations – their current professions rarely coincide with those of their ancestors (*badanari*, paintbrush makers; *ursari*, bear tamers; *caramidari*, brickmakers, etc.). A number of Roma call themselves *țigan romanizat* (Romanized gypsy), underscoring their belonging to a group that has been strongly assimilated into the majority population, especially during the Romanian socialist regime (Achim 2004). The Romanian Roma of Turin live in fairly small family groups made up of parents, children and sometimes grandparents. Some Roma families have a transnational organization, with some members living in Italy and others in Romania. Moreover, the size of the families may vary over time, because, depending on the opportunities, some members return to Romania while others arrive in Italy.

The conditions within the camp where I conducted my research were precarious for several reasons. The camp was on land polluted by industrial waste material. There was no drinking water, to the extent that families took this from public fountains outside the camp. Electricity was produced using transformers and the heating by burning plastic or other rubbish on stoves. All of these characteristics negatively affected residents' state of health, especially that of the children, who often suffered from bronchitis, respiratory diseases and dermatitis.[6] As Sigona (2015) points out, life in the camp leaves permanent traces in the bodies of the inhabitants, who become 'the sites of incorporated history'. The camp was also located in a peripheral area of the city with few public connections to the centre and without nearby health services, such as doctors' surgeries and hospitals.

From all these points of view, the camp was an exceptional space. It was isolated but, at the same time, had multiple ties to the external space (Solimene 2017): for years, helpers from volunteer associations, journalists, researchers, social workers and police attended the camp, building networks of control but also conveying information and resources.[7] The camp was also connected, both materially and symbolically, with many places in Romania. The inhabitants of the camp sent money earned home to Romania, as well as various objects such as materials collected from the refuse or bought at second-hand markets. Their presence and lives in the camp therefore took place within dense transnational networks which, as will be seen, were also relevant in the choices they made about health care.

Legal Status and Access to Treatment in Italy and in Romania

The legal status of the Roma has been crucial in determining their relationship with health-care services. The Roma immigrants of Romanian origin that I interviewed have had different legal statuses over the years. Until 2007, they were non-EU citizens and, therefore, because the vast majority of them resided in Italy without residency permits, the only possibility of gaining access to public health services was linked to their possession of the STP (Temporarily Present Foreigner) card.[8] Later, with the entry of Romania into the EU, their legal status changed. Some have succeeded in obtaining residency in Italy and therefore enrolment in the national health system with the assignment of a general practitioner; many others now have the right to health care thanks to the ENI (European Person Not Registered) card. In the transition from one system to another, many people found themselves living in a state of bureaucratic limbo for long periods; even after 2007, STP cards were still being issued to Romanian citizens even though the cards were no longer recognized. In Italy, health services and their financial management are delegated to the regions – the twenty governmental units lower than the state. Essential care should always be guaranteed in equal measure throughout the national territory but, in practice, there are significant differences, and many regional systems do not apply the principle of fairness to the most fragile groups (Geraci, Bonciani and Martinelli 2010). For this reason, in addition to the problems outlined above, all citizens, not just migrants, find themselves having different experiences depending on area where they live.

In accessing services, the Roma experience forms of exclusion that are not linked to their legal conditions, but are often due to lack of information, distrust and sometimes to discriminatory attitudes on the part of the health-care workers (Ricordy, Motta and Geraci 2014). For example, research has shown that many Romanian Roma, although residing in Italy for a long time, do not possess STP or ENI cards, and thus are totally excluded from the public system of provision of care.

The experiences that my interviewees had in Romania is certainly not better than in Italy. Access to care in Romania is guaranteed, at least formally, for all citizens, by a compulsory insurance system that is regulated by a national health insurance fund. The structure remains highly centralized, despite recent attempts to decentralize the regulatory functions; 86 per cent of the Romanian population is formally covered, while the rest of the uninsured population is entitled to a minimum level of assistance covering life-threatening emergencies, epidemic-prone/infectious diseases and care during pregnancy (OECD/European Observatory on Health Systems and Policies 2017). The costs for the patients will increase again because a new tax reform calls for a fixed monetary contribution, even from the unemployed and Romanian citizens who have emigrated abroad.

All persons covered by insurance are entitled to the same level of care regardless of their economic conditions and place of residence, but there are profound differences in the quality of the services provided – for example, between rural and urban areas. The healthcare system has been experiencing a strong privatization process for more than ten years, especially for large hospitals and specialized treatment centres, which are becoming increasingly expensive for patients (Vlădescu et al. 2016). To all these negative elements is added profound corruption in the system; doctors and health professionals often demand payment of a bribe from patients in order to provide them with health-care services – basic as well as specialized services. This fact emerged in many of the interviews conducted during my research, and is also confirmed by several studies on the Romanian health system.[9] Many Roma are in the segment of the population most affected by the shortcomings of the public health system (Roth and Toma 2014). Many of them come from depressed and marginal areas of Romania where the services are worst. Often, they are not registered in any form with the health system because they lack residence documents or have expired identity cards, and this further worsens their condition. A survey conducted by FRA in 2011 showed that only 45 per cent of Roma claimed to possess health insurance, while among the non-Roma population the proportion was 85 per cent (FRA 2011). These characteristics of the Romanian public health system make it clear why and how many Roma deal with their health-care issues by seeking treatment options in both Italy and Romania, and in some cases also in other European countries.

The Complex Relationship between Roma and Health-Care Workers

The relationship between the Roma living in the camp and the health services of Turin is quite complex. There were many contacts with health-care workers. First, there were several projects in which doctors or volunteer health workers entered the shanty town to provide assistance and information to the inhabitants. Second, many camp residents attended free-access clinics providing assistance at no charge. These clinics were run by private associations and did not require identification documents.

There were several cases of emergencies in which people came to the emergency service departments of city hospitals. To understand the therapeutic pathways of the Roma it is essential to understand the perception that health-care professionals have of Roma patients. Among the workers I have found different approaches, which I define here as 'expulsive', 're-educational', 'generalizing' and 'culturalist'.

A first, rather recurrent approach was the 'expulsive' one. The Roma patient is considered to be the bearer of a diversity that cannot be understood or managed. One doctor stated:

> Many of my colleagues do not want to get their hands dirty; they would never go to a Roma camp. Better to receive them in their nice, clean offices. It is a question of status; working with Roma and with immigrants is not prestigious. Imagine that in the competition to work in the clinic with the immigrants there were three free places and only twenty candidates presented themselves. Incredible, when they say that there is no work. And then the health director sent a message asking who wanted to voluntarily participate in a project in the Roma camps. Not one doctor showed up, just me. Not even my colleague – who has been in the clinic for much longer than me – wanted to do it. I accepted because I [had] worked in African countries for many years and these realities do not scare me.

This testimony discloses a widespread attitude of refusal because working to help to treat the poor does not interest many health professionals, especially when the poor are also Roma.

A second approach that emerged among the workers is the 're-educational' one. Roma patients are infantilized and considered to be in need of guidance and care. These are the words of a paediatrician working in a public health clinic:

> There are big problems, especially with prevention. We often have to repeat to Roma mothers that they should not give fried or fatty foods to young

children; many women do it because they have never received any health education. We need to explain everything from zero because they have lived in such an isolated way and with no possibility of discussing these issues. There is a lot of work to do, but this is the best part of our work.

This attitude of care and attention emerges above all towards female patients. In fact, women are considered to be vulnerable subjects par excellence, and special assistance programmes are dedicated to them in both the social and health fields. But at the very moment when women are included in these programmes, they enter a path of control and evaluation that is based on a highly normative view of social intervention. The beneficiaries are considered victims, but if they do not meet the standards for 'good patients', they are punishable (Vrăbiescu and Kalir 2018). The following testimony was given to me by a doctor who works as a volunteer in a clinic:

> Many Roma women do their own thing. There is an instrumental relationship because they think: 'I do it only because I have an immediate advantage'. And then many women do not turn to doctors because they are afraid of communicating with social workers. Social workers can bring material help but at the same time they have the reputation of taking away children.

This testimony highlights a tension often experienced by the Roma. They try to present themselves as good and diligent patients, but they are also afraid of the sanctions available to the institutions. These fears have not facilitated, over the years, the building of relationships of trust with health-care workers.

There are two other ways in which Roma patients are represented. In the 'generalizing' approach, health-care workers place the inhabitants of the camps into a single group and create an anonymous community. The camp transforms its inhabitants and eventually determines their identity. This aspect explains why assessments of Roma patients are also expressed by those who, for different reasons, have never entered the camps and therefore base their evaluations on an imagined space. These are the words of a nurse from the maternity ward of a hospital:

> I've never been there, but I think the conditions in the camps make them all more or less the same. Many Roma choose to live in irregular camps; they are used to staying there because their idea is to spend as little as possible in Italy and build a house in Romania. In my opinion they could also rent a house, but for them it is not a priority, and so they come to the hospital in the conditions that I see.

Other health professionals, when analysing the behaviour of Roma in the health sphere, adopt a 'culturalist' approach, and make a strict distinction between 'modern Roma' and 'traditional Roma'. This classification is based on various elements, such as clothing or the degree of knowledge of the Italian language, but also on the methods adopted in the therapeutic relationship. In some cases, the workers have also highlighted a generational difference, underscoring how younger patients are progressively moving away from the 'traditional' norms that are respected by their parents. For example, younger women are much less resistant than older women to visits by male doctors. The modern Roma, according to the health-care workers encountered, are able to understand the logic of the proposed health interventions, have a greater adherence to the treatment pathways and are more reliable. The traditional Roma are seen as more resistant to the proposals of doctors because of the influence of premodern conceptions that for doctors are difficult to decode. A health-care worker explained it to me this way:

> There are traditional Roma that we also call colourful Roma because the women dress in big long skirts. It is much more difficult to work with them because they have a special relationship with the body, they have very strong customs and traditions. And then there are the other Roma, who are like any other patient, accustomed to the relationship with doctors, and with them it is much easier to understand one another.

These categories are used by the workers but are also reproduced by the patients to legitimize themselves in the eyes of those health workers. In particular, the contrast between traditional and modern Roma is often used by Roma when interacting with health workers. In a clinic run by volunteers where, during paediatric visits for children, diapers and milk powder were distributed free, I observed a Roma woman from the camp commenting on how it was becoming more and more complicated to receive these free goods. She claimed that those like her who attended the scheduled visits, were punctual and respected the rules should be rewarded: 'I pay close attention and listen to the doctor, because I am civilized. That is, I am Roma, but not like the colourful ones, who come here when it suits them. For this reason, I should receive something more'.

The rigid contrast between assimilated Roma and traditional Roma is found not only in the representations of the workers and in the self-representations of the Roma, but it also partly occurs in the scientific literature. On the one hand, there are scholars who focus on the description of Roma groups strongly anchored to traditions, emphasizing how cultural difference is the basis for explaining all their behaviours and choices in the field of health. This literature focuses on the concepts of 'modesty and purity', 'fear of contamination' and beliefs in spiritual or magical entities (Sutherland 1992; Von Hausen 1992; Liegeois 1994; Smith 1997; Hancock 2002; Vivian and Dundes 2004). On the other hand, there is a literature that explains Roma health almost exclusively in terms of material disadvantage, and which gives little relevance to the existence of other cultural factors (Parekh and Rose 2011). The boundaries between these categories are much more nuanced than this literature suggests; in many situations, the Roma combine biomedical solutions with traditional medicine. To sum up, the following factors influence Roma in their decisions on their health: their legal conditions; the material conditions of their lives; and the perception and the representations that the health-care workers have of them. In the following section, I analyse how some transnational strategies implemented by the Roma in everyday life are a response to these.

Transnational Mobility and Immobility in the Health Environment

The conditions of vulnerability experienced in Italy or Romania have led to the activation of links or strategies of transnational mobility, with different outcomes. In some cases, people manage to solve their problems by combining solutions from various geographical and cultural spheres; in others, they find only partial or temporary answers; in others still, people remain trapped within their transnational paths, without finding a real solution. The four stories I describe below represent four different transnational behaviours that Roma living in the camp have developed in response to conditions of discomfort and disease.

The Story of Csoran: Transnationalism as a Double Exclusion

Csoran is a 57-year-old Roma from a rural village in western Romania. He arrived in Italy in 2004, lived in several Italian cities, and from 2009 he went to live in the Lungo Stura camp in Turin, from where he was evicted at the end of 2015. In Turin, Csoran worked occasionally as a bricklayer while his wife retrieved material from amongst rubbish and resold it at market. For many years Csoran had no contact with

Italian health facilities. His first experience was in the summer of 2011, when he showed up at the accident and emergency department because of a cyst on his neck that he had long neglected. The cyst had suddenly broken and caused a large infection. The accident and emergency Csoran went to belonged to a large hospital in the north of Turin. Csoran described his first contact with the institution: 'Until that day I had never gone to hospital. Because in hospitals there are only sick people and it's better to stay away from them. I went to that hospital because they say the nurses are kind and do not leave you until last, even if they see you're a gypsy'.

Csoran was medicated and the doctors arranged for antibiotics and a replacement bandage every two weeks. When he started therapy, Csoran discovered to his surprise that it was not totally free because every intervention involved payment for a ticket. Csoran was convinced that, with the mediation of social workers working in the camp, he could have avoided that expense. Thus, he commented: 'These workers are good but take care of too many things at the same time. Their duty is to help us to solve problems. They take money from the European Union in our place, money that we should have received. Thirty euros for each treatment is too much for me'.

Csoran abandoned the prescribed therapy after the first visit. This decision was determined by the high cost of the medicine and by the perception that social and health workers had denied him a right to which he believed he was theoretically guaranteed.

The situation of Csoran in the following months worsened because the infection spread. In the meantime, the project to clear the camp had begun. When social workers assessed his situation, they proposed an assisted voluntary repatriation process to Romania for him and his family, where travel expenses and a financial contribution would be made for the first six months spent at home. Csoran accepted because at that time he hoped to be able to heal more effectively in Romania.

I met Csoran again in the summer of 2014 in his home town, where he had arrived a few months before. The situation was even more difficult than the one he had encountered in Turin. Csoran told me that he felt a lot of distrust, especially from health-care professionals whom he had asked to solve his cyst problem. Romanian nurses and doctors made many financial demands of him, which he compared to the money for the treatment he would have had to pay in Italy at the hospital:

> Here it is worse than in Italy, everyone wants to get paid, nothing is free. They always ask me the same questions: What did I do to be sent away?

How much money did they give me? This happened especially with the doctor. I didn't believe everything had stayed the same in Romania. In Italy there was a ticket that was paid at the hospital cash desk and here in Romania it's the same thing, although they don't give you a receipt.

The only alternative Csoran had was to seek treatment at an expensive private hospital in the nearby city, but the financial contribution he had received from the repatriation project was not sufficient to meet the expenses. The contribution, which should theoretically have guaranteed a path towards social reintegration in Romania, allowing him to search for a job and manage the costs for health and other social services, was just enough to cover the expense of repairing his house. Csoran, who in Italy had not found a solution to his health problem, had become involved in a project that resulted in bankruptcy, such that now back in Romania he wanted to go abroad again. In his case, transnationalism between Italy and Romania revealed non-inclusion, from both a social and a health point of view, in both contexts.

Marinela's Story: Transnationalism as a Creative Option

Marinela is a 40-year-old Roma woman who arrived in Turin in 2011. She lived in the Lungo Stura camp with her elderly parents and her ten-year-old daughter, Adina. In Italy, Marinela supported herself by begging in front of the entrance to churches and supermarkets in the centre of Turin.

From our first meeting, Marinela defined herself as a 'Romanized Roma', and repeated this on many occasions, both to me and other non-Roma. From the end of 2012, after a severe bout of bronchitis, she began attending a clinic run by volunteer doctors. The clinic also offers a paediatric consulting service, and Marinela took Adina there because her daughter had problems with hearing in her right ear.

When she told me about this problem, Marinela connected it to a problem the child had had when she was very young:

> I remember when Adina was a year old in Romania and it was winter. We were very cold and she had a problem: her ears became swollen. In the country there are no hospitals, and in our village, which is completely inhabited by Roma, the government never wanted to build a clinic. It was snowing a lot, I could not get to the hospital and when I called the doctor he told me it was nothing serious.

The Italian doctor diagnosed permanent damage to the ear caused by untreated otitis. The doctor suggested a hearing aid for Adina and put Marinela in contact with another Italian association that provides these devices for particularly poor people free of charge. After receiving the news, Marinela was constantly worried about her daughter's situation because the conditions of cold and humidity present in the camp had worsened the situation, but in 2013 Adina finally received the hearing aid.

In 2014 Marinela returned to Romania with her daughter. When I met them both in their village, Marinela told me the reason for the trip. Not convinced by the solution she found in Italy, she wanted to take her daughter to an elderly Roma woman, who carried out some traditional practices in order to heal her: 'Everyone trusts this woman, we call it *babeste* care. Only women can do it because they know many things. This woman told me that Adina does not hear because someone wished evil on her when she was little and that we need to solve this problem'. The woman prepared hot compresses of herbs repeatedly applied to the ear for several weeks, accompanying these interventions with the recitation of oral formulas to remove the negative influence still present. On her return to Italy, Marinela returned to the doctor to check the hearing aid but did not make any reference to the therapeutic sessions in Romania. When I asked her about this behaviour, Marinela told me that it would not make sense to talk about it because the doctor would not understand. With these words, Marinela referred to the fact that her choices in Romania were linked to what Kleinman (1999) defined a 'local moral world'. In every cultural context, people adopt ways of reasoning and local codes of judgement that determine what is acceptable and what is unacceptable from the point of view of actions and choices in their social sphere. A widely shared and approved behaviour in rural Romania, one belonging to the sphere of traditional medicine, would hardly be accepted by a Western medical specialist.

For Marinela, Romania was the place to look for solutions that she had not found in Italy. An unsatisfactory response in Italy, from the biomedical point of view, pushed this mother to follow an alternative path, demonstrating the extent to which some imaginary and healing practices are still alive, especially in the rural areas. Adina's hearing problems did not disappear, but her mother remained firmly convinced that the chosen solution would bring beneficial effects in the future.

This second case has its roots in a situation of marked vulnerability and denial of rights initially experienced in Romania (the lack of basic health services, the doctor who did not intervene when called). This was followed by a complex experience with the health-care system in Italy, from which only a partially accepted solution emerged. Transnational contacts were important, in this case, in the search for compensation in another area, one different from the biomedical. Not disclosing to the doctor in Italy the therapy that had been carried out in Romania indicates how, among Roma patients, there is a strong fear of misunderstanding and of negative judgement regarding their choices. The resistance of doctors to recognizing forms of care different from those of Western biomedicine is still very strong, and the initiatives of immigrant patients in this direction are often discouraged (Zanini et al. 2013).

Sorina's Story: Transnationalism as an Emotional Dimension

The third story I present does not concern the mobility of a Roma patient between Italy and Romania, but rather the transnational flow of medicines. This movement of medicines can be explained within the power relationships between the majority society and the Roma minority living in the camps (Alunni 2013). Sorina is a 35-year-old Roma woman who lived in the camp with her husband and three children. She faced many problems over the years in Italy, which severely affected her emotional stability. Her youngest child, Gabriel, was taken away from his family following a report from primary school teachers to social services, and he was temporarily placed in a community for minors.

In addition to the problem with her son, a strong conflict developed with another family in the camp over a loan of money that Sorina's family could not pay back; Sorina was finally abandoned by her husband, who moved to live with another woman. All of these circumstances generated a state of strong anxiety in Sorina:

> If I had stayed in Romania all this would not have happened. Life in the camp is difficult; there is never enough money and if you ask for help from those who seem to be friends… There are social workers who should help us, but instead they take the children away. All the weight of this situation has been on my shoulders.

Sorina did not want to talk about her discomfort to the psychologist who followed her son's placement in the community, because she considered her a threat.

Every month Sorina received some packages from Romania containing medicines, which she took in large quantities. They were restoratives that her elderly mother bought in the village pharmacy and then sent by the buses that travel every week between Romania and Italy. These restoratives are also found in Italy – they have a different name but the same active ingredient – but Sorina preferred to buy them in Romania. The choice did not depend on an economic evaluation but on an exclusively emotional evaluation. As other scholars have shown, there is a 'social efficacy of travelling medicines' (Pribilsky 2008), because the effectiveness of the medicine depends on the intention as much as the efficacy (Van der Geest and Hardon 1996). The link between the elderly mother and her daughter was strengthened by sending these medicines that had a calming effect.

> We use these things for many different problems, because we were used to doing so in Romania. Here the doctors say we use too many, but they are fine. My brother had problems with his memory, he forgot everything, and he used them too, and everything went better, especially because he wanted to get his driving licence and he just couldn't. I have these other problems, and it works with me too. But only the Romanian ones work – we send the money and our mum buys and sends them!

In this case it is not a question of therapies that fall within the sphere of traditional care, as was the case with Marinela, but of medicines that acquire curative power because they are linked to the social meanings attributed to them within the migratory experience.

Banu's Story: The Rejection of Transnational Ties

Banu is a 35-year-old Roma born and raised in Bacau, a city in eastern Romania. Banu had long travelled between Romania and other European countries – Sweden, France and Spain – until he settled in the camp in Turin in 2007. In Italy, Banu did not have an opportunity to practise the trade he had learned from his father, blacksmithing, and so he begged in the central areas of the city. In 2010 he had a serious accident, falling at night from an abandoned building in the camp. The fall caused an injury to the vertebral column that caused him permanent paralysis in his legs. Immediately after the incident he was admitted to a section of the largest city hospital, the Unipolar Spinal Unit, where he stayed for two years to follow a long rehabilitation path. In 2012, when he was released from the hospital, he received accommodation thanks to a religious volunteer association, and he moved there with his entire family. Until the day of the accident, neither Banu nor his family had had any contact with the Italian health services.

A support network of many non-Roma people has been set up around Banu to meet various needs, both social and financial. This network includes the attending physician who provides him with free health material, such as catheters and gauze. There are volunteers from the association who, in addition to finding the house and paying the costs, have donated other useful material, such as a pram and a bed. There is a social worker in the municipality who works in a disability assistance office and who helps Banu resolve different paperwork issues – for example, to complete the disability pension application. When I met Banu in his lodgings, he told me that the incident had made him feel suddenly visible, in a positive sense, to people working in Italian institutions:

> Before having the accident, I didn't know that here in Italy everything was so organized. I didn't even think there were such generous people. It was a nice surprise and all this is free. If this had happened to me in Romania, I would be dead: there was no possibility, there was no money. Of course, if you have money you can do everything in Romania, but otherwise the doctor will not even look at you. The bribe opens all the doors.

In Banu's testimony he strikes at the continuous opposition between Romania, where only economic power matters, and Italy, where he believes the system is organized and people are 'generous'. The incident provided Banu and his family with the opportunity to leave the camp and find a house, and it also allowed them to send their children to elementary schools in the area.

Prior to the accident, Banu had led a life with a high degree of geographical mobility and strong transnational ties. The incident was the reason he greatly reduced these ties. He was forced into a state of physical immobility; but he also decided to limit his contacts with Romania for a symbolic reason: 'In the family they took my disease very badly. Everyone looked at me with pity. Other people went away because in Romania when you see a case like mine you run away, scared. I have no reason to go back'.

The story of Banu is very interesting in this context as, precisely because it is so extreme, it highlights the paradoxical aspects found in many experiences of the Roma. The camp is a space for social and power relations where many rights, particularly in terms of health, are not recognized or are negotiated with the institutions within a framework of exceptionality. In the case of Banu, the encounter with the health system took place outside the context of the camp. Healthcare workers approached him as a patient and not a 'Roma patient';

they did not apply the cultural prejudice that has been presented in many other interactions. Thanks to this inclusion, Banu did not develop transnational practices in the health field because he felt fully recognized in Italy while, at the same time, evaluating his condition in Romania negatively.

Conclusions

In this chapter, the concept of structural vulnerability is fundamental to understanding the health-care pathways of the Roma population in Italy and to understanding whether the right to health can be fulfilled in conditions of high social marginality. The case of the Roma is particularly relevant because this is a minority that, historically, has been the object of forms of violence exercised through specific models of governmentality.

Camps are one of the most obvious forms in which this governmentality has been achieved. The camps are physical and social spaces, created and reproduced by institutions, within which the person must live with a permanent suspension of rights. It is therefore into this framework that any reflection on the right to health and on the social determinants of health must be inserted. The camp produces poor health conditions among its inhabitants, and at the same time it is the symbolic reference point often used by health professionals when thinking about their Roma patients.

The Roma, even before meeting the doctors, are inserted into an explanatory framework that conditions all of their relations with the institutions that deal with their health. The approach that health-care practitioners adopt varies: from a refusal to treat Roma patients, to a desire to re-educate them; from not making any distinctions, to applying rigid cultural categories. The health workers expect the Roma to behave like good patients and end up attributing any difficulties to their unwillingness to integrate. These same mechanisms are repeated in many interventions designed for Roma populations in housing, education and work.

Interventions conceived with the aim of helping the Roma have been a failure because they have not addressed the causes of social exclusion, but rather have maintained a differentialist approach. These interventions have not brought Roma populations closer to the services, but have ultimately moved them farther away, and they have not resolved misunderstandings between health-care professionals and patients.

My ethnographic analysis of what happened inside and outside a large spontaneous camp in the city of Turin has allowed me to disaggregate this imagined community, and to understand how the Roma subjects reacted in different ways to representations and to the health practices they received when they had health problems.

Transnationalism is one of the strategies frequently adopted by individuals in response to their health needs. Although some of these strategies can be viewed as acts of resistance with respect to dominant practices experienced in Italy, inequalities are often reproduced and perpetuated along transnational paths. The four stories presented above do not exhaust the multiplicity of experiences, but rather represent a variety of possible paths: transnationalism as geographical mobility that produces a double exclusion (Csoran); transnationalism as a creative combination of different therapeutic pathways (Marinela); transnationalism without geographical mobility but as a symbolic and affective link (Sorina); and finally integration and rejection of every possible form of transnationalism (Banu). The conditions of structural vulnerability experienced in a given social and territorial context cannot be understood except in relation to the conditions experienced in even the initial contexts. Much research remains to be done. At the same time, policies aimed at the real protection of the right to health should take this transnational dimension into account.

Pietro Cingolani teaches anthropology of media, and is research fellow at the Department of Culture, Politics and Society, University of Turin. His research topics are anthropology of migration; urban ethnography; inter-ethnic relations; Roma migration and labour integration in destination countries; and transnationalism. In the last few years he has taken part in several EU-funded projects. On the issues of migrants' health, he has collaborated with the Fundamental Rights Laboratory in Turin.

Notes

1. Within the European Union, Italy is therefore considered an exemplary case – in a negative sense – for the conditions of housing segregation in which the Roma populations live. Even today, most of the housing solutions adopted consist of nomad camps.
2. The same observation can be made regarding other indicators of the level of social inclusion, such as data on levels of schooling. Data on the school attendance of Roma minors in Italy are based on counting pupils who are identified as such by the teachers themselves, often because they are

followed by social services or reside in camps. Nothing is known of the other Roma children, who attend school but are not identified as such (Associazione 21 Luglio 2016).
3. This is the project 'Health as a Fundamental Right. Research on Migrants in Turin', conducted on behalf of the Fundamental Rights Laboratory and financed by the Compagnia di San Paolo. The research group consisted of Eleonora Castagnone, Pietro Cingolani, Laura Ferrero and Cristina Vargas. Other considerations on the health experiences of the Roma in Romania are derived from previous field observations in 2011.
4. The latest data produced by the Nomad Office of the Municipality indicate a reduction in the presence of the Roma in 2016 compared to 2014; in particular, the number of Roma present in the camps decreased by three hundred (Prefecture of Turin 2017).
5. The Nomad Office emphasizes that, despite the closure of the spontaneous camp, around six hundred Romanian Roma have moved to other such camps in the city.
6. There are no detailed analyses of the health conditions of the inhabitants, except for the reports produced in the context of specific interventions, such as the research report drawn up by a doctor who attended the camp for more than a year on behalf of a voluntary association (Terra del Fuoco 2009).
7. My own presence was welcomed without too much surprise and without suspicion by the inhabitants, who were accustomed to numerous foreigners passing through. Within the camp, for more than a year, there was a film crew that made a documentary called *I ricordi del fiume* [Memories of the River], directed by Gianluca and Massimiliano de Serio.
8. The STP card entitles its bearer to: outpatient and urgent or essential treatment for illness and accident; pregnancy and maternity services; services to protect the health of minors; vaccinations; preventive care; and diagnosis and treatment of infectious diseases.
9. For all of these reasons, in 2016 Romania was last in the Euro Health Consumer Index, which measures the quality of European health-care systems.

References

Achim, V. 2004. *The Roma in Romanian History*. Budapest: Ceu Press.
Alunni, L. 2013. 'La morale delle avvertenze: Circolazione, uso e manipolazione dei farmaci nei campi rom di Roma'. *AM – Rivista della Società Italiana di Antropologia Medica* 35/36: 41–63.
———. 2015. 'Securitarian Healing: Roma Mobility and Health Care in Rome'. *Medical Anthropology: Cross-Cultural Studies in Health and Illness* 34(2): 139–49.
———. 2017. *La cura e lo sgombero: Salute e cittadinanza nei campi rom di Roma*. Rome: Argo.

Associazione 21 Luglio. 2016. 'Ultimo banco: Analisi dei progetti di scolarizzazione rivolti ai minori rom a Roma'. Rome.
Bell, D., et al. 2015. 'Transnational Healthcare, Crossborder Perspectives'. *Social Science & Medicine* 124: 284–89.
Canzler, W., V. Kaufmann and S. Kesserling. 2008. *Tracing Mobilities: Towards a Cosmopolitan Perspective*. Aldershot: Ashgate.
Cingolani, P., and L. Ferrero. 2015. 'La salute che attraversa i confini', in E. Castagnone et al. (eds), *La salute come diritto fondamentale: esperienze di migranti a Torino*. Bologna: Il Mulino, pp. 231–58.
Cresswell, T. 2010. 'Towards a Politics of Mobility'. *Environment and Planning D: Society and Space* 28(1): 17–31.
Dell'Agnese, E., and T. Vitale. 2007. 'Rom e Sinti, una galassia di minoranze senza territorio', in A. Amiotti and A. Rosina (eds), *Identità e integrazione: passato e presente delle minoranze nell'Europa mediterranea*. Milan: Franco Angeli, pp. 121–42.
European Roma Rights Centre (ERRC). 2006. 'Ambulance Not On the Way: The Disgrace of Health Care for Roma in Europe'. Budapest.
European Commission. 2014. 'Roma Health Report: Health Status of the Roma Population. Data Collection in the Member States of the European Union'. Brussels.
Fundamental Rights Agency (FRA). 2011. 'The Situation of Roma in 11 EU Member States: Survey Results at a Glance'. Vienna.
Geraci, S., M. Bonciani and B. Martinelli. 2010. *La tutela della salute degli immigrati nelle politiche locali*. Rome: Caritas Diocesana.
Hancock, I. 2002. *We Are the Romani People*. Hatfield: University of Hertfordshire Press.
Hannam, K., M. Sheller and J. Urry. 2006. 'Editorial: Mobilities, Immobilities and Moorings'. *Mobilities* 1(1): 1–22.
Kleinman, A. 1999. 'Moral Experience and Ethical Reflection: Can Ethnography Reconcile Them? A Quandary for the New Bioethics'. *Daedalus* 128(4): 69–97.
Levitt, P., and N. Glick Schiller. 2004. 'Conceptualizing Simultaneity: A Transnational Social Field Perspective on Society'. *International Migration Review* 38(3): 1002–39.
Liegeois, J.-P. 1994. *Roma, Gypsies, Travellers*. Strasbourg: Council of Europe Press.
Mainil, T. 2012. *Transnational Health Care and Medical Tourism: Understanding 21st Century Patient Mobility*. Nieuwegein: Nrit Media.
Monasta, L., et al. 2012. 'Review of the Scientific Literature on the Health of the Roma and Sinti in Italy'. *Ethnicity and Disease* 22(3): 367–71.
Nacu, A. 2011. 'The Politics of Roma Migration: Framing Identity Struggles among Romanian and Bulgarian Roma in the Paris Region'. *Journal of Ethnic and Migration Studies* 37(1): 135–50.
Nguyen, V.K., and K. Peschard. 2003. 'Anthropology, Inequality and Disease: A Review'. *Annual Review of Anthropology* 32(1): 447–74.

OECD/European Observatory on Health Systems and Policies. 2017. 'Romania: Country Health Profile 2017'. Brussels.
Parekh, N., and T. Rose. 2011. 'Health Inequalities of the Roma in Europe: A Literature Review'. *Central European Journal of Public Health* 19(3): 139–42.
Piasere, L. 2004. *I Rom d'Europa: Una storia moderna*. Rome: Laterza.
Prefecture of Turin. 2017. 'Osservatorio interistituzionale sugli stranieri in provincia di Torino: rapporto 2016'. Turin.
Pribilsky, J. 2008. 'Sending Energías from the Andes: The Social Efficacy of Travelling Medicines'. *Anthropology News* 49(5): 13–14.
Quesada, J., L.K. Hart and P. Bourgois. 2011. 'Structural Vulnerability and Health: Latino Migrant Laborers in the United States'. *Medical Anthropology* 30(4): 339–62.
Ricordy, A., F. Motta and S. Geraci. 2014. *SaluteRom: Itinerari possibili*. Bologna: Pendragon.
Roth, M., and S. Toma. 2014. 'The Plight of Romanian Social Protection: Addressing the Vulnerabilities and Well-Being in Romanian Roma Families'. *The International Journal of Human Rights* 18(6): 714–34.
Sigona, N. 2015. 'Campzenship: Reimagining the Camp as a Social and Political Space'. *Citizenship Studies* 19(1): 1–15.
Smith, T. 1997. 'Racist Encounters: Romani "Gypsy" Women in Mainstream Health Services'. *The European Journal of Women's Studies* 4(2): 183–96.
Solimene, M. 2017. 'Challenging Europe's External Borders and Internal Boundaries: Bosnian Xoraxané Xomá on the Move in Roman Peripheries and the Contemporary European Union'. *Social Identities* 24(4): 1–15.
Sutherland, A. 1992. 'Gypsies and Health Care'. *Western Journal of Medicine* 157(3): 276–80.
Terra del Fuoco. 2009. 'Analisi socio-sanitaria dei campi rom abusivi di Lungo Stura Lazio e Via Germagnano'. Rapporto di attività. Turin.
Trevisan, P. 2004. 'La salute dei rom: una questione piuttosto ingarbugliata. Riflessioni antropologiche sulla letteratura medica riguardante gli zingari'. *La Ricerca Folklorica* 50: 53–63.
Van der Geest, S., S.R. Whyte and A. Hardon. 1996. 'The Anthropology of Pharmaceuticals: A Biographical Approach'. *Annual Review of Anthropology* 25: 153–78.
Villa-Torres, L., et al. 2017. 'Transnationalism and Health: A Systematic Literature Review on the Use of Transnationalism in the Study of the Health Practices and Behaviors of Migrants'. *Social Science & Medicine* 183: 70–79.
Vitale, T. 2010. *Rom e sinti in Italia: Condizione sociale e linee di politica pubblica*. Milan: ISPI.
Vivian, C., and L. Dundes. 2004. 'The Crossroads of Culture and Health among the Roma (Gypsies)'. *Journal of Nursing Scholarship* 36(1): 86–91.

Vlădescu, C., et al. 2016. 'Romania: Health System Review'. *Health Systems in Transition* 18(4): 1–170.
Von Hausen, W. 1992. *Gypsy Folk Medicine*. New York: Sterling Publishing Co.
Vrăbiescu, I., and B. Kalir. 2018. 'Care-full Failure: How Auxiliary Assistance to Poor Roma Migrant Women in Spain Compounds Marginalization'. *Social Identities* 24(4): 520–32.
Zanini, G., et al. 2013. 'Transnational Medical Spaces: Opportunities and Restrictions'. MMG Working Paper, 13–16. Göttingen.

6

Mental Health as Politics

Exploring Mental Health Services among Syrian Refugees in Lebanon

Hala Kerbage and Filippo Marranconi

Introduction

Since the beginning of the Syrian war, Lebanon has hosted more than one million displaced Syrians who have fled violence and armed conflict, according to the last official estimations of the United Nations High Commissioner for Refugees (UNHCR 2017).

Even if the word refugee is today employed to define Syrian presence in Lebanon, Syrians lack the official juridical status of refugees, since Lebanon has not yet ratified the Geneva Convention (UNHCR 1951). Instead, Lebanon and the UN had an informal agreement to entail the formation, on the Lebanese side, of a High Committee, whose aim is to coordinate its action with local and international agencies and NGOs (Geisser 2013) to aid Syrian 'displaced' people. In 2003 there was an attempt to formalize UNHCR presence in Lebanon through a Memorandum of Understanding. The category of refugee was at the core of the negotiation of this memorandum between UNHCR and Lebanon's General Security Office, the latter refusing to use it in order not to legitimize Lebanon as a country of asylum (Janmyr 2017).

We cannot enter deeply in the political or historical reasons[1] that underlie this choice, but the consequences are relevant. Today, in fact, refugees registered at UNHCR receive a registration certificate that entitles refugees to international protection and humanitarian assistance. But this document does not confer a formal status recognized by the Lebanese government, nor does it protect refugees who do not fulfil the legal procedures in order to receive a residence permit. As Janmyr points out, 'being a registered refugee is increasingly being directly linked to being allowed to live legally in Lebanon; yet … UNHCR's registration of Syrian refugees is one of the more contentious issues in its Lebanon operations. The situation for Syrian refugees in Lebanon has in consequence become legally more complex and piecemeal, with different systems of law and policy being applied on both a global and a local level' (Janmyr 2017: 411–12).[2]

This situation contributes to the precarious and difficult situation of Syrian refugees in this country. Syrian refugees do not have civic or political rights, rendering their administrative and bureaucratic situation fragile and unstable. Structural conditions – like lack of access to health care, poor housing, restrictions on employment and movement, discrimination, restricted legal status, random arrests by police and a fear of being detained by groups involved in the conflict – are also important sources of distress and instability for Syrian refugees. Furthermore, most of the refugees live in an irregular situation, as they are not able to afford to renew their papers because of the new conditions put by the Lebanese government in 2015, which require paying very high fees and finding a Lebanese sponsor (Harissi 2015). Moreover, children of Syrian refugees who are born in Lebanon are usually not registered, making them stateless (NRC 2015), and deaths are not recorded (Kassatly 2017). Therefore, key life milestones become complicated and challenging in this displacement setting.

Concerning the access to health care, Syrian refugees registered at UNHCR benefit from a partial health coverage. Through the network of primary health-care centres of the Ministry of Public Health (MoPH) and the Ministry of Social Affairs (MoSA), refugees can access primary health-care centres managed by NGOs, often in partnership with UNHCR and the MoPH (UNHCR 2017). However, since the Lebanese health system relies heavily on the private sector, the cost of secondary and tertiary health care is not covered, and this constitutes an important limitation to its access for refugees.[3] The UNHCR endorses a public health approach that reproduces the Lebanese system, where the possibility of benefiting from health services is strongly determined by the social, financial and juridical status of patients, and where the costs of care constitute one of the major obstacles to health care access (Blanchet,

Fouad and Pherali 2016). Moreover, many reports in the literature emphasize the challenge in access to health care for Syrian refugees in Lebanon (Coutts, Fouad and Batniji 2013): constant fluctuation of funds; lack of a strong national health policy; and a weakened public sector unable to respond to the health needs of the Syrian refugee population. Finally, health politics create a hierarchy of eligibility for access to services, not only in regard to Lebanese citizens but within humanitarian structures and among Syrians refugees themselves. This hierarchy depends on different factors, such as the type of pathology or intervention needed, their financial instability, the bureaucratic situation, security check points and the geographical fragmentation of families (Parkinson and Behrouzan 2015).

This context of displacement in a post-war setting as well as the social adversity that refugees are exposed to have been associated with mental health problems, mainly depression, anxiety and post-traumatic stress disorder (PTSD) (Karam et al. 2016). Beyond these diagnostic categories, qualitative studies in this context revealed that refugees may suffer from the loss of role and social networks, isolation, feelings of helplessness and hopelessness, loss of a sense of meaning and purpose, and an inability to imagine a future (Miller and Rasmussen 2010; Hassan et al. 2016; Wells et al. 2016). Therefore, the Inter-Agency Standing Committee (IASC)[4] emphasizes that the displacement situation following a war setting can lead to mental and social problems (IASC 2007), and that Mental Health and Psychosocial Support Services (MHPSS) are needed in this regard.

In this context, various local and international NGOs, in collaboration with the Lebanese MoPH and MoSA, are providing MHPSS for Syrian refugees in Lebanon. These services are free of charge for Syrian refugees and include non-specialized psychosocial support as well as specialized mental health consultations (psychiatry and/or psychotherapy). Most of them provide psychotropic medications, and the referral to those services is done through various ways: either at the UNHCR registration, or through the primary health-care centres of the MoPH and MoSA. Since the Lebanese mental health system is mostly led by the private sector, local and international NGOs working in the humanitarian field try to fill the lack of public mental health services by functioning in coordination with the government. In 2014, the MoPH, in partnership with the World Health Organization (WHO), the United Nations Children's Fund (UNICEF) and the International Medical Corps (IMC), established the National Mental Health Program (NMHP) and developed a national mental health strategy for the country with the primary aim of 'scaling up mental health services' (El Chammay and Ammar 2014). In line with this strategy, and in response to the massive influx of Syrian refugees to Lebanon, the NMHP established a Mental Health and Psychosocial Support Task Force (MHPSS-TF), co-chaired by WHO and UNICEF. The aim of this task force is to 'coordinate the work of more than 62 mental health and psychosocial support staff actors working within the Syrian crisis response in Lebanon through a common annual action plan for all' (Karam et al. 2016). Therefore, the MHPSS-TF is trying to implement MHPSS evidence-based interventions that would be homogeneous across all NGOs, providing services for Syrian refugees in Lebanon, even though not all NGOs have yet adopted the model suggested by the task force. On one side, there is the MHPSS-TF related to the MoPH, which has its own agenda of interventions, and on the other side, there are numerous NGOs in the field that are part of the MHPSS-TF, however for now each NGO has its own programme of interventions. The International Medical Corps is the main partner of the MoPH and NMHP, and is systematically adopting the interventions suggested by the MHPSS-TF. To date, there is no information available on the impact of the MHPSS established, or whether they are tailored to the needs and expectations of the Syrian refugee community. This chapter will focus on a critical and analytical description of the MHPSS services for Syrian refugees in Lebanon, following a study conducted during 2016 that explored the functioning and organization of these services from different perspectives: health-care providers, policymakers and Syrian refugees. In particular, we analyse the organization of the MHPSS services and the discourses mobilized by mental health professionals, in order to show how these actors construct and perceive the Syrian refugees and their experience of suffering, as well as the perceptions of the Syrians themselves. We argue that even though all recommendations stress the community-based approach to mental health, MHPSS services are, in practice, based on a medical and diagnostic approach, and we explore the meaning of evidence-based interventions in this particular setting. In particular, we show how by making the suffering of refugees a matter for the humanitarian and the medical fields, MHPSS services might pathologize ordinary human suffering in reaction to horrifying events, and hinder important aspects like social history and political justice.

We ultimately show how the therapeutic relationship encounters several difficulties due to the context in which it occurs and the emphasis it puts on the individual level. In particular, through our analysis of the matter of 'lying' among refugees, we show how lying, far from being a specific characteristic or personality trait of the Syrian refugee as some professionals seem to believe, is a result of the humanitarian system itself and of its bureaucratic violence. Finally, these services, while emphasizing the medical and individual rather than the social aspect of suffering, through their practice of healing and the discourse and stereotypes mobilized by professionals of mental health, assign a particular place to the refugee subject and his suffering, and carry specific politics of care.

Brief History of MHPSS Interventions in Humanitarian Settings and the Current Inter-Agency Standing Committee Guidelines

This psychologization of war exposure has its roots in the introduction of PTSD as an official psychiatric diagnostic category in the early 1980s. Proponents of PTSD were part of the anti-war movement in the United States, and they lobbied for veterans to receive a distinctive diagnosis, which would help them to access compensation (Young 1997; Bracken, Giller and Summerfield 1995). Therefore, PTSD was as much a sociopolitical as a medical response to the problems of a particular group, at a particular moment in time. Yet, the mental health field rapidly endorsed it as a universal response to war for entire populations, with specific diagnostic criteria and specific interventions, including antidepressant medications and cognitive behavioural therapy (Young 1997; Bracken, Giller and Summerfield 1995). The generalization of this diagnostic category led to an assumption that all refugees and war survivors are a particular psychological category, at risk of developing PTSD or other psychiatric disorders, justifying the urgent need for psychiatric interventions in war and post-war settings (Summerfield 1999; Fassin and Rechtman 2009). Therefore, the first mental health programmes in war emergencies were mainly based on individual and trauma-focused approaches (Agger et al. 1995; Young 1997; Summerfield 1999). However, in the last two decades, evidence has begun to emerge against the use of exclusively trauma-focused and individual counselling services in war or post-war settings (Argenti-Pillen 2003; Almedom et al. 2004; Giacaman et al. 2011). One important critique was that these programmes were mostly imported from a Western context, without previous exploration of the perceptions of locals on mental health and illness, or of the refugees' patterns of social strengths and weaknesses. This has been described by American psychiatrist and anthropologist, Arthur Kleinman, as a 'category fallacy': applying a category that makes sense for one particular sociocultural group to another group, for whom this category may not make sense (Kleinman 1991). Another important critique of trauma-based programmes is that arguably they might impair the long-term rebuilding after the war, by shifting resources and energy away from the reinforcement of local capacities, advocacy for peace, and the quest for social justice (Summerfield 1999; Giacaman et al. 2011). Other critiques described these interventions as disempowering for refugees, ascribing them to the sick role, while pathologizing ordinary human suffering and eradicating any social or historical context in which this suffering takes place (Summerfield 1999; Fassin and Rechtman 2009).

In an attempt to address these contradictory data and theories, the IASC developed guidelines for MHPSS services in war and crisis settings. Experts agreed that exposure to distress is a risk factor for social and mental health problems, but there was no agreement on the public health value of diagnosing or treating PTSD (IASC 2007; Van Ommeren, Saxena and Saraceno 2005). They recommended that first-line psychosocial interventions in an acute setting should be community-targeted rather than individual-targeted: covering basic needs, providing safety, and organizing social networks – religious, political, social and cultural – that re-establish systems of meaning and cohesion. These community-based interventions were recommended as a priority over specialized interventions (psychotherapy and/or psychiatry consultations). The guidelines coined the term Mental Health and Psychosocial Support Services instead of the then usual 'trauma-focused services'. The authors emphasized, though, the term 'mental health problems' instead of 'disorders', moderating the paradigm (IASC 2007) that perceives refugees as being systematically at risk of developing psychiatric disorders, while, however, continuing to perceive their living experience as pertaining to the medical field.

Overview of the Current Research on the Mental Health of Syrian Refugees in Lebanon: The Emphasis on the Diagnostic and Biological Approach

To date, there is no data on the experiences of Syrian refugees with the MHPSS services or more generally on their expectations or perceived needs in terms of psychological well-being, mental illness, or resources for surviving. A recent literature review led by the

UNHCR aimed at informing on cultural specificities and idioms of distress of the Syrian community, in order to have more 'culturally sensitive interventions' (UNHCR 2015), but did not implicate Syrian refugees themselves as participants. In a paper summarizing the report (Hassan et al. 2016), the authors point out the importance of avoiding medicalizing social distress. However, they end with recommendations to improve the screening and treatment of mental health disorders through the 'Mental Health Gap Action Programme', or 'mhGAP'[5] (WHO 2016), thus emphasizing the medical and diagnostic approach within MHPSS services. Other epidemiological studies have explored rates of psychiatric diagnosis among the Syrian refugees' population in Lebanon, especially rates of PTSD and depression (Karam et al. 2014; Souaiby et al. 2016; Naja et al. 2016; Kazour et al. 2017). Those studies report a high prevalence of psychiatric disorders: for example, 27 per cent of PTSD in a sample of 452 participants (Kazour et al. 2017); 44 per cent of depression in a sample of 310 adults (Naja et al. 2016); and 26 per cent of PTSD in a sample of children and adolescents exposed to war (Karam et al. 2014).

These results can be misleading, however, and should be interpreted with caution as the tools used to diagnose these disorders were not validated in the Syrian context. Moreover, by emphasizing symptoms rather than the individual and collective experience of suffering, the daily lives and struggle of refugees are reduced to a list of symptoms isolated from their context that are assumed to be easily quantified and measured in order to constitute a mental disorder. Obviously, rates of symptoms will be high, with overdiagnosis of PTSD and depression, thus hindering a recognition that these manifestations can be a normal reaction to extreme life circumstances, ultimately medicalizing ordinary human suffering and creating a need among refugees for MHPSS services.

Another trend in the current research about the mental health of Syrian refugees is the search for a genetic marker of resilience (Karam et al. 2016). This kind of study can have serious ethical and political considerations: by individualizing to that extent the reaction to war events, there is a marked tendency by international donors to depoliticize collective and social suffering, and to shift resources away from the restoration of basic rights, social justice and human security. Collecting saliva and hair samples from Syrian refugee children in order to 'unravel the role of biological markers' (ibid.) and how much it contributes to their coping mechanisms and ways of adapting to social adversity poses moral dilemmas: submitting them to such protocol experiments can be harmful and deleterious, while not benefiting them in their current living conditions. Furthermore, it can be disempowering to reduce the struggle for survival to genetic factors at play that would favour some children over others in facing extreme hardship. Moreover, the current international mental health trend among specialists is to insist on the importance of training fieldworkers and NGO staff on MHPSS interventions, especially on the psychiatric diagnosis by mhGAP, because of the increase in psychiatric disorders following war and displacement (ibid.). There seems to be an assumption that rates of psychiatric disorders are higher among the refugee population, not because of the social adversity they are exposed to, but simply because they are refugees; the juridical category of a refugee is therefore treated as a psychological category.

Exploring MHPSS Services in Lebanon, and the Experience of the Syrian Refugees

Methodology

As well as our own experience with MHPSS services in Lebanon,[6] we have explored the functioning of MHPSS services in Lebanon taking into account three levels: the conceptualization of the services; the discourse of mental health professionals and policymakers involved in the field of mental health; and the experience of Syrian refugees with these services. Data was gathered over the course of nine months during 2016.

First, we reviewed and analysed official documents published by UNHCR and NGOs providing MHPSS services in Lebanon, detailing the type and organization of the services. We contacted ten NGOs that were providing specialized services for adult Syrian refugees (psychiatry and psychotherapy consultations). The list of NGOs was taken from a service mapping published by the Ministry of Public Health (MoPH 2015). Only two international NGOs, based respectively in the regions of Bekaa and Beirut, allowed us access to the Syrian refugees benefiting from their services. The eight other NGOs evoked strict confidentiality policies, as well as expressing concerns about exposing their 'vulnerable beneficiaries to the risk of interviews with strangers'.[7] However, all NGOs accepted that we would interview staff and/or mental health programme coordinators under the cover of anonymity. An ethical approval was obtained from the ethics committee of Saint-Joseph University and a verbal consent was obtained from all participants; data was anonymous and confidential.

We conducted sixty semi-structured interviews with informants from different organizations, governmental and non-governmental: programme coordinators (at the regional and national level), service providers (psychologists, psychiatrists, social workers), and representatives from UNHCR, the Ministry of Social Affairs and the Ministry of Public Health. All informants interviewed were of Lebanese nationality. When possible, we accompanied the social workers during their daily work in the refugee camp and in people's houses. Finally, we conducted interviews with Syrians who were benefiting from the services, and with their families; we could visit some of them several times at their place of living, participating as we could in their daily lives. The selection of Syrian participants as well as the consent gathering were completed by the psychologists working for the two NGOs. Inclusion criteria were the largest possible in order to constitute a diverse sample, but they had to be over 18 years old and benefiting from MHPSS services. In total, we met fifteen refugees living in the Bekaa region (five men and ten women), and ten refugees living in the Beirut region (two men and eight women). Our fieldwork concentrated on patients and families who had access to psychiatric services, mainly in the west Bekaa region (the valley that traverses the east part of Lebanon from north to south, where the majority of Syrians are settled) and in Beirut's suburbs. The Syrian participants' ages ranged between 24 and 43, with a mean age of 35, reflective of the population of Syrian refugees who were most likely to use MHPSS services, according to the two NGOs' records. All were married and had children. Fourteen among them had been displaced in Lebanon for more than three years, while eleven had been displaced for between one and three years. They came from different regions in Syria: three were from Aleppo, four from Damascus, five from Homs, one from Deraa, six from Rif Damascus, one from Hama, two from Latakia, and three from Deir Ez Zor. Three of them had a graduate degree and five an undergraduate degree; six had completed high school, three complementary school and eight primary school. Refugees from Beirut lived in rented apartments shared with other family members; the ones from Bekaa lived in tents or shacks, which are a form of informal refugee settlement, since the Lebanese government has forbidden the establishment of official refugee camps. They were grouped together with family members or people from the same original region.

The Meaning of Evidence-Based Mental Health Interventions in the Syrian Refugee Context and the Medicalization of Suffering

In May 2016, the head of the National Mental Health Programme described the aim of the MHPSS Task Force as follows:

> We aim at implementing cost-effective and evidence-based strategic mental health interventions, like integration of mental health care into primary health care using the WHO Mental Health Gap action programme in primary care centres, training of trainers on Inter-Personal Therapy,[8] ... with the aim of scaling it up to all professionals working in the humanitarian response, training of more than six hundred frontline staff on psychological first aid for persons in distress, and agreeing on a set of mental health and psychosocial indicators for all actors to report. We aim at homogenizing all mental health interventions for actors working in this field.

Q: Why did you choose IPT?

A: Actually, it could have been IPT or Trauma-Focused Cognitive Behavioural Therapy, because these interventions have proven to be effective in the refugee settings, but we chose IPT because we found it more convenient for refugees – it focuses more on daily life. We want to promote evidence-based interventions and randomized controlled trials have proven the efficiency of these interventions.

Q: How is IPT evidence-based in the Syrian context?

A: Not specifically in the Syrian context, but there was a study of IPT in Uganda with refugees and it was validated and proven effective.

He emphasized the role of promoting evidence-based mental health interventions in his programme. He assumed that an intervention studied in Uganda (Bolton et al. 2003) could be transposed to the Syrian refugee context and be effective, as if all refugees belonged to the same category, and had the same psychological condition, independent of the social history and sociopolitical context. What is the meaning of evidence-based medicine in this context? By assuming that this model of therapy can generate a universally valid knowledge base, and retaining international psychiatric categories as the basic framework of understanding human suffering and struggling for survival, the relevance of this type of intervention becomes questionable as it fails the 'fundamental test of scientific validity' (Summerfield

2008: 992). As Summerfield states, validity is 'a concept meant to assess the nature of reality for the people being studied'. This very nature of reality for the people with whom we are intervening is bound up with local forms of knowledge systems that were not explored prior to implementing the 'evidence-based interventions'. For example, many Syrians do not talk about 'depression' or express that they are 'depressed' as if they have a psychological condition; they rather speak about 'being tired' (*ta'ban*), having 'tired nerves' (*A'sabe ta'bane*), or a 'heavy head' (*rase t'il*). These expressions are not only metaphors of a diagnostic category (depression) but a specific collective language that allows them to express to others their suffering, to make their suffering collective or shared. These expressions can be understood by mental health professionals, however, as symptoms of depression, but expressed in a different way. This ultimately depoliticizes the Syrian refugee subject, rendering him similar to all refugees, and eliminating the social history as a major determinant of health and mental health.

All programme directors of the NGOs interviewed, as well as the head of the NMHP/MHPSS-TF and the UNHCR representative, confirmed that they followed the IASC model of interventions. Therefore, it was striking to note the inconsistency between the IASC recommendations, on the one hand, and the action plan of the MHPSS-TF on the other. Indeed, according to the IASC pyramid, MHPSS services must be directed in priority to community and family interventions (levels 1 and 2), before referral to individual psychosocial support (level 3) or specialized consultations of psychiatry and psychotherapy (level 4) (IASC 2007: 20).

However, the discourse of professionals and policymakers, as well as all the recommendations published by UNHCR and MoPH, put most of the emphasis on the individual-focused levels, even more so on the specialized level 4 (psychiatry/psychotherapy consultations) than on the level 3, which includes non-specialized psychosocial support. The term 'psychosocial support' remains vague and poorly defined by the various actors. It can include diverse and non-specific activities: child-friendly spaces, awareness sessions, occupational activities. The level 3 includes more than 50 per cent of the totality of MHPSS activities according to the MoPH mapping of services (MoPH 2015), while level 4 constitutes 10.3 per cent, and level 2 constitutes 34.2 per cent. There is no mention or information about level 1, even though the IASC guidelines recommend that levels 1 and 2 must be a priority.

An evaluation of the MHPSS services in Lebanon by UNHCR in 2013 revealed that most of the needs noted were at levels 1 and 2: Syrian refugees struggled to ensure adequate shelter, health services, food and education for their children (UNHCR 2013). The majority did not feel safe circulating. Most of them were isolated within their own community and perceived the host community as rejecting. They also reported prostitution and domestic violence. Yet, at the end of the report, the recommendations only targeted specialized interventions at level 4 (implicating a psychiatric diagnosis), which constitute less than 11 per cent of the MHPSS services, and completely ignored the social needs found by the evaluation. The same was found in a document published by the MoPH (2015) on the mapping of MHPSS services for Syrian refugees in Lebanon. An example of these recommendations is to homogenize psychotherapeutic interventions of all NGOs by promoting IPT as an effective therapy to be used, or to establish a unified list for psychotropic medications.

The discourse of the MHPSS task force is focused on the individual medical aspect, even though it claims to be a community-based approach. It promotes 'evidence-based' interventions, as being a universal knowledge that needs to be transposed to all refugee contexts and that presents the 'contemporary Western way of being a person' (Summerfield 2008: 992) and of dealing with stressors as the model of coping to be followed. The needs of the community itself are overlooked or dismissed, and no exploration is done on how the community perceives its strengths and weaknesses, or how people cope with their situation. Instead, refugees are viewed as people with a 'lack of mental health literacy, [who] need to be educated about the reality of psychiatric disorders'.[9] This has been described by Summerfield as a form of 'medical imperialism, similar to the marginalization of indigenous knowledge systems in the colonial era, and is generally to the disadvantage of local populations' (ibid.).

Perceptions of Mental Health Professionals: Recruiting Beneficiaries, Educating on Mental Health and the Limits of the Target

The recruitment of beneficiaries by the MHPSS services is done in various ways. They can be referred by the UNHCR at the level of registration: 'When a refugee comes to register, and we see that he/she is in distress, or that he/she is taking psychotropic medications, we will refer him/her to a UNHCR-funded NGO providing MHPSS services'.[10] A sign of distress is therefore considered immediately as pertaining to MHPSS services. Sometimes the refugees hear about the services from other refugees. However, the most frequent way of recruiting beneficiaries is through NGO social workers or case managers, while doing outreach visits to the camps and informal settlements, or through awareness sessions at the primary health care centres of the Ministry of Social Affairs or the Ministry of Public Health in the International Medical Corps. All case managers are trained on the mhGAP, in order to 'detect symptoms that would necessitate an intervention'.[11] After screening of mental health symptoms, social workers will refer to the psychologist or the psychiatrist for a diagnosis, which is the distinctive function of the specialist; the diagnosis is based on international diagnostic classification criteria. Detecting symptoms is one of their most important tasks, but they also link to other NGOs who can provide social and basic needs when necessary. With time, they may get to know, maybe even more than the psychiatrist, the refugee's life in its complexity, as they will often make home visits and get to know the details of the patient's life while supporting him on a daily basis. However, the symptoms, as they are categorized in the mhGAP, remain the priority for the referral to the psychologist/psychiatrist, and to justify or explain the referral to the user himself:

> We will explain to the person what is depression, what is PTSD, what is psychosis, how to detect and recognize them; most of the time they have the symptoms of depression but they don't know it is a depression. So we tell them that it is a disease like any other, that they should not be ashamed of it, that it can be treated and we explain to them what we can do.[12]

This social worker, like many other professionals, emphasizes the lack of education of Syrian refugees on mental health disorders, and their need to be 'educated' about it, as if it was a universally valid knowledge. These awareness sessions are usually conducted in the waiting rooms of the primary health-care centres, where social workers would recruit patients by explaining to Syrians about different mental health disorders, how they can recognize that they suffer from one, and what can be done about it. They usually have with them information sheets about each disorder, as well as short stories, describing cases of mental health conditions that were successfully treated or what they refer to as 'success stories'. The production of psychiatric knowledge is therefore done through a medical legitimization ('it is a disease like any other') and a universalizing process ('depression is one of the most frequent illnesses in the world'). As another social worker of IMC described it:

> In a way, we have to convince the refugees that they need the service. You should tell them that it will be helpful for them if they took some medications that they should try, but sometimes you have to try hard before they accept, because they don't consider that this is a priority, they want a job, clothes, material aids; but we tell them we cannot help them materially but psychologically.[13]

Even though the basic needs of the beneficiaries are clearly recognized by the case managers and social workers, the lack of education about mental health disorders is considered a priority over the expressed needs. The social workers in this international NGO focus on letting the person 'know' or 'recognize' that he/she has a 'mental health disorder', sometimes even at the expense of addressing the social adversity that obviously is contributing to the psychological distress. Policymakers and professionals also frequently evoke the concept of stigma surrounding mental health among refugees that might explain the refugees' lack of knowledge in this area:

> They [the refugees] often think the cause of a delusion, for example, is a bad spirit or a possession. They don't know about psychosis. They will hide the person who has psychosis, fear of being embarrassed. There is a lot of stigma around mental health that we should fight, explain that this is a disease, that there is nothing to be ashamed of, that the solution is not to go to a religious healer but to take a medication.[14]

The services end up creating a need among refugees. The awareness sessions seek to catch patients and convince them of the services, but can only do so to a certain extent: indeed, there is a specific number of patients to see, a target to reach, that is established by donors. All professionals mentioned the limits of funding and the concept of the target: they have a fixed number of consultations they should attain by the end of each month, which is fixed by donors:

> Sometimes there are not enough patients but sometimes there are many more than the target number fixed but we cannot take everyone, because we work in an emergency context. These numbers are predetermined by donors and do not reflect the needs. Sometimes we are obliged to refer to other NGOs. The target is fixed for psychologists and psychiatrists because the social workers can see as many as possible. Sometimes there is even a fluctuation in funding, and we run out of some medications, for example.[15]

The politics of donors and funding of services are pre-established before the services are implemented, and without prior exploration of the people's needs or expectations: at IMC, for example, a specific number of patients is fixed every month for the psychiatrist and the psychotherapist, with a limited duration for treatment and follow-up, as the services are submitted to the logic of the emergency state:

> We work in an emergency context, so we cannot take everyone and we have a fixed duration for the follow-up, which is three to six months. We are currently promoting brief therapy like IPT or trauma-focused therapy, as we want short-term outcomes, just to deal with the emergency before referring to a primary health-care centre.[16]

The logic of the emergency context determines the type and nature of interventions, and is adopted by NGOs funded by UNHCR. Many contradictions, however, emerge from this discourse: the Syrian refugee crisis has been evolving for more than five years now, and considering it in an emergency context rather than as a chronic and structural situation is controversial. Moreover, creating a need through awareness sessions and outreach among Syrian refugees but then stopping the services abruptly, as the time allowed for 'emergency context' has elapsed, can be experienced by refugees as yet another contradictory discourse by the humanitarian actors, and can leave them in a state of need and request. If the emergency context is so important to the main actors in the field (NMHP, MHPSS-TF and IMC), then why are level 1 interventions of the pyramid (basic and security needs), which should be prioritized in emergency contexts, the least documented and the least described, and sometimes even practically ignored in recommendations?

A further problem frequently mentioned by professionals is the non-sustainability of funding in terms of psychotropic medications. There can be a sudden and unexplained shift in funding, leading to a shortage of certain medications, which may provoke serious relapses in patients who were previously stable (especially patients suffering from psychosis or bipolar disorder). Therefore, priorities seem to be fixed by donors more than by the actual needs of the people concerned.

Another implication of funding in an emergency context is the difficulty of requesting biological or radiological exams, like blood tests or cerebral imagery when an organic disease is suspected. Psychiatrists are limited in their clinical activity, and the number of consultations for psychiatrists and psychotherapists can vary from one month to another, depending on the target fixed by donors, creating instability of income for these specialists, which they cite as an inconvenience. Indeed, in IMC for example, psychiatrists are paid per consultation, and so by limiting the number of consultations the psychiatrist's income is also limited. On the one hand, the humanitarian system is based on the 'economy of charity' (Moghnie and Marranconi 2017), with fluctuations in funding and a logic of emergency context, while on the other hand it is sought as a source of employment for freshly graduated specialists seeking fixed incomes.

This exploration of the perceptions of mental health professionals and coordinators of NGOs and the MHPSS-TF reveals that there is a certain representation of the Syrian subject as being 'ignorant', or 'lacking education about mental health'. Even though we observed during our study that Syrians attending the MHPSS services come from different religious, economic and social backgrounds, and do not all have the same level of education, they are generally viewed by Lebanese mental health professionals as a homogeneous category: lacking education in general (as Syrians) and more specifically on mental health disorders (as patients). Most of the mental health professionals report that a minority of Syrians, especially those who come from cities like Damascus and Aleppo, are 'rich, educated, and constitute an elite, but they are not the ones we see in our services, as they can afford to see a private psychiatrist'.[17] Therefore the Syrians that they refer to are the ones who attend the NGOs services, which are free of charge. Those Syrians are perceived by professionals as necessarily poor, and this low socio-economic background is associated with a rural background, allowing the construction of a stereotype of the Syrian subject by Lebanese mental health professionals that seems to be based ultimately on an ingrained class prejudice. It is as if the 'rich and educated' Syrians from the big cities do not fit the profile of the poor refugee from a rural background, who needs humanitarian assistance, and who is viewed as lacking education in general, and on mental health disorders in particular.

More importantly, the discourse of the professionals reveals an underlying assumption that Syrians of this particular profile seem unable to identify their true needs (because of their lack of education as patients, and their low socio-economic backgrounds – hence, they attend MHPSS services rather than private consultations), while those needs are detected by the professionals. The implementation of evidence-based interventions therefore naturalizes the mental health needs of the Syrians: symptoms (physical and psychological) constitute the reality of the disorder, the reality of the Syrians, and reflect the needs to be addressed. These particular needs are not necessarily felt or thought by the Syrians themselves. It is indeed through this naturalization of the refugee's needs that psychiatry applied in the humanitarian field becomes a discipline in Foucauldian terms (Foucault 1975).

Therefore, we think that addressing the 'lack of mental health knowledge and literacy of Syrian refugees' should be replaced by efforts to address the lack of knowledge of policymakers, professionals and NGOs directors about the Syrian refugee context, systems of knowledge, idioms of distress, and community resources. Indeed, examples from the field reveal that mental health interventions can be much more efficient when they are coupled with other types of interventions, mainly communal and/or social: strengthening community resources and support that can help to alleviate feelings of isolation and sadness, rather than employing psychological counselling for individuals; coordinating with local healers or figures of authority who are important for the refugee patient can help him/her to accept treatment; and engaging Syrians in community activities or relief efforts in helping other Syrians from the community can help them to regain a sense of meaning and purpose. Moreover, increasing community resources also involves promoting access to education, employment and community engagement by enabling activity, creating new social roles, acquiring new skills, and increasing refugee involvement in the design and implementation of psychosocial programmes. This community ownership of projects may help to overcome the effects of structural inequalities, and promote social justice while responding to the requests and perceived needs of refugees.

In this context, and after exploring the conceptualization of services as well as the perceptions of mental health professionals, the question now is what happens in practice to the therapeutic relationship, since it is supposed to be at the core of any mental health intervention. On the one hand, as we have just seen, professionals mention the ignorance of the Syrians, which prevents them from understanding their disorder. On the other hand, the Syrian refugees are also perceived as resorting to lying and manipulation in order to obtain benefits. These lies of the Syrians (if the assumption is true), beyond constituting a character trait, reveal a power relationship system to which the UNHCR contributes. We will analyse in the coming section the significance of these lies as well as the therapeutic relationship in the context of the MHPSS services as described above; we will show that in the Lebanese context of the humanitarian field, an approach based on the individual – rather than on the community – structurally undermines the possibility of a therapy.

The Instability of the Therapeutic Relationship

When asked about the challenges and frustrations linked to their work with Syrian refugees, practitioners often spoke about the difficulties of establishing a long-lasting relationship with them. They complained about the fact that their patients do not easily accept taking medications for a long period, and that they miss the appointments that are given to them.

Practitioners expressed two main concerns: firstly, the need to convince the refugee patients of the importance of following therapeutic procedures; and secondly, they have a feeling of being manipulated, which in some cases they ascribe to a tendency Syrians have to lie to them. A psychologist told us:

> Lies… you can say they are liars… But you can't begin a therapy like this. Once, a young girl – 17 years old – came, and she started telling me things, but she was lying; there were things she didn't want to say.
>
> Q: Maybe she wanted to obtain something?
>
> A: Yes, OK. But I'm a psychologist, and she can't obtain material goods from me … There are some people who try to manipulate you, and they provoke you. It happened to me once that a woman told me: 'If you don't help us, I'm going to tell my husband to go and fight with Daesh'. Madam, I'm a psychologist, I can't help you with material aid! And you know, they already receive aid, every month, and they receive the rent. … They receive everything, but they continue to ask.[18]

During our work in the clinic, some people would come and ask for a medical report that they could then give to the UNHCR, hoping to obtain resettlement; the same happened during our fieldwork, when people would sometimes show us wounds or parts of their bodies, so that they could prove to us that they needed medical assistance[19] – that is to say, they might then obtain a priority in the UNHCR procedures. Some of the professionals complained about the fact that refugees were constantly asking for reports stating that they suffer from a psychological condition that needs specialized treatment abroad, hoping this would influence the UNHCR's decision in selecting them for resettlement. Professionals also complained that they kept asking about material aid while in therapeutic settings. These attitudes were understood by some professionals as intemperance and a lack of honesty, in contrast to their own humanitarian attitude, which they saw as moral per se and, therefore, legitimated.[20]

Some other professionals, when pointing out what they perceive as being patient manipulation, express their profound frustration about the sense of their work and the crisis of their role as therapists:

> There's a woman who came back to the clinic after a long absence, because a taxi driver had tried to harass her sexually. She told me she wanted to go back to Syria because she felt she wasn't safe here. When she arrived here, she was in a state of distress. She told me she went to the UNHCR – she's waiting restlessly to travel, she's obsessed with this: she wears the earplug of her cellphone non-stop, because she's afraid of missing the call of UNHCR. At the UNHCR office, they told her that a group had just been accepted for resettlement to Germany, but that she was not part of it. She started telling me they were liars, and that she couldn't bear all of this anymore. She took off her veil and started beating herself, saying she wanted to commit suicide. … Sometimes I get angry because I feel manipulated, particularly when they think we work for the UNHCR.[21]

During our fieldwork outside the therapeutic setting, we faced similar situations that can help us to reframe the behaviours of the refugees described in the previous quotes.

In the next section, we will show that what the professionals often consider as lies can be understood as an ambiguous way of the refugees to cope with the situation they are in, and, ultimately, as an eminently political practice. The lying, rather than showing us an attitude or a personal characteristic, as some of the professionals seem to explain it, allows us to explore the consequences of humanitarian agencies on shaping the lives of refugees, and reveals how these agencies arguably participate in bureaucratic violence.

The Moral Economy of Lying, the Bureaucratic Violence and the Issue of Resettlement: Case Studies

Nour and Bilal[22] are a Syrian couple that we met in a psychiatric clinic of an NGO in August 2016. They both come from Daraa, a city in the south-west of Syria. Nour had arrived in Lebanon three years before with their two children. Her husband Bilal had recently joined her, after being imprisoned and tortured by Assad's regime for several months, partially losing the mobility of one leg. During his absence, Nour had begun to beg, sweeping Beirut suburbs with her eldest daughter. She told us she had twice avoided the kidnapping of her daughter in the streets, and she was a victim of sexual abuse. Nour and Bilal did not have any income, and the UNHCR aid had been stopped after Bilal arrived in Lebanon and registered with the UNHCR. They did not know the reason for this, but they supposed it was because they have only two children, and since Bilal had rejoined the family he was assumed to be able to work. Since the return of Bilal, there were many problems at home. On the one hand, Nour's sister and brother, who hosted them in their respective homes, started complaining that Bilal – who should take care of his family – was not working. On the other hand, Bilal was experiencing extreme anxiety and irritability that led him to beat Nour and the children. When sitting alone with him, he told us about the torture he had been subjected to, the insomnia he suffered from, and the frustration he had from not being able to find a job. Because of his leg injury, he could not stand up for a long period, and so no one would accept him for a job; the thought of not being able to provide for his family was fretting him. When we went to visit the family in the house of Nour's sister, she and Nour's brother took us aside to tell us their stories: her sister's husband had been tortured, and now he had just lost his job; her brother had been beaten the year before by some men of Hezbollah, in retaliation for a car bomb in the southern suburbs of Beirut. He showed us his hand: there was a big red sign on it, and he told us it was a scar caused by the beating; but it was easy to understand that it was not a scar. Just before we left their home, the sister and the brother gave us their telephone numbers, and on another piece of paper they wrote the number of their file at the UNHCR. Once we left, we received a phone call from Nour. She apologized for the behaviour of her brother and sister, because she said, 'the half of what they told you is not true. A few weeks ago, they were refused for resettlement by the UNHCR, and they hoped they would change their situation through you'. Nour wanted to make sure that their behaviour did not have negative consequences: she might have thought that we had some authority and that we could inform the UNHCR.

Roberto Beneduce suggested the concept of the 'moral economy of lying', while exploring the narrative strategies used by migrants in order to face the arbitrary and the bureaucratic violence of the evaluation procedures for obtaining asylum. This concept provides 'analytic pathways to understand the meaning of behaviours or narratives that are often trivialized as being simple deceit or tactics aimed at gaining an immediate advantage', and 'helps us interpret practices whose political value is difficult to determine' (Beneduce 2015: 562). In our case, it is not only a matter of procedures that the Syrians have to deal with in order to obtain the resettlement, but this concept can also be extremely useful for understanding the world that the Syrian refugees live in, and the attitude they adopt towards institutions – and, in our case, towards mental health professionals.

The relationship with the UN agencies and humanitarian organizations, as well as the interaction with the apparatuses of the Lebanese state, punctuate the daily life of Syrian refugees; it is a world traversed by the tension between repression and compassion, as analysed by Didier Fassin (2012: 16). The refugees' life conditions appear precarious, and everything can become a source of danger, preventing any projection in the future: the majority of refugees lives in a situation of illegality and cannot afford to pay for the renewal of the residence permit.[23] The daily life of the refugee is a besieged time, without a possibility of imagining a future, marked by exploitation, relations of personal dependence, discrimination, a lack of basic needs like food and money, debts, the impossibility of sending children to school, and a lack of access to health services. Daily concerns revolve around searching for a job, for means of subsistence and for humanitarian aid: this generates some form of contradiction for humanitarian agencies, as refugees tend to hide their occupation, in order for their UNHCR aid not to be cut down. It was only after several home visits that we discovered that Marwan[24] – father of five children, who told us he was unemployed – in fact worked as a waiter in a restaurant in a suburb of Beirut, where he earned 450 US dollars per month (50 dollars more than what he spent for the rent). He feared that if the UNHCR knew about that, they would cut down the monthly aid he received.

The decision to grant aid to a refugee seemed to be related to his capacity to prove his situation and needs to the institutions in charge. The UNHCR organizes a hierarchy of suffering by establishing certain criteria that have to be fulfilled by the individual (or the family) in order to stand a chance of getting the means of subsistence or access to health care. The medical certificate, the exposition of wounds, the display of a state of morbidity: everything becomes a way of legitimating their request in front of NGO employees or in front of the authorities in charge of the procedures for resettlement.

During our fieldwork the dialogue around UNHCR was pervasive, and tended to replace the dialogue around MHPSS services, who were seen as a mediator or a potential link to the UNHCR, rather than as services for mental health. The UNHCR is perceived as an organization that can offer some advantages, but its logic remains unfathomable, and it is experienced as being arbitrary and hypocritical. The UN is perceived as a remote and unattainable presence, but one that, at the same time, is the master of their destiny, who can intervene in their favour and save them: 'If the situation doesn't change, I'm going to light myself and my children in front of the UN in Beirut';[25] 'we did the interview at the UN, and they told us they were going to call again. In the meanwhile, our neighbours have been accepted. But they live in a better situation than us!' – we heard such sentences many times from our interlocutors.

In this precarious situation, without any possibility of building something stable in the present and with an obfuscated horizon, Syrians are constantly forced to become mimetic creatures. During our interviews, participants told us about many strategies they use to 'adapt': changing their accent or their vocabulary according to the zones they live in (*'merci, madame, monsieur'* in French are words they quickly learn to use);[26] trying to avoid the check points of the Lebanese army who control their papers, or taking with them a child in the hope not to be imprisoned; not wearing *shahata*;[27] taking off the veil; tactically converting to another religion hoping to get access to the aid of the churches; and letting the woman instead of the man circulate outside the house in order to avoid his arrest and imprisonment (and losing the only source of income for a family). All these elements are parts of a repertoire of tactics of avoidance and adaptation, with the aim of keeping a 'low profile', negotiating with the gaze of the other who is in a position of strength, and corresponding to expectations of the agencies or other NGOs. Their life, indeed, is marked by the daily performance of the representation of themselves, and by a position of extreme dependency on the aid they receive. They are forced to different narrations of themselves towards the donors, and to constantly play with their politics of identification. On the other hand, and paradoxically, institutions require from them stability, the possibility to be identified and to express a truthful and credible story and narration of self.

When talking about Syrian refugees, one social worker told us: 'Some of them, they receive the aid and then they sell them… There are some people who are in need, and others who sell them! Sometimes they do it to buy some medicines, but sometimes only for money!' A second social worker said: 'You can't take your right, and the right of the other too… Here lies the limit of your right!'[28]

The image conveyed by professionals of the refugee as a liar is, in a certain way, coherent with the only possible legitimization of his presence, the one who depicts him as a victim in need of help. In fact, when the refugee stops inhabiting this only legitimated space – the one defined by the right to survive granted by humanitarian organizations – he becomes liable to control procedures, moral judgements and, paradoxically in the case of lying, he is excluded from the possibility of resettlement.

The lying, we believe, can be understood as a resistance to, or a way to cope with, a universe of arbitrary and impenetrable procedures, dissimulated under humanitarian reasons, whose legitimization from the refugee remains very problematic. In this space, indeed, the social pact between refugees and humanitarian agencies – and it is the same for the therapeutic relationship – remains a reality that is structurally uncertain. The lying, more than revealing to us a personal or social trait, discloses a field of power relationships, the humanitarian space, in which the refugee is embedded. Lying is charged with ambiguity, and it appears as a result of the paradoxical conditions in which the refugees are forced to live; however, we believe that it can also be seen as a sign of a living context that crashes every possible horizon of life, and where the only way out appears to be resettlement in another country.

Conclusion

Through the representation of the Syrian refugee as being ignorant and unable to identify his own needs, professionals and policymakers involved in MHPSS services in Lebanon produce a discourse on the refugee that places him/her at the margin of history and of politics. This leads to a crucial implicit question: what does healing mean, in these situations? The answer most commonly reported by the professionals we met – psychologists, psychiatrists, social workers – is the following: to help the refugee to reinforce his coping strategies, and give him the capacity to adapt to adverse living conditions; in other words, to become 'functional' again, by reinforcing his ability to 'deal with' the situation he is facing. But what does it mean to 'adapt to the context', when this same context forces the person into a perpetual struggle for survival, from which the only way out appears to be resettlement to a third country? Furthermore, what coping strategies are the MHPSS services hoping to reinforce, when the actual coping strategies that the refugees resort to while facing this adversity are seen by most professionals as manipulation and lying?

In this context, we can also wonder: is the 'discourse of neutrality', which some researchers find among Syrian refugees concerning the political situation in their country, the result of the long duration of the conflict as well as the inability to identify with either the opposition or the regime (Dot-Pouillard and Pesquet 2015: 65)? Or is it a depoliticized discourse created and enhanced by humanitarian agencies? In other terms, what expression is possible, and what explanation of one's own situation is legitimate, in a humanitarian regime?

The refugee lives in a humanitarian space, a space of tension (Agier 2003: 76), in which he has to submit to the humanitarian regime that wants him to be a victim. He also has to submit to its identification mechanisms and its arbitrary bureaucratic procedures that make him a suspect and that force him to play with his identity: 'Because it is a systematic negation of the other, an entrenched decision to refuse to the other all attributes of humanity, colonialism corners the dominated people into constantly asking themselves: Who am I in reality?' (Fanon 2002: 240). Paraphrasing Fanon, one can wonder: if mental illness is also the result of social dynamics (Basaglia 2000: 99), could humanitarian agencies and organisms be themselves a source of production of suffering and mental illness, as they contribute to, and participate in, the establishment of this daily regime. The suffering of refugees is reframed by humanitarian agencies as being an individual mental disorder, depoliticized and isolated from all the bureaucratic violence and context described above. Besides the political exclusion due to the position of the Syrians as refugees, the therapeutic encounter in a humanitarian setting, as we have tried to analyse it, may not legitimate the knowledge and experience of the patient, while not being able to 'think their suffering and their doubts as the reflection of an incorporated history' (Taliani and Vacchiano 2006: 123). Solutions offered are therefore specialized short-term technical 'evidence-based' interventions, targeted at the individual. This psychiatric discourse, by individualizing to that extent social suffering, regards the category of refugees as being a psychological rather than a political one, eroding the role of history and the political context, and ignoring that the refugee lives in a present that is full of obstacles, bureaucratic violence and arbitrary procedures, and, in this regard, participates in the wider humanitarian setting and agencies in eroding the political dimension of suffering. In response to this erosion of the political dimension in the humanitarian space, the only way out that the refugee seems to perceive is through individual solutions, such as changing narratives, or resettlement.

In conclusion, if humanitarian agencies cannot be other than spaces of tension, it is within these spaces that mental health professionals should be able to reach the refugee, legitimate his experience and support him, going beyond the logics that we tried to describe above but without dehistoricizing him, and without overlooking his own knowledge and expressed needs.

Hala Kerbage, MD, MSc, is an attending psychiatrist at the Psychiatry Department of Hotel-Dieu de France Hospital in Beirut, and an instructor at the School of Medicine, Saint-Joseph University. She is a clinical consultant for the International Organization of Migration. Dr Kerbage is involved in several research projects using a participatory approach to highlight the emic perspective of mental health conditions among marginalized communities, and to explore their attitudes to, and perceptions of, mental health and well-being.

Filippo Marranconi is an anthropologist, a former PhD candidate at EHESS (École des Hautes Études en Sciences Sociales) Paris, and former fellow at Ifpo (Institut français du Proche-Orient, Beirut). He was awarded with the Michel Seurat prize, 2017. He has conducted fieldwork in Lebanese psychiatric care devices, mental health and the production of subjectivities.

Notes

1. For a description of the political and historical reasons for this choice, see Geisser 2013: 72.
2. The author specifies: 'In such blurred circumstances, the level and quality of protection inter alia differ among those individuals whom UNHCR considers refugees but who are not registered; those who are registered refugees; those who are not registered but are recorded refugees; and those who are registered refugees but may at some point have renewed their residency in Lebanon under the sponsorship system. An additional layer of uncertainty is added when the starting point for many of UNHCR protection interventions is vulnerability, by which certain categories of people are perceived to be, by definition, vulnerable' (Janmyr 2017: 412).
3. We cannot here explain in detail the condition of eligibility for access to health care for refugees. It is enough to point out that generally the cost of the consultation in primary health-care centres is around 3,000–5,000 Lebanese pounds. Instead, for the secondary and tertiary health care, UNHCR stipulated a convention with fifty-three public and private hospitals, but covers only the 75% of the costs, and only under specific conditions: there must be an immediate danger to the life of the person – a broad and blurry categorization – and the prognosis must be positive (UNHCR 2014). The eligibility to this kind of service is only possible for people owning a valid ID or registered to UNHCR.
4. As stated in the guideline, 'the Inter-Agency Standing Committee (IASC) was established in 1992 in response to General Assembly Resolution 46/182, which called for strengthened coordination of humanitarian

assistance. The resolution set up the IASC as the primary mechanism for facilitating inter-agency decision making in response to complex emergencies and natural disasters. The IASC is formed by the heads of a broad range of UN and non-UN humanitarian organisations' (IASC 2007: ii).
5. The Mental Health Gap is a tool elaborated by the World Health Organization (WHO), designed for primary health-care professionals, in order to train them to detect, screen, diagnose and treat mental health conditions, according to 'evidence-based' interventions. It is promoted in low- and middle-income countries, as stigma around mental health is assumed to be more important in these countries due to a 'lack of mental health literacy' and a 'need for education' in terms of mental health, while universalizing the treatment of mental health illness, without always taking into account the context in which those interventions are applied.
6. Kerbage has worked as a consultant psychiatrist for several NGOs providing MHPSS services for Syrian refugees. Marranconi is currently conducting a PhD on psychiatry in Lebanon, looking specifically at the case of Syrian refugees.
7. Director of a UNHCR funded NGO, April 2016.
8. Interpersonal psychotherapy (IPT) is a brief, attachment-focused psychotherapy developed in the 1970s in the United States that centres on resolving interpersonal problems and symptomatic recovery. It is an empirically supported treatment (EST) that follows a highly structured and time-limited approach, and is intended to be completed within 12–16 weeks.
9. An international NGO programme coordinator, April 2016.
10. A UNHCR representative, May 2016.
11. Social worker at IMC, April 2016.
12. Social worker for an international NGO, May 2016.
13. Ibid.
14. Programme coordinator of an international NGO, May 2016.
15. Ibid.
16. Mental health advisor at IMC, April 2016.
17. Social worker at IMC, May 2016.
18. Interview with a psychologist working for an international NGO, October 2016.
19. When we conducted our research, we pointed out the fact that we were working for a university, not for the UNHCR. But many people seemed not to 'trust' us, or they thought they could obtain something from our presence at a UNHCR level. This is particularly meaningful, because it shows us, in some ways, the uncertainty of the world these people live in and, most of all, the opacity and instability of the UN presence for them.
20. This could be viewed as a phenomenon coherent with humanitarianism as a practice that legitimizes itself aprioristically (Fassin and Rechtman 2009).
21. Interview with a psychologist, April 2016.

22. The names have been changed.
23. Since 5 January 2015, the residence permit for Syrian refugees must be renewed every six months at the cost of 200 US dollars. The ones registered in UNHCR must also provide an official pledge not to work. These are only a few of the conditions with which they have to comply in order to get the permit (cf. Janmyr 2016).
24. All names in the chapter are changed to keep anonymity.
25. In March 2014, a woman set herself on fire in front of the UN building (*Al Jazeera*, 4 April 2014. 'Syrian Self-immolation Case Reflects Tragedy'. Retrieved 18 July 2017 from http://www.aljazeera.com/news/middleeast/2014/04/syria-self-immolation-case-reflects-tragedy-20144216034370957.html). There is no official data available on how this was managed by the UNHCR, but an informal source from an international NGO providing specialized MHPSS for Syrian refugees in Lebanon reported to us that she was diagnosed as 'mentally ill' (psychotic depression) by the psychiatrist, as well as the neurologist, who were sought by UNHCR to evaluate her after the incident, while she was being treated in the hospital. This story reveals the power that the psychiatrist can have in a humanitarian setting in transposing a political message into a psychiatric disorder. The woman died of her wounds in the hospital a few days later, as the UNHCR could not fund the rest of her treatment. Furthermore, they declared they did not want to encourage this kind of behaviour by giving her family what she was requesting, as it could become 'contagious' with other Syrians resorting to the same death threats to obtain more aid.
26. In Lebanon, the French language is still used by a part of the population living in some neighbourhoods. Sometimes the use of French can be seen as a sign of distinction, or in the case of the Syrians, it can be a way to present themselves to the population of the neighbourhood, avoiding some 'typical' form of greeting that could refer them directly, in the mind of their Lebanese interlocutor, to stereotypes linked with their Syrian origin.
27. Arabic word for 'slippers'. In Lebanon, a stereotype about Syrians is that they wear slippers, with the connotation, in the eyes of some Lebanese, of provincialism, underdevelopment, countryside origin, simplicity, etc.
28. Interview with social workers from an international NGO, April 2016.

References

Agger, I., et al. 1995. *Theory and Practice of Psychosocial Projects under War Conditions in Bosnia-Herzegovina and Croatia*. Zagreb: ECHO/ECTF.

Agier, M. 2003. 'La main gauche de l'empire: Ordre et désordres de l'humanitaire'. *Multitudes* 11(1): 66–77.

Al Jazeera, 4 April 2014. 'Syrian Self-immolation Case Reflects Tragedy'. Retrieved 18 July 2017 from http://www.aljazeera.com/news/

middleeast/2014/04/syria-self-immolation-case-reflects-tragedy-20144216034370957.html.
Almedom, A., et al. 2004. 'Mental Wellbeing in Settings of "Complex Emergency": An Overview'. *Journal of Biosocial Science* 36(4): 381–88.
Argenti-Pillen, A. 2003. *Masking Terror: How Women Contain Violence in Southern Sri Lanka*. Philadelphia: University Pennsylvania Press.
Basaglia, F. 2000. *Conferenze Brasiliane*. Milan: Raffaello Cortina.
Beneduce, R. 2015. 'The Moral Economy of Lying: Subjectcraft, Narrative Capital, and Uncertainty in the Politics of Asylum'. *Medical Anthropology* 34(6): 551–71.
Blanchet, K., F.M. Fouad and T. Pherali. 2016. 'Syrian Refugees in Lebanon: The Search for Universal Health Coverage'. *Conflict and Health* 10(12). Retrieved 17 January 2017 from https://conflictandhealth.biomedcentral.com/articles/10.1186/s13031-016-0079-4.
Bolton, P., et al. 2003. 'Group Interpersonal Psychotherapy for Depression in Rural Uganda: A Randomized Controlled Trial'. *Journal of American Medical Association* 289(23): 3117–24.
Bracken, P., J.E. Giller and D. Summerfield. 1995. 'Psychological Responses to War and Atrocity: The Limitations of Current Concepts'. *Social Science & Medicine* 40(8): 1073–82.
Coutts, A., F.M. Fouad and R. Batniji. 2013. 'Assessing the Syrian Health Crisis: The Case of Lebanon'. *Lancet* 381(9875): e9. Retrieved 18 July 2017 from http://www.thelancet.com/journals/lancet/article/PIIS0140-6736(13)60863-6/fulltext.
Dot-Pouillard, N., and J.B. Pesquet. 2015. 'Les réfugiés syriens au Liban: l'émergence progressive d'un discours de neutralité ?' *Confluences Méditerranée* 92(1): 61–72.
El Chammay, R., and W. Ammar. 2014. 'Syrian Crisis and Mental Health System Reform in Lebanon'. *Lancet* 384(9942): 494.
Fanon, F. 2002. *Les damnés de la terre*. Paris: Editions La Découverte.
Fassin, D. 2012. *Humanitarian Reason: A Moral History of the Present*. London: University of California Press.
Fassin, D., and R. Rechtman. 2009. *The Empire of Trauma: An Inquiry into the Condition of Victimhood*. Princeton, NJ: Princeton University Press.
Geisser, V. 2013. 'La question des réfugiés syriens au Liban: Le réveil des fantômes du passé'. *Confluences Méditérranée* 87(4): 67–84.
Giacaman, R., et al. 2011. 'Mental Health, Social Distress and Political Oppression: The Case of the Occupied Palestinian Territory'. *Global Public Health* 6(5): 547–59.
Harissi, M.A. 2015. 'Lebanon Imposes Visas on Syrians for First Time'. Retrieved 15 July 2017 from http://www.unhcr.org/cgibin/texis/vtx/refdaily?pass=52fc6fbd5&id=54aa2ef98.
Hassan, G., et al. 2016. 'Mental Health and Psychosocial Wellbeing of Syrians Affected by Armed Conflict'. *Epidemiology Psychiatric Sciences* 25(2): 129–41.

Inter-Agency Standing Committee (IASC). 2007. 'IASC Guidelines on Mental Health and Psychosocial Support in Emergency Settings'. Geneva. Retrieved 30 March 2017 from http://www.who.int/mental_health/emergencies/guidelines_iasc_mental_health_psychosocial_june_2007.pdf.

Janmyr, M. 2016. 'Precarity in Exile: The Legal Status of Syrian Refugees in Lebanon'. *Refugee Survey Quarterly* 35(4): 58–78.

———. 2017. 'UNHCR and the Syrian Refugee Response: Negotiating Status and Registration in Lebanon'. *The International Journal of Human Rights* 22(3): 393–419.

Karam, E.G., et al. 2014. 'Outcome of Depression and Anxiety after War: A Prospective Epidemiologic Study of Children and Adolescents'. *Journal of Traumatic Stress* 27(2): 192–99.

———. 2016. 'Lebanon: Mental Health System Reform and the Syrian Crisis'. *British Journal of Psychiatry* 13(4): 87–89.

Kassatly, H. 2017. 'Enterrer son mort c'est l'honorer'. *Hommes & Migrations* 1319: 105–13.

Kazour, F., et al. 2017. 'Post-traumatic Stress Disorder in a Sample of Syrian Refugees in Lebanon'. *Comprehensive Psychiatry* 72: 41–47.

Kleinman, A. 1991. *Rethinking Psychiatry: From Cultural Category to Personal Experience*. Cambridge: Free Press.

Miller, K.E., and A. Rasmussen. 2010. 'War Exposure, Daily Stressors, and Mental Health in Conflict and Post-Conflict Settings: Bridging the Divide between Trauma Focused and Psychosocial Frameworks'. *Social Science & Medicine* 70(1): 7–16.

Moghnie, L., and F. Marranconi. 2017. 'Mental Health Strategy in Lebanon: An Anthropological Critique'. *The Legal Agenda*, 24 April 2017. Retrieved 8 July 2017 from http://legal-agenda.com/en/article.php?id=3635.

MoPH. 2015. 'The "4Ws" in Lebanon: Who's Doing What, Where and until When in Mental Health and Psychosocial Support'. Retrieved 31 March 2017 from https://www.rcpsych.ac.uk/pdf/4Ws-in-Lebanon-2015%20(2).pdf.

Naja, W., et al. 2016. 'Prevalence of Depression in Syrian Refugees and the Influence of Religiosity'. *Comprehensive Psychiatry* 68: 78–85.

Norwegian Refugee Council (NRC). 2015. 'Birth Registration Update: The Challenges of Birth Registration in Lebanon for Refugees from Syria'. Retrieved 15 January 2017 from https://www.nrc.no/globalassets/pdf/reports/the-challenges-of-birth-registration-in-lebanon-for-refugees-from-syria.pdf.

Parkinson, S.E., and O. Behrouzan. 2015. 'Negotiating Health and Life: Syrian Refugees and the Politics of Access in Lebanon'. *Social Science & Medicine* 146: 324–31.

Souaiby, L., et al. 2016. 'Impact of the Syrian Crisis on the Hospitalization of Syrians in a Psychiatric Setting'. *Community Mental Health Journal* 52(1): 84–93.

Summerfield, D. 1999. 'A Critique of Seven Assumptions behind Psychological Trauma Programs in War-Affected Areas'. *Social Science & Medicine* 48(10): 1449–62.

———. 2008. 'How Scientifically Valid is the Knowledge Base of Global Mental Health?' *BMJ* 336(7651): 992–94.

Taliani, S., and F. Vacchiano. 2006. *Altri corpi: Antropologia ed etnopsicologia della migrazione*. Milan: Edizioni Unicopli.

UNHCR. 1951. 'Convention and Protocol Related to the Status of Refugees'. Geneva. Retrieved 17 April 2017 from http://www.unhcr.org/3b66c2aa10.

———. 2013. 'Assessment of Mental Health and Psychosocial Support Services for Syrian Refugees in Lebanon'. Geneva. Retrieved 17 April 2017 from http://daleel-madani.org/sites/default/files/MentalhealthserviceassessmentDec2013.pdf.

———. 2014. 'Guidelines to Referral Health Care in Lebanon'. Geneva. Retrieved 15 January 2017 from data.unhcr.org/syrianrefugees/download.php?id=4277.

———. 2015. 'Culture, Context and the Mental Health and Psychosocial Wellbeing of Syrians'. Geneva. Retrieved 18 April 2017 from http://www.unhcr.org/55f6b90f9.pdf.

———. 2017. 'Syrian Regional Refugee Response'. Geneva. Retrieved 16 September 2006 from http://data.unhcr.org/syrianrefugees/regional.php.

Van Ommeren, M., S. Saxena and B. Saraceno. 2005. 'Mental and Social Health during and after Acute Emergencies: Emerging Consensus?' *Bulletin of the World Health Organization* 83: 71–75.

Wells, R., et al. 2016. 'Psychosocial Concerns Reported by Syrian Refugees Living in Jordan: Systematic Review of Unpublished Needs Assessments'. *British Journal of Psychiatry* 209 (2): 99–106.

WHO. 2016. 'mhGAP Intervention Guide for Mental, Neurological and Substance Use Disorders in Non-Specialized Health Settings'. Geneva. Retrieved 13 April 2017 from http://apps.who.int/iris/bitstream/10665/44406/1/9789241548069_eng.pdf.

Young, A. 1997. *The Armony of Illusions: Inventing Post-traumatic Stress Disorder*. Princeton, NJ: Princeton University Press.

7

Intercultural Mediation in the Italian Health-Care System

Ana Cristina Vargas

Intercultural Mediation and the Politics of the Encounter

Intercultural mediation is one of the strategies promoted by the European Union[1] to favour migrants' access to public services. In the health-care sector, intercultural mediation aims to facilitate the clinical encounter between foreign patients and health professionals. 'Health-care interpreter', 'intercultural mediator', 'culture broker', 'link worker': there are many such terms used in various countries, in various operational contexts and in the literature to refer to social operators who play an intermediary role, in which two main features converge: on the one hand, the practice of linguistic interpretation, and on the other, the ability to deal with cultural diversity and to communicate in cross-cultural contexts (Theodosiou and Aspioti 2016).

This chapter analyses the role of intercultural mediation in the protection of immigrants' right to health, with particular reference to the case of Turin, Italy. As I will demonstrate, intercultural mediation plays a major role in facilitating access to health-care services for foreign patients, it promotes mutual understanding and, in clinical practice, it allows the co-construction of a common ground of meaning and of a therapeutic alliance between migrants and health professionals. However, there are many uncertainties surrounding the role of the mediator and no lack of critical issues, which can be understood by taking into account the contradictions and inequalities that characterize the current Italian immigration policies.

These reflections have as their starting point the research project 'Health as a Fundamental Right: Experiences of Migrants in Turin', coordinated by the Fundamental Rights Laboratory (Castagnone et al. 2015). The research focused on an analysis of the experiences encountered by immigrants in their relationship with the health services of Turin. Ethnographic methodologies have been favoured, particularly (a) participant observation in the hospitals and outpatient settings of the national health system, and (b) narrative interviews.[2] Another important source of information was my active participation as an anthropologist in health education, preventive medicine interventions and social inclusion projects focused on immigration and health. This participation, which continues today, has made possible a continuous process of dialogue with the workers and the intercultural mediators on the potential of their role, and on the difficulties they encounter in their work.

Intercultural mediators (male and female) in the health-care sector, defined by Verrept as 'persons who are employed in health-care institutions to cross the language and culture barrier and to increase responsiveness to the needs of ethnic minority patients' (Verrept 2008: 188), represent a fundamental means of support in the relationship between foreign users and professionals in the field of health. The mediators who work in Turin are mostly immigrants who have experienced first-hand the difficulties of immigration and who, in addition to knowing the language and culture of their geographical area of origin, have a wealth of knowledge and skills acquired in Italy, in the complex process of interacting with the host society. Theirs is therefore a 'participative knowledge', which allows the development of an awareness of the obstacles in the migration path and of the complexities of the process of integration.

A particularly thorny issue is to define the professional profile of the mediators. In Piedmont, as in many other Italian regions, there is no specific rule that regulates the scope of intercultural mediation, and there are no mandatory criteria for accessing this professional area. A significant number of the mediators, but not all of them, followed training courses recognized by the Piedmont region, which comprise six hundred hours divided between theory and practice. These courses are free, and are open to laid-off or unemployed foreigners who have resided in Italy for at least two years and who have a level of education equal to at least a high school diploma. These are courses that offer basic skills on issues related to equal opportunities, migratory phenomena, the asylum system, integration policies and other issues connected to the operational scope of intercultural mediators. Often included in the total number of hours are Italian language modules and lessons on civics, communication sciences, sociology and anthropology.

Despite the generic nature of these paths, mediators may find themselves having to perform their function in radically different contexts: from prison to hospital; from schools to public offices; and from the police headquarters to third-sector associations. The acquisition of specific skills, in general, happens 'on the job' and in an informal way. In these contexts, only those most sensitive to the problems of the migratory encounter have designed targeted processes and developed working models tailored to the needs of each sector.[3] The generic nature of training paths is a long-standing problem (Beneduce 2008), one for which there are no structural solutions yet.

In Italy, intercultural mediation (also called cultural mediation, or linguistic-cultural mediation) began as an experiment in the 1990s, coinciding with the intensification of international migration, which until then had only marginally affected this country. The arrival of people from distant social, linguistic and cultural worlds was a strong challenge for unprepared public services, and it was necessary to create collaborative networks with people who were able to act as intermediaries with the newcomers. These were mostly foreigners with a good cultural background behind them, who worked in a mainly informal way with public institutions and associations that, in the most varied environments, were involved in the first reception phase.

In these early experiences, intercultural mediation proved to be an effective operative tool and soon began to acquire a more stable and structured character, in the regulatory framework given by law n. 40 of 6 March 1998 – better known as the Turco-Napolitano Law[4] – an organic law on immigration in which, for the first time, migration was regarded as a structural social phenomenon.

In the field of social policies, at least on paper, intercultural mediation has been an important resource from the early stages to promote the integration of migrants, to facilitate access to public services and to generate greater social cohesion in the various areas of everyday life. In the diffusion and consolidation of intercultural mediation, in addition to the initiatives of local authorities, the work of the mediators was central, through associations such as A.M.M.I. (Multi-ethnic Association of Intercultural Mediators).[5]

Intercultural mediation was spotlighted within the political world around 2009, when the document *Riconoscimento della figura pro-*

fessionale del mediatore interculturale [Recognizing the Professional Figure of the Intercultural Mediator], was approved by the Conference of Regions and Autonomous Provinces. The intercultural mediator, defined as an 'agent active in the integration process', had the role to 'put itself between foreigners and institutions, public services and private structures, without substituting either one or the other, to favour instead a link between subjects of different cultures'.[6]

The expected goal of recognition, paradoxically, was reached in a phase characterized by a general tightening of immigration rules, by the contraction of integration policies and by the strong presence of political currents hostile to the presence of foreigners (if not openly xenophobic). In an attempt to explain why intercultural mediation had not been 'targeted' by political decision makers, Lorenzo Luatti highlighted three misunderstandings about intercultural mediation and the positioning of this resource in the context of integration policies:

> (a) the idea that it was sufficient to count on a 'handyman' (the intercultural mediator) to whom the institutions could delegate the reception of foreign users, rather than 'rethinking in depth the methods and times of dialogue' and reformulating the methods of service delivery according to the needs of increasingly diversified users;
>
> (b) the emphasis on the 'cultural specificity' of the migrant, within a rigid and reified conception of culture, and a substantial lack of attention with respect to the social, historical, political and subjective factors that condition the well-being of migrants; and
>
> (c) the uncritical acceptance of mediation as an 'impartial' technique, and of the mediator as an individual who 'should position herself as a neutral third among immigrants and services', which contradicts a de facto positioning of the mediator who, working within a given context, is required to act 'mainly in an integrationist and assimilationist perspective, which propels the adaptation of the immigrant user'. (Luatti 2009: 81–84)

These reflections (Luatti 2009, 2010), together with the works of authors such as Ceccatelli Gurrieri (2003) and Baraldi (2009), without diminishing the potential of intercultural mediation, highlight the risk of considering it a 'shortcut' to the complex issue of the integration of migrants, which would require far-reaching structural and social inclusion policies. Intercultural mediation in Italy must therefore be contextualized within a set of immigration policies, which are fraught with unresolved tensions, pervasive inequalities and more or less veiled forms of institutional violence towards migrants.

Political favour and the guidelines of the State–Regions Conference gave momentum to intercultural mediation for a few years, but the positive trend that arose in the early 2000s was not destined to last long. A systematic survey coordinated by Allasino, which had the objective of evaluating the results of the Piedmont region's policies aimed at promoting intercultural mediation, highlighted a fragmented and uneven set of mediation services, a lack of knowledge of the potential of this health-care resource by health workers, and a global lack of mediation services (Allasino et al. 2006).

This situation worsened after 2012, when the economic crisis began to erode public investment in integration. Although intercultural mediation is still held in high regard by political decision makers, the economic crisis, the systematic reduction of resources for welfare (euphemistically called 'rationalization of expenditures') and austerity policies have led to a serious and widespread impoverishment of the network of mediation services in many areas, including health care.

Mediation in the Health Sector

One of the areas in which the need for intercultural mediation has clearly emerged is that of health protection. The Italian national health service (SSN), operating through its regional units, is public and guarantees universal access to urgent and essential care, which must also be provided to undocumented foreigners.[7] In the National Health Plan of 2006–08 the need to implement 'social-health services more attentive to the complex problems of people in respect of different dignities and cultures' is in fact explicitly recognized, and for the first time mention is made of the importance of the 'linguistic-cultural mediator' (PSN 2006–08: 80).[8]

Many mediators describe their role using the metaphor of a 'bridge that connects two worlds' and that 'helps thoughts to pass from one bank to the other'. The intercultural mediator, in fact, operates on trajectories of meaning that should be constantly traversed 'to ensure a satisfactory exchange between members of different cultures, between logical and distinct representations of health and therapy, between distinct universes of thought' (Beneduce 2004: 235). How are these tasks accomplished in the different operating situations of health services in Turin?

The work of mediators is different depending on the context, and it is not easy to make generalizations. We can, however, outline some of the most salient features of the work of mediators, taking into consideration three particularly representative areas: the large hospitals; public and private community clinics operating in the region; and ethno-psychology and ethno-psychiatry centres.

The Hospital

In large hospitals, the mediation service is usually contracted out to an external cooperative and is managed by an office in the hospital, which collects the requests sent by the workers and, depending on the degree of urgency, defines the priority and sends the mediators. These requests are almost exclusively linked to the presence of linguistic barriers which make communication impossible and which are perceived by workers as the main obstacle to assistance (Biglino and Olmo 2014). I will return to this subject in the next pages.

In hospitals, intercultural mediators often also carry out welcoming and orientation tasks, as they know in depth the regulations governing access to the health of foreigners, particularly if they are undocumented, as well as the often complicated bureaucratic procedures to access particular services in a health system that is hardly user friendly:

> I do not follow just the Albanian patients, but also those of other nationalities if they speak the language, because there are so many bureaucratic things and nobody knows the laws for foreigners ... the clerks, the secretaries ... they all call us. Almost no Italian employee knows the legislation, and, to make matters worse, the laws change constantly, so when a patient is in an irregular situation, they call us. Sometimes I even accompany Nigerian patients, sometimes I help them because they don't know the hospital, they don't know where to go. So we explain to the patient that, if he is undocumented, he must get an STP code, and also how to do it because there are so many foreigners who have been here for six years or more and who have never got an STP code. Among foreigners you feel closer. We also arrived here without speaking the language. That's why you think that whatever you did, the other person can do also. (Albanian cultural mediator)

Overall, the presence of the mediator in the hospital is limited to specific moments, such as the start of the treatment path, appointments with medical specialists and important check-ups in which it is essential to understand the language, or when making significant decisions with respect to the therapeutic procedure and the signing of informed consent is required (Quagliariello and Fin 2016). The latter is one of the areas in which the mediator's role entails greater legal responsibilities.

The presence of the mediator, therefore, is not continuous, and for hospitalized patients their everyday life often runs without the support of people who can translate basic information or facilitate communication. In these situations, recourse to informal mediation is prevalent: the help of family members, friends and acquaintances is fundamental. On some occasions even complete strangers, by virtue of their linguistic competence, wind up by chance 'lending a hand'. As Ahmed, a 30-year-old Moroccan worker who had lived in Italy since 2014, recounted during an interview in the Obstetrics and Gynaecology Ward, shortly after his wife gave birth:

> My wife never felt badly treated as a foreigner. She only tells me that she's sorry because she sometimes doesn't understand what they're trying to say. To ask for information about pregnancy and breastfeeding, she managed to make herself understood with gestures or she had to wait for me. If there were urgent things, they would call me and I would translate over the phone. We had done the same with our first child, when she needed to know something about how to breastfeed.

In the daily life of the hospital wards observed in the course of the research, in particular those concerning maternal and infant health and infectious diseases, contact between foreign patients and health-care workers, such as nurses and health-care assistants, takes place mostly without any intermediation. This compromises the possibility of dialogue on matters concerning the operation of the ward (hours and rules, the flow of family visits, who to contact in case of need, the distribution of meals, etc.) and the management of the illness or condition that has led to the admission (administration of the therapy, management of catheters or medical instruments, lactation, postpartum care, etc.).

In often rigid contexts such as hospital wards, it is not always easy to manage the diversity that manifests itself at many levels. This can include nutrition, the way in which important life-cycle events such as birth and death are accompanied, gender roles and the involvement of the extended family. Many of the misunderstandings, misconceptions and mix-ups that hinder the helping relationship relate precisely to practices in which bodily experience and cultural meaning are inseparably connected. In these sensitive areas, in which the body is at once tool, agent and object (Csordas 1994), embodied differences (Lock and Scheper-Hughes 1987; Csordas 1990) can easily be read in negative terms.

The case of Li, a young Chinese mother, is a clear example of how mediators can act as intermediaries and as negotiators between different representations of body and health. Li had had a natural birth without complications and, as foreseen by the care protocol, she was discharged after two days and had been given instructions to present herself the following day for a midwifery and neonatal visit at the hospital. Moreover, in the following two weeks, Li would have to make an outpatient paediatric visit to the public paediatrician (*pediatra di libera scelta*), and she had been sent to the paediatric community clinic (*consultorio pediatrico*) in her area, where, if she wanted to, she could have set up further check-ups. The first month of the newborn's life is considered a very delicate phase and, consequently, women are strongly urged to attend the hospital and outpatient services. Li, however, did not show up for the first visit and this gesture, often considered 'typical of Chinese women', was attributed by health-care workers to a lack of interest in the Western-biomedical system and to a certain inattention to her own health and to that of the child.

When asked to recontact the woman and reschedule the visit, the Chinese mediator managed to create a channel of dialogue and to offer the team a different interpretation of Li's absence. Like many other Chinese women, Li was observing the days of *zuo yuezi*, also known as 'sitting the month', a widespread practice both in China and among Chinese women living abroad, which calls for women to stay at home for about a month after birth, avoid any kind of physical exertion, avoid contact with water, keep the body warm, adopt a 'hot' diet, which contrasts with the postpartum cold, and to carefully avoid wind, rain and other environmental elements. Leaving home, therefore, was perceived by Li as something that would endanger her health and that of her child.

The task of mediators, in cases like Li's, is to contextualize the actions and motivations of patients, bringing out the meaning of a given practice from the perspective of those who carry it out. Although *zuo yuezi* is in sharp contrast with the care procedures for the puerperium, it is a practice oriented towards the protection of well-being, and in this sense it has the same goal as the postnatal care: the therapeutic alliance can be built around this common goal if the possibility of reaching a compromise or exploring alternative routes is accepted. In Li's case, the visits were simply postponed, but contact was made with the local community services, which could have intervened at the home level in a case of need.

In some hospitals, mediators work in conjunction with social services in an attempt to fill an institutional gap between the possibility of access to medical care, guaranteed (albeit within certain limits) even to undocumented foreigners, and access to support from regional social services, which is available for Italian citizens but only for foreigners who are in the country legally and are permanent residents. The case of Rashid is a clear example of this disconnection between health protection and social protection. Rashid was a 46-year-old Moroccan man who had arrived irregularly in Italy in 2010. His migratory path, though difficult, initially seemed to be moving towards equilibrium: he had managed to find a job, relatively adequate accommodation and had obtained a temporary residency permit. During the economic crisis, however, he was laid off. As with many migrants, the loss of work triggered a series of consequences that completely disrupted his life: Rashid was no longer able to renew his residency permit or to pay his rent. He ended up living on the street, and gradually his physical and mental health deteriorated. He became ill with tuberculosis, contracted hepatitis and, in general, his whole body suffered the impact of a life in conditions of extreme social marginality:

> Now I sleep at the Red Cross 'cold emergency' shelters. In every room there are eight people, a tremendous cold, too cold. If one [person] is sick, everyone is sick. You cannot wash the blankets, you cannot wash yourself. Understand? No, no, no … I swear, a real humiliation. Some time ago I went to the hospital and I was hospitalized for five days … I've been better, but it was only five days, maybe four days. You go there … do you understand? … and they treat you well, but don't solve anything, because then everything starts all over and there are many people who are sick. When you're in the hospital you don't have to worry about anything else … the important thing is that you go to the doctor, then the doctor knows how to do his job. The problem is outside.

Situations like that of Rashid are frequent, and would require the activation of social and health intervention routes articulated on several fronts, which, at present, are rarely possible to predict.

In a panorama of complex needs, which should be addressed using a systemic approach, the mediator's intervention represents an important step for giving voice to the experiences of migrants and creating bridges with the regional organizations that are able to offer some form of support. However, these are attempts to help that have to come to terms with important structural limitations. In many cases, organizations linked to the world of religious charity and private social associations are the only ones able to offer relief to users who are structurally excluded from the public system.

In recent years, problems related to the economic crisis, the reduction in public investment in health, and the increasing privatization of health services have led to a weakening of the intercultural mediation service in hospitals: there have been cuts to staff; the mechanism for the procurement of mediation services to cooperatives external to public health companies has been generalized; the 'hours' of mediation available to the workers have been reduced, with a consequent fragmentation of the work contexts of the mediators; an 'on-call' work mechanism[9] has been implemented; and, in general, the contractual and working conditions of the intercultural mediators have worsened. Many of these problems emerge in the narration of Olga, an Albanian mediator:

> I work mainly in the 'immigration and health' centre. At the beginning it was basically a new idea. It was about setting up, inside the hospital, a clinic only for foreigners that was not just a clinic but also a reference point, where they could come and ask for information, guidelines … In the first few years there were many mediators, of many languages. Then with the budget cuts … now only we three poor people remain: a Nigerian, a Somali and me. We have had a drastic cut in all staff, but the clients have not decreased at all, they remain the same … We have always worked through a cooperative system. The cooperative hires the mediator, but our dream is that the hospital [Azienda Ospedaliera] will say: 'For sixteen years you have worked with us, come … we will hire you'. We are only dreaming, though.

In the context of a contraction of mediation services, mediators are often forced to operate under conditions that hinder, rather than facilitate, the construction of an effective health-care worker–mediator–user triangulation. In some hospitals, for example, telephone translation methods have been implemented; in these cases, the company stipulates an agreement with a call centre that, remotely, offers an interpreting service by speakerphone. These strategies, which have reduced costs and can be a resource for solving emergency situations, should not, however, be a generalized mechanism because they strip clinical communication of any relational connotation, and deprive the user of the possibility of finding in the mediator a bridge to resources present in a specific local situation.

Community Clinics and Private Social Services

In the community health-care centres, as in the outpatient facilities in hospitals, the presence of mediators tends to be more constant than in hospital wards, and the recognition of the importance of these figures is greater. Because these services are linked to specific areas, or to the management of specific conditions or illnesses, the choice of mediators is generally carried out on the basis of the characteristics of the users of each service. In general, mediators have fixed weekly hours, announced through posters and other information channels. Many of the outpatient clinics, in particular family and paediatric counselling centres,[10] provide programmed access channels and free access channels, with no reservations required. This facilitates the coordination of services and also a certain degree of self-organization by users.

In these structures, both in the public sector and in the second welfare, the presence of the mediator transcends the circumscribed moment of the medical examination, and there are frequent occasions for direct contact between the mediator and the client. The sharing of language, of cultural origin and, above all, an empathic knowledge of life circumstances and the migratory experience, open the door to a relationship based on trust and closeness, which often proves relevant in identifying needs and in building a therapeutic alliance:

> Sometimes a person with a headache arrives and manages to say two things in Italian or he makes himself understood with gestures; as a health worker you do your job, you give him a Tachipirin (acetaminophen) and he goes home, but maybe the headache was just a small part of the problem and there were many other things he wanted to talk about ... so his problem was not solved and it may be that no one noticed it. So there is something more we can do as mediators – we can listen. (Jordanian cultural mediator)

Often the mediator facilitates the interaction with local resources and specific associations of the migrant's country of origin,[11] helping to create an intertwining of bonds that can support him or her in times of difficulty; in some cases, this can have a therapeutic value too. The mediator is also an important link with respect to the neighbourhood, and is a fundamental support in the planning of initiatives in the area.

The involvement of the mediator allows for a better understanding of the client's living conditions and biography, thus facilitating the construction of a targeted path upon which to address specific health problems. These dimensions clearly emerge in the experience of Halima, an Egyptian cultural mediator:

> The responsibility for following Arab women who have difficulty with the Italian language and urging them to show up for the scheduled exams, both the prenatal and the postnatal ones – such as appointments with the paediatrician, a visit to the gynaecologist for a prescription for contra-

ceptive pills compatible with breastfeeding, and others – is mine. I am convinced that our presence can give added value to what is otherwise the work of doctors and nurses. Without the mediators, many health-care workers would find it difficult to create a 'therapeutic contract', to share objectives, to obtain informed consent [or] to carry out interventions involving the patients in an active way, making them not only compliant, but also aware of, and in agreement with, the proposed treatments. For us, however, this is possible because women trust us. I try to bring myself closer to them, I give them advice based on their needs, their history. Then they trust me. Maybe the woman does not dare show others her discomforts or problems. Maybe a woman comes to give birth who has another child at home and does not know who to leave it with. Maybe I'm dealing with a woman who has a low level of culture, who does not understand the meaning of some specialized examinations, and I try to simplify these.

In some contexts, moreover, the mediator must perform tasks that are outside the scope of the mediation, such as planning for check-ups and diagnostic tests. However, the direct involvement of mediators in the services' operational dimension can create confusion among users and can place the mediator in situations of conflict.

The intrinsically liminal position of the mediator can result in a difficult oscillation between solidarity with the users and their duties towards structures that have to make do with limited resources that are often insufficient to cope with a client with complex needs. The story of Asma, a Moroccan mediator, highlights this dimension:

> I feel guilty because I cannot listen to everyone, and I cannot even satisfy everyone's requests. Sometimes I meet people I know are needy, but I have to say no because those are the resources we have … Sometimes we hear 'you are racist with your countrymen' … someone accuses you of being 'a traitor to your community', but I am really very sorry. At that moment the person probably just throws you two words because she is angry and then goes away, but I constantly live through the suffering of saying no. I can describe myself as a good listener but I cannot always do what I would like … so, sometimes I can't even listen … because, above all, there is a lack of time.

This sense of powerlessness reflects the real impossibility of responding to needs that often transcend the operational capabilities of a single structure, and which refer to deeper and more pervasive social inequalities.

Finally, it is worth noting that the general practitioners, also known as family doctors, who represent the first and most important link between the individual and the health system, have no available channels to make use of the intercultural mediation services: informal mediation, carried out by friends, relatives or other countrymen, is therefore the client's only resource to overcome the linguistic and cultural barriers in the encounter with the doctor.

The Ethno-Psychology and Ethno-Psychiatry Centres

Perhaps the area in which intercultural mediation has achieved the greatest level of recognition, and the working methodologies of mediators have been formulated in a more complex and articulated way, is that of the ethno-psychiatry and ethno-psychology services. In Turin, organizations such as the Frantz Fanon Centre and the Mamre Association, which have inherited and reinterpreted the tradition of French ethno-psychiatry, have developed pioneering work with mediators, who are considered an integral part of the team. This inclusion has allowed the development of treatment trajectories in which the intervention of the therapist and the mediator act in a synergistic way. The mediators, writes Roberto Beneduce, ethno-psychiatrist and director of the Frantz Fanon Centre, can become constituent elements of the therapeutic system, as people capable of acting as 'guides' to the use of culture as the nucleus for generating change (Beneduce 2007: 241–43).

At the base of this approach to intercultural mediation there is a critical reflection on the concept of culture and on the way in which psychic realities and cultural realities are articulated. The ethno-psychiatric mechanism starts with recognition of the connection between forms of suffering (in particular, mental, but also physical) and the historical-cultural context in which the subject's life has unfolded. It follows that only an in-depth exploration of this context, and of its transformations, makes it possible to search for the roots of the intelligibility of a symptom and to understand the processes that underlie the experience of the disease.

Culture is therefore caught up in its incessant dynamism and intrinsic conflict, two dimensions that, in the migratory experience, manifest themselves in the constant tension between: (a) adhesion or rebellion with respect to the norms and values of the environment of origin; (b) the difficulty of recognizing oneself in a new country and the desire for new roots; (c) external forces that devalue the meaning or actively erode the degree of symbolic relevance of the cultures of origin and the often traumatic experience of the encounter with the new culture; and (d) social suffering and attempts to adapt and build new horizons of life.

A Situated Process

The word 'mediation' is derived from the Latin *mediatio*; *-ōnis* is attached to the word *medius*, 'in the middle, central', but also 'intermediate', 'ambiguous', 'neutral'. *'Mediare'* refers to the process of constructing meeting points between opposing positions, the art of reconciling divergent needs in a creative way, the possibility of generating relationships and finding compromises in situations of conflict, and accepting the ambiguities and contradictions inherent in this precarious game of equilibrium.

Mediation is usually represented as a neutral technique and the mediator as an individual who is placed in an equidistant position by the parties, regardless of the context in which the mediation takes place. This image, however, is misleading, because it obscures the influence that power relations (in social, economic, political, cultural and professional terms) have on *every* relationship, including the clinical one.

From the perspective that I intend to develop here, intercultural mediation is seen as a social process situated within an area of non-neutral sociopolitical forces. Although it is outside the field of medical anthropology, the work of Morgan Brigg (2003, 2008), mediator and expert in the field of conflict resolution, is interesting in this regard. Analysing a number of experiences of intercultural mediation in situations of conflict between Australian aborigines and non-Aboriginal Australians, Brigg points out a substantial difference in the way in which the conflict itself is defined, and therefore managed, by the social actors involved. In the Aboriginal view, this not only represents a constructive and necessary social process, but also a mechanism through which interpersonal bonds, subjectivities and political communities are shaped. This difference, however, is not taken into account in the mediator's intervention: 'Explicit and implicit mediator techniques lead disputants in intercultural mediations to behave in ways consistent with the goals of mediation and Western norms around conflict and selfhood' (Brigg 2003: 288). Intercultural mediation is therefore not a 'culturally neutral' mechanism, but one that bases its own assumptions on a specific vision of the world and thus reproduces the asymmetries and inequalities of power present in a given social whole.

Even in the health sector, there is an unequivocal power dimension in intercultural mediation, because the meeting does not take place on an equal footing. Intercultural mediators are called to act within services that operate according to precise organizational and health logics, which provide for access and ways of taking charge that are regulated by pre-established norms and criteria. Mediators and operators also follow health protocols (guidelines) which are not easy to modify and which cannot always be adapted to needs that are sometimes radically different from those of the Italian population. Intercultural mediation in Italy does not therefore act from the perspective of building a medical pluralism, one capable of integrating different systems of care. Rather it is aimed at facilitating the integration of migrants within a system in which the differences in the conceptions of the body, health and treatment are more often perceived as obstacles to the implementation of an appropriate care option than as potential resources for the individual and for the system.

The relationship with otherness – and with the body of the 'others' – is etched into social and political relationships of domination-subordination (Beneduce 2004, 2007; Taliani and Vacchiano 2006), which translate into a hierarchy of knowledge in which the only fully legitimate horizon is the biomedical one. In parallel, recognition of the historically situated character of the gnoseological categories, therapeutic techniques and languages of biomedicine is limited, if not absent; the importance of 'culture' is emphasized in the 'other', but is not recognized in its own system of reference.

In fact, ethnographic research shows a widespread tendency to explain the health problems of migrants by emphasizing the dimension of cultural otherness, which can make people lose sight of the social problems by which foreigners are measured. The migratory experience is often characterized by poverty, marginalization, the absence of solid social networks, unfavourable housing conditions, poor social recognition and inclusion in subordinate, irregular, precarious and poorly protected jobs. In the life stories of many foreigners, regular and above all undocumented social suffering (Kleinman, Das and Lock 1997) is clearly embodied, and translates into medically pathological situations. As Paul Farmer has repeatedly written, discrimination, social inequality and marginalization are vectors of structural violence and are the underlying reason behind most human rights violations (Farmer 1999).

One of the most fundamental and radical criticisms of culturalism can be found in the works of Didier Fassin, who, in an open controversy with French ethno-psychiatry, writes:

> In the first place, culturalism deprives others of their universality and blocks their culture, whether it be ethnic, religious or national ... The Bambarity of Bambara is the only horizon for their humanity. Secondly,

it deprives the others of their diversity. Immutable and naturalized, as a dead animal would be, culture only allows a single and standardized expression of every self. It is believed that all Soninké must act in the same way, like Soninké. Thirdly it deprives the others of their rationality. It does not say that the other is necessarily irrational, but it confines him/her to the rationality of an exotic imaginary ... And finally, the most serious thing, culturalism deprives others of their social condition. The reduction of the individual to his/her culture, especially when it comes to an immigrant, involves the denial of his/her concrete existence, of the legal, economic and social difficulties s/he encounters in everyday life. (Fassin 1999: 168–69)

Intercultural mediation was considered an instrument that 'can contribute to the reduction of health-care disparities', but, as Hans Verrept (2008), one of the leading scholars and advocates of intercultural mediation, affirms, there is a significant distance between the theoretical potential of health mediation and the real capacity of mediators, in the absence of adequate integration policies, to influence complex and multifactorial problems concerning integration and social recognition.

Translating Words, Mediating Meanings

While preparing this chapter, I had the opportunity to take part in the D.I.S.Co.R.S.I. Migranti project,[12] in which a focus group was organized on intercultural mediation in the health sector. It involved mediators, health professionals, people who hold institutional decision-making roles and groups of researchers representing the other two countries involved in the project: Catalonia (Spain) and Auvergne-Rhône-Alpes (France).

The project, in addition to representing a constructive moment of transnational sharing of good practices, allowed some unresolved issues to emerge. One of the most interesting ideas from the discussion referred precisely to the objectives of the mediator's intervention, which should intersect the linguistic and the sociocultural sphere but, in practice, is very often reduced to the 'translation of words'. In the heat of the debate, one of the mediators present, addressing the health workers, asked in a somewhat provocative manner if any of them had ever asked for the presence of an intercultural mediator during a clinical encounter with a client who could communicate, even in a very limited way, in Italian. The silence with which her words were received was more eloquent than any answer.

Among the health workers, the idea is that, with patience and willingness, the physical examination, clinical tests and a minimal dialogue – made possible through gestures, drawings, applications, and IT tools such as Google translator or (in the best cases) specially designed graphic materials – are sufficient for 'understanding each other', identifying the disease and guaranteeing, if not qualitatively excellent, at least effective assistance.

The case of Fatima, however, shows how erroneous this representation can be and is an eloquent testimony to the way in which communication difficulties condition the clinical encounter. Fatima, a 42-year-old Moroccan widow, claimed to be in 'good health', but said she has been suffering from pains in the lower part of her abdomen, which have required a long series of investigations:

> Fatima: They first took a picture, a photograph of me here [indicating the point where she feels pain], then again I did another ... Then I came here to the clinic and then back to the hospital, for other tests. There they took a picture again.
>
> *An X-ray? An ultrasound?* Yes, yes ... a photograph.
>
> *Why did they do these exams?* I do not understand.
>
> *Why did you take the picture?* For the pain, for the pain 'here' [shows, once again, the point where there is this pain that is never identified].
>
> *But did they explain to you what the exams were for?* No, I do not understand.
>
> *Then they gave you the results?* Yes ... later they made me take another, another photograph. Maybe I'm going to have a surgery, they told me so.
>
> *But did you understand what the problem is? Do you know why do you need a surgery?* Always for the pain ... for the same pain I told you about.

The lack of vocabulary and the limited ability to formulate complex sentences made it impossible for the patient to clearly explain the discomfort she felt, to talk about the symptoms, to ask questions and ask for possible explanations. Her overall understanding of what 'the doctor' said was poor, which not only created uncertainty and anguish, but also reduced the woman's autonomy and decision-making power. In fact, Fatima had no clear indication of the significance of the investigations to which she had been subjected, nor the overall clinical picture. Even if she had signed a number of informed consent documents, at the time of the interview she could not even tell what was leading the diagnostic process or explain the clinical reasons for an invasive medical procedure such as a surgery.

For the doctor, too, it was difficult, if not impossible, to reconstruct the patient's medical history, collect her experience of illness, know anything about her migration path, provide clear and comprehensive information, explain the motivations of the diagnostic tests or give treatment options.

Fatima, like many of the migrants interviewed, had never explained her difficulties in linguistic comprehension, or expressed her need for a mediator. In fact, not all foreigners know of the existence of this resource; often they do not know the word 'mediator', nor are they familiar with the role of this professional figure. In addition to having to request the intercultural mediation service, health professionals therefore have the responsibility of identifying the need for this intervention, even in appointments with patients who know 'a few words' of Italian.

Still, as we have already noted, recourse to mediators in these cases is sporadic, if not altogether absent. The decision not to resort to mediators is motivated by pragmatic organizational difficulties (such as the low number of hours of mediation available), but also by the lack of knowledge of the potential for mediation as an instrument in the clinical encounter and by the tendency to focus on the biological aspects of therapeutic communication, a bodily disease that is thought to be somehow 'shown' with a gesture or with a few words, dismissing the narrative elements that allow to explore what Arthur Kleinman has called illness (1988): the patient's experience of symptoms and suffering. Illness, as Cristiana Giordano accurately notes, is both culturally shaped and rooted in the complex biography of the migrant:

> Medicine and psychiatry take translation as transparent. Symptoms can be translated into pathologies, and pathologies into forms of treatment. For the anthropologist and the ethno-psychiatrist, on the other hand, symptoms can be the language of dissent and critique; they speak of a larger history and are always inscribed in a cultural and political context. (Giordano 2014: 1)

Pathology, from the perspective of medical anthropology, represents not only an organic dysfunction, but calls into question the dimension of subjective experience of illness (Kleinman 1988, 1997) and the social and cultural horizons into which this experience is inscribed. The therapeutic relationship, from this point of view, should deal with both the strictly biomedical dimension and the processes of signification that confer intelligibility onto a symptom, an unease, a knowledge or a gesture of care. In the case of foreign patients, the co-construction of a treatment relationship (Good 1994) not only requires sharing a linguistic code, but also requires a shared meaning and knowledge, at least partial, of the cultural, social, historical and autobiographical context that shapes individual experience.

In this perspective, the intercultural mediator's role has three levels: first, she allows a linguistic exchange that is otherwise impossible; second, she contributes to placing words in a broader horizon, which restores their cultural density; and third, she has the task of facilitating the establishment of a positive clinical relationship between people who do not share the same symbolic-cultural background (or, therefore, the same values) or the same communicative pragmatics. Using the words of Sergent and Larchanché, which describe in detail the French experience, the task of mediators is therefore 'literally to translate, on the one hand, but also (and perhaps more significantly) to bridge social worlds' (Sergent and Larchanché 2009: 7).

While presenting some areas of overlap, as the intercultural mediators themselves point out, their role is not the same as that of the interpreter. An effective example, in my opinion, of the complex oscillation between linguistic translation and facilitation of the relationship was recounted to me by Lida, then an Arab mediator in a large obstetric-gynaecological hospital. In her role, Lida often accompanied women during scheduled specialist visits and, on one of these occasions, a gynaecologist, referring to a young Moroccan woman, said dismissively to her: 'Can you ask the lady why she *still* wears the veil?' How can you translate this kind of sentence? If he wanted a literal translation, the weight of the prejudice against the veiled women behind that '*still*' would have been obvious and would probably have led to a communication shutdown. At the same time, given her role, she could not escape the task of asking what was required of her. She then chose to paraphrase: 'The doctor would like to know why you wear the veil ... why don't you explain what it means to you?'

Her strategy had a positive effect; the woman explained to the doctor her choice to wear the veil, and the encounter managed to proceed without a hitch. In carrying out her intervention, the mediator had implicitly taken note of the stereotypes that conditioned the reciprocal representation and, by modifying the way in which the question was asked, had acted as a facilitator of the relationship, allowing the patient's point of view to emerge.

From an anthropological point of view, cultural difference cannot be seen as a given fact, but as a social construction. In this perspective, one of the most important aspects of the intercultural mediation intervention is the awareness of how social representations and stereotypes of the 'other' can condition the relational setting. In this regard, a second anecdote serves as an example; it is taken from one of the many training courses for health workers and professionals who deal with the theme of interculturality, which I had the opportunity to take part in as an anthropologist.

One of the proposed activities called for participants to use coloured post-it notes to write questions, comments and curiosities to be submitted to 'foreigners'. The latter were represented by life-size white shapes, marked with labels that displayed the most commonly used appellation to refer to a certain group: 'Moroccans', 'South Americans', 'Africans', 'Roma', 'Chinese', and so on. The post-it notes had to be placed on the corresponding figures that gradually filled with the thoughts expressed anonymously by the workers. The idea was to allow the expression of all opinions, even those that were 'not politically correct'.

The next day, a group of mediators from each of the areas indicated on the outlines were asked to introduce themselves, to briefly tell their story and to respond to what was written on the post-it notes. It was a radical upsetting of the initial situation: the messages, addressed to a hypothetical generic and collective subject, were 'taken in hand' by real people – men and women in flesh and blood, who had to deal with the stereotypes attributed to their community of origin. One of the questions sounded something like this: 'Why are pregnant Arab women almost always accompanied by their husband? How can we rid ourselves of these men?' The tone of the question caused a lot of laughter among those present, partly because it reflected a widespread feeling, partly because, for a health worker with an adequate 'cultural competence', it transgressed a sort of 'prohibition' against expressing negative opinions about 'others'.

The Arabic language intercultural mediator, a very experienced and competent individual, instead of trying to answer, asked the group a question: 'If the husband were Italian,' she asked, 'how would you perceive his presence?' Those present were forced to admit that they would read it positively, as a sign of paternal involvement, of his support for the woman and of overcoming the traditional division of roles in favour of greater equity. Why then was the presence of an Arab husband so disturbing? From the discussion it emerged that at the base of this negative view was a widespread perception of Muslim women – and, by extension, of Arab women – as needing help to be emancipated, saving them from the oppression of a closed, extremist and patriarchal culture.

This representation has many implications, both on the more immediate level of the clinical relationship and on the geopolitical level (Abu-Lughod 2013). Images of oppressed Muslim women or of those liberated – thanks to the West – from the veil and traditional obligations, have indeed played a central role in the construction of rhetoric based on the ontological opposition between the European–Christian world, characterized by the presence of civil and democratic liberties, and the Muslim world, represented in terms of fanaticism, the absence of individual rights, and backwardness (Said 1978; Yegenoglu 1998; Salih 2008).

Without addressing all of these questions explicitly, the mediator's question and her subsequent reflections, which aimed to reconstruct the possible points of view of Arab women, led the group of health professionals to reflect on the way in which cultural difference is constructed within social interactions.

This approach represents an interesting attempt to engage culture in its relational, fluid and dynamic dimension, avoiding the reductionism that is found even in notions such as that of 'cultural competence'. It is not possible to reconstruct the rich debate or the numerous criticisms that this notion has raised in medical anthropology (Taylor 2003; Carpenter-Song, Nordquest Schwallie and Longhofer 2007), but it is worth briefly problematizing the 'culture' category within the area of biomedicine.

'Culture', in a context that represents itself as 'non-cultural' (Taylor 2003), is seen above all as something that the patient 'has', which homogeneously characterizes a human group, does not change over time and exists apart from actions and subjective choices. Despite attempts to overcome this way of understanding the notion of 'culture',[13] in the working realities we observed it is still a reified, essential and static understanding of culture that prevails, and transforms cultural competence into 'a series of "do's and don'ts" that define how to treat a patient of a given ethnic background' (Kleinman and Benson 2006: 1673).

In the above example, the full potential of intercultural mediators shows them not to be 'representatives' of a given culture or of a specific community, but people capable of dealing with a process by which 'cultural individuals creatively appropriated collective repertoires of knowledge and practices' (Quaranta and Ricca 2012: 31), bringing out the dynamic and dialogical character of culture, without losing sight of the irreducibility of the individual dimension.

The ability of mediators to problematize the way others are perceived, and the way perception transforms subjects into 'others', also emerges along with the ability to focus on different points of view and on ways, sometimes radically different, of reading and interpreting the phenomena.

Conclusions

The centrality of the mediator is recognized by researchers, health workers and clients alike, who all consider mediators to be a fundamental element in the construction of better clinical communication and a more effective therapeutic alliance. Despite this, there are some critical issues that need to be identified and addressed in order to formulate in a more coherent and effective way the professional profile of a figure who represents a resource for the individuals involved in the treatment relationship.

The reduction of mediation services is closely linked to the increasing privatization of health services and a general reduction in public welfare spending: crises, as has been demonstrated on many occasions, more seriously affect those social groups that are under conditions of structural vulnerability (Quesada, Hart and Bourgois 2011). The difficult moment that intercultural mediation in Italy is undergoing today is not at all linked to a decrease in the 'need for mediation'. On the contrary, the forms that migratory flows have taken on in recent years – the increase in arrivals by sea, the presence of significant numbers of refugees with traumatic histories behind them, the risk of trafficking, the high numbers of unaccompanied minors and the overall worsening of living conditions and levels of integration – have all made the presence of qualified, competent and recognized mediators even more urgent.

Intercultural mediation has been understood here as a socially located process, which allows a dialogue between the foreign user and health workers. It favours the emergence of cultural forms of experience and of sense-making processes; it also contributes to building bridges between people, each with their own cultural background and positioning, who enter into a relationship in a context traversed by political, social and historical forces. From this perspective, intercultural mediation can only be effective within a broader set of immigration and integration policies: no matter how important, mediation alone is not sufficient to guarantee adequate protection of the foreign patient's health.

As we have noted, one of the most common risks in the intercultural encounter is that of culturalism, which places culture, understood in the abstract and reified sense, in the forefront, thus hindering recognition of the impact of individual variables, the role of socio-economic inequality and the weight of migration in the structuring of new forms of social marginality. At the same time, we have stated that opening a space for the cultural dimension to emerge in the clinical encounter is essential for understanding the profound meaning of the experience of illness. How then do we deal with the question of cultural difference? More than starting from an idea of culture based on stereotypical representations, it is necessary 'to open oneself to an intersubjective exploration of which scenarios of collective sense emerge as relevant in the context of a specific experience' (Quaranta and Ricca 2012: 49). In this process, which is eminently based on dialogue, intercultural mediation helps us to overcome linguistic barriers and to generate a common ground of meaning that allows for co-construction of a shared therapeutic itinerary.

Ana Cristina Vargas, PhD in anthropological sciences, is Adjunct Professor of Cultural Anthropology at the University of Turin. Since 2012 she has been the scientific director of the Ariodante Fabretti Foundation, and is also research fellow at the Fundamental Rights Laboratory, a research unit of the European Human Rights Research Network. Her main research and publication topics include Colombian armed conflict, intercultural communication, human rights, medical anthropology and fundamental rights.

Notes

1. Whereas migration and integration policies remain a national topic, in 2006 the European Economic and Social Committee issued an opinion on 'Immigration in the EU and Integration Policies: Collaboration between Regional and Local Governments and the Civil Society Organisations' (2006/C 318/24), where it states that 'Intercultural mediators should be available and teaching resources should be boosted in order to resolve linguistic and cultural difficulties' (§ 6.9), and that 'access to health and healthcare for immigrants should be promoted', including through the 'collaboration of intercultural mediation services' (§ 6.11).
2. During the project, ethnographic observation was accompanied by the use of semi-structured narrative interviews. A total of 75 in-depth interviews were carried out with the migrants using the services, 24 with

intercultural mediators and volunteers from foreign associations, and 24 semi-structured interviews with selected witnesses.
3. As an example, we can mention the project MediaTo (www.piemonte immigrazione.it/mediato), active in Turin since 2011 with the aim of offering training in various fields to mediators and social workers involved in reception, integration and the protection of health. This project, funded by the Compagnia di San Paolo, is promoted by the Observatory on Immigration in Piedmont – IRES Piemonte; ASGI (Association for Juridical Studies on Immigration); and A.M.M.I. (Multi-ethnic Association of Intercultural Mediators) and CCM (Medical Collaboration Committee).
4. The intercultural mediating role is also included in articles 38 and 42 of Legislative Decree no. 286 of 25 July 1998, Consolidation Act of the provisions concerning immigration regulations, the main regulatory reference at the national level. The regulatory framework was subsequently integrated into the Conference of Regions and Autonomous Provinces document, *Riconoscimento della figura professionale del Mediatore interculturale* [Recognition of the Professional Figure of the Intercultural Mediator], Rome, 8 April 2009.
5. Further information on this association is available at http://www.media toreinterculturale.it/, last accessed 31 July 2020.
6. This definition incorporates the one previously elaborated by the 'Policies for Cultural Mediation: Training and Employment of Cultural Mediators' working group of CNEL – the national coordinating body for policies on the social integration of foreigners.
7. The procedure for accessing this system depends, in large part, on legal status. In a nutshell, it is compulsory to register with the national health service in Italy, which gives equal rights and duties with respect to Italian citizens, resident Europeans and non-EU foreigners legally residing for work reasons, for family reasons, for political asylum or other forms of international protection. Students and other foreigners legally present, but who do not fall into the first category, can voluntarily enrol in the national health service by paying the scheduled rates. Undocumented foreigners can access urgent or essential care whether they are non-EU citizens (Temporarily Present Foreigner or STP) or EU citizens who do not meet the requirements for enrolment in the service (ENI – European Person Not Registered). Preventive medicine programmes are also extended to foreigners.
8. Title 5.7, 'Interventions on the Health of Immigrants and Marginal Social Groups', Ministry of Health, *National Health Plan 2006–2008*: 78–80.
9. The 'on-call' mediators are contacted on an occasional basis, and do not have continuous working relationships with health-care companies.
10. Family and paediatric counselling centres are public and free structures offering integrated outpatient social and health services, with the aim of promoting the health of women and children of paediatric age. They represent points of coordination of the birth plan.

11. See Ferrero, in this volume.
12. Project 'D.I.S.Co.R.S.I. Migrants: Interregional Dialogue on Services in the Field of Employment, Residence and Health for the Integration of Migrants in Piedmont, Auvergne-Rhône-Alpes and Catalonia', carried out by the Consortium of Piedmont NGOs in partnership with EnAIP Piedmont, CICSENE, CCM, RESACOOP, laFede.cat and SOS Racisme Catalunya, and funded by the 2014–2020 Asylum, Migration and Integration Fund.
13. Among the works on this subject, it is worth mentioning 'Beyond Bias: Exploring the Cultural Contexts of Health and Well-being Measurement', the report of the first experts' group meeting convened by the WHO Regional Office for Europe on 15–16 January 2015; and 'Focus on Culture: Developing a Systematic Approach to the Cultural Contexts of Health in the WHO European Region', the report of the second meeting, held in Copenhagen, Denmark, on 4–5 April 2016.

References

Abu-Lughod, L. 2013. *Do Muslim Women Need Saving?* Cambridge, MA: Harvard University Press.

Allasino, E., et al. 2006. *Promuovere la mediazione culturale in Piemonte: La valutazione di una politica regionale per diffondere la mediazione culturale nelle amministrazioni pubbliche Piemontesi.* Turin: Ires.

Baraldi, C. 2009. *La mediazione interlinguistica e interculturale: Una prospettiva sociologica.* Perugia: Guerra.

Beneduce, R. 2004. *Frontiere dell'identità e della memoria: Etnopsichiatria e migrazioni in un mondo creolo.* Milan: Franco Angeli.

———. 2007. *Etnopsichiatria: Sofferenza mentale e alterità fra storia, dominio e cultura.* Rome: Carocci.

———. 2008. 'Migrazione e disagio psichico: le sfide dell'ambivalenza'. *Psychiatry on line Italia.* Retrieved on February 5 2018 from http://www.psychiatryonline.it/node/3623.

Biglino, I., and A. Olmo. 2014. *La salute come diritto fondamentale: una ricerca sui migranti a Torino.* Bologna: Il Mulino.

Brigg, M. 2003. 'Mediation, Power, and Cultural Difference'. *Conflict Resolution Quarterly* 20(3): 287–306.

———. 2008. *The New Politics of Conflict Resolution: Responding to Difference.* Basingstoke and New York: Palgrave Macmillan.

Carpenter-Song, E.A., M. Nordquest Schwallie and J. Longhofer. 2007. 'Cultural Competence Re-examined: Critique and Directions for the Future'. *Psychiatric Services* 58(10): 1362–65.

Castagnone, E., et al. 2015. *La salute come diritto fondamentale: Esperienze dei migranti a Torino.* Rome: Il Mulino.

Ceccatelli Gurrieri, G. 2003. *Mediare culture: Nuove professioni tra comunicazione e intervento.* Rome: Carocci.

Csordas, T.J. 1990. 'Embodiment as a Paradigm for Anthropology'. *Ethos* 18(1): 5–47.
———. 1994 (ed). *Embodiment and Experience: The Existential Ground of Culture and Self*. Cambridge: Cambridge University Press.
Farmer, P. 1999. 'Pathologies of Power: Rethinking Health and Human Rights'. *American Journal of Public Health* (89)10: 1486–96.
Fassin, D. 1999. 'L'ethnopsychiatrie et ses réseaux: L'influence qui grandit'. *Genèses, L'Europe vue d'ailleurs* 35: 146–71.
Giordano, C. 2014. *Migrants in Translation: Caring and the Logics of Difference*. Oakland: University of California Press.
Good, B. 1994. *Medicine, Rationality and Experience: An Anthropological Perspective*. Cambridge: Cambridge University Press.
Kleinman, A. 1988. *The Illness Narratives: Suffering, Healing, and the Human Condition*. New York: Basic Books.
———. 1997. *Writing at the Margin: Discourse between Anthropology and Medicine*. Berkeley: University of California Press.
Kleinman, A., and P. Benson. 2006. 'Anthropology in the Clinic: The Problem of Cultural Competency and How to Fix It'. *PLoS Med* 3(10): 1673–76.
Kleinman, A., V. Das and M. Lock (eds). 1997. *Social Suffering*. Berkeley: University of California Press.
Lock, M., and N. Scheper-Hughes. 1987. 'The Mindful Body: A Prolegomenon to Future Work in Medical Anthropology'. *Medical Anthropology Quarterly* 1(1): 6–41.
Luatti, L. 2009. 'Una nuova stagione per la mediazione linguistico-culturale?'. *Africa e Mediterraneo* 18(68): 80–87.
———. 2010. 'La mediazione frammentata: Pluralità di modi di intendere e agire una professione in cerca di futuro'. *Africa e Mediterraneo* 19(72–73): 14–22.
Quagliariello, C., and C. Fin. 2016. *Il consenso informato in ambito medico: Un'indagine antropologica e giuridica*. Milan: Il Mulino.
Quaranta, I., and M. Ricca. 2012. *Malati fuori luogo. Medicina Interculturale*, Milan: Raffaello Cortina Editore.
Quesada, J., L.K. Hart and P. Bourgois. 2011. 'Structural Vulnerability and Health: Latino Migrant Laborers in the United States'. *Medical Anthropology* 30(4): 339–62.
Said, E. 1978. *Orientalism: Western Conceptions of the Orient*. New York: Pantheon Books.
Salih, R. 2008. *Musulmane rivelate: donne, islam, modernità*. Rome: Carocci.
Sergent, C., and S. Larchanché. 2009. 'The Construction of "Cultural Difference" and its Therapeutic Significance in Immigrant Mental Health Services in France'. *Culture Medicine and Psychiatry* 33(1): 2–20.
Taliani, S., and F. Vacchiano. 2006. *Altri corpi: Antropologia ed etnopsicologia della migrazione*. Milan: Unicopli.
Taylor, J. 2003. 'Confronting "Culture" in Medicine's "Culture of No Culture"'. *Academic Medicine* 78(6): 555–59.

Theodosiou, A., and M. Aspioti (eds). 2016. 'Research Report on Intercultural Mediation for Immigrants in Europe'. TIME – Train Intercultural Mediators for a Multicultural Europe, project partnership. Retrieved 24 June 2020 from http://www.mediation-time.eu/images/TIME_O1_Research_Report_v.2016.pdf.

Verrept, H. 2008. 'Intercultural Mediation: An Answer to Health Care Disparities?', in C. Valero Garcés and A. Martin (eds), *Crossing Borders in Community Interpreting: Definitions and Dilemmas*. Amsterdam: Benjamins, pp. 187–202.

Yegenoglu, M. 1998. *Colonial Fantasies: Towards a Feminist Reading of Orientalism*. Cambridge: Cambridge University Press.

8

'Community Welfare'
Community-Based Networks as Migrant Health Promoters

Laura Ferrero

Introduction

In the field of health, talk of the essential value of the relationship between doctor and patient is increasing. Research has shown that the quality of the relationship has consequences for compliance and therefore, ultimately, on the effect of the treatment (Eisenberg and Kleinman 1981; Good 1994). In this regard, it should be noted that the relationship between doctor and patient does not take place in a neutral context, first of all because it takes shape within precise cultural systems, which condition the patient's interpretation, understanding and explanation of symptoms as much as the actual medical practice (Good 1994). Secondly, it should be kept in mind that both the doctor and the patient are part of social networks.

The aim of this chapter is to propose some reflections on how social networks of migrants affect the possibility of accessing health services, thus protecting a fundamental right and ultimately improving their health conditions. To do this, I situate the analysis of the relationship between social networks and health conditions in the intersection of two traditions of study: one on social capital and the other on inequality, both elements having strong effects on the health status of individuals. On the one hand, social capital – understood as the resources that derive from civic participation, relationships of trust and the rules of reciprocity that characterize social networks – is closely related to the health of individuals (Minelli 2007), so much so that some even claim that this relationship is of a causal nature; that is, greater social capital corresponds to a better degree of health (Kawachi 1999). In fact, social capital increases people's ability to perform certain functions or to achieve certain objectives, given equal resources and individual skills. On the other hand, the study of social inequalities has received much attention in the analysis of the distribution of pathologies, to the extent that the impact on health of social class, economic resources (Lynch et al. 2004) and level of education (Geyer and Peter 2000), among other social, political and economic factors, is now taken as a given by medical anthropology (Farmer et al. 2013) and beyond. The role that social factors play in the process of the promotion or deterioration of the health of individuals is also recognized by the World Health Organization when it affirms that inequalities – understood as objective and systematic disparities over the possession of resources and skills useful for obtaining a result (Tognetti Bordogna 2008: 10) – often translate into social determinants of health (Fassin 2009; Aïach 2010).

In particular, social determinants of health and inequality dominate the literature dealing with health and migration (Leclerc et al. 2000; Marmot 2005; Fassin 2009). Looking at the experience of migrants, I will highlight in this chapter the strong link between inequality and social capital when the latter is understood as 'relational inequality' (Rocco and Suhrcke 2012), an inequality that is often embodied by migrants as uprooted people. The displacement of migrants is visible at different levels because the moment of departure from the home country coincides as much with the loss of social capital that was rooted there as with removal from the social contexts in which collective and shared meanings related to health belong (Beneduce 2004). I will focus in particular on the loss of social capital, bearing in mind that the transnational ties and networks that one possesses in the context of arrival are often not strong enough to compensate for this loss (Sayad 1999). The perspective adopted suggests that social networks are the context in which social capital grows, and that the networks influence the practices of the people who are part of it – including practices linked to health and well-being – and that the absence of networks is a factor that leads to an increase in risks in general, and to those related to health in particular (Kawachi 1999; Tognetti Bordogna 2008; Rocco and Suhrcke 2012), because the absence of networks hinders access to treatment.

Case Studies

The study presented was conducted in Turin, a city of just under one million people located in north-western Italy. At the end of 2017, there were 132,806 people of foreign origin residing in Turin,[1] a proportion greater than the national average. Previous research has shown that in Turin there is a system where public health structures are seen 'as operating in synergy, although not always with the best coordination, with private social and voluntary bodies. It refers to a set of reference points that now respond to a criterion of subsidiarity, although this is within the context of a specifically Turin-based nineteenth-century tradition' (Biglino and Olmo 2014: 10). Turin is therefore characterized by a living social fabric created by a particularly dynamic and proactive civil society. The effects of this vitality impact the health conditions of migrants, as there are non-profit organizations in the city that voluntarily take care of irregular, destitute migrants and others who, for whatever reason, do not resort to the Italian national health system.[2]

In recent years, alongside local associations, migrant associations have emerged as foreign citizens have begun to create collectives that carry on heterogeneous activities and that almost always pursue the ultimate goal of encouraging and supporting the paths of immigrants in their new life context, looking for ways to encourage cultural, identity and symbolic recognition. Often these associations have been co-founded or are supported by Italians with specific skills or interests in a specific national group. Several associations manage information desks aimed at collecting a wide variety of questions about city services, documents and legal assistance. Despite the difficulty these organizations have – such as weak organizational stability, scarcity of funds and high staff turnover – some of them have begun to take action, in a formal or informal way, to meet the health needs of migrants who turn to them. Through a mapping of the migrant associations present in the city, I have identified four entities that share the following two characteristics: (a) the presence of a statute, and therefore formalization of their activity; and (b) an active involvement in health issues. They are the following:

> A.M.E.C.E. (Association Maison d'Enfant pour la Culture et l'Education [Children's home association for culture and education]): an association founded in 2000 with an educational mission. Active projects are related to the education, sports, arts and social arenas, and are mainly based on the work of volunteers. Since 2003, the association has become part

of a regional network where its knowledge and promotional activities take place through institutional channels: the Foreign Office, the Youth Information Centre and the Intercultural Centre of the City of Turin, and the Culture Office and Social Services of the Moroccan consulate.

ANGI (Italian–Chinese New Generation Association): an association of young Chinese and Italians with particular interests or skills regarding the Chinese community. It was founded in 2007 by a group of Chinese people whose goal was to intervene in situations that could have turned into social conflicts. The association is active in various areas of social life, and boasts numerous agreements with formal and informal enterprises in the region.

San Lorenzo dei Romeni: the Turin branch of the association was founded in 2011 and is part of the national association of charities of the Romanian Orthodox Diocese. In March 2011, the association officially started its listening centre activity, which takes place in church spaces and is based on the work of volunteers active in the association.

Zhi Song (Italo-Chinese sociocultural association): a sociocultural association that defines itself as a democratic, nonpartisan, nonpolitical and nonprofit. Its purpose is the development of social solidarity and the promotion of intercultural relations between Chinese citizens and Italian society, with particular attention to young people, women and people with disabilities.

In these associations, I conducted a total of twenty interviews[3] with three categories of people: representatives, workers (in most cases volunteers, sometimes mediators[4]) and users who have contacted them in order to solve health problems. Associations have therefore been chosen not because they are 'representative' of a certain community or valued 'better' than others, but by virtue of action they have taken that is sensitive to the issues of well-being and to access to health services, and for their significant and innovative practice in health matters.

Formalization Paths

As Tognetti Bordogna says, 'in addition to a third historical and consolidated sector, there remains a third, less formal sector in the health sector, which has less continuity in interventions and collaborations but is capable of being activated in response to particular needs' (Tognetti Bordogna 2008: 200).[5] This observation applies well to the Turin case, because it is precisely in the context of this 'third less-formalized sector' that the action of the associations I have investigated has been placed. Accompanying the children to a language class or an after-school course, or going to pray or meet with fellow countrymen to celebrate a holiday linked to their country of origin, can also be crucial opportunities in which networks can be forged; these can then provide valuable resources in the field of health and welfare. In the next paragraph, I turn my attention to how associations that were not established to work in the health sector have begun to take an interest in it.

The work of two of the associations was involved with Chinese immigrants – a community that is described as having a deep distrust of the Italian national health service (SSN), and not just in Turin (Osteria, Carrillo and Sarli 2013). The associations involved and the studies conducted in other contexts converge to observe migrants' improper use of emergency services. Distrust of a health system that works differently from what the migrants are familiar with is often accompanied by their lack of competence in Italian and by equally poor health literacy.

> They don't know that they are entitled to a general practitioner and a paediatrician. When the baby is sick – for example, if he has a fever of 39 – they go directly to the emergency room. Many come from the villages of the countryside, where these services don't exist ... then they are afraid of not understanding and not being understood by the doctor. (Mediator, Zhi Song)

The fear of not understanding, the worry about not being understood, and the sense of mistrust of an unknown institution all underlie requests for help from those migrants who turn to the associations – places that they frequent for different activities:

> The association was founded in 2009 to give Chinese lessons to children ... The families who came to the meetings brought us many other problems of communication and culture: at school, in the hospital, at work, on documents ... Requests exploded. ... The mediator receives all kinds of requests: once she was called by a woman who was at an Italian class when her waters broke. She called us instead of her sister, as she trusted us 100 per cent. Another woman had taken an Italian class but then moved to Milan, and after a year had gynaecological problems and called to ask for help. There is a lot of word of mouth; they come to ask for anything. (Volunteer, Zhi Song)

Deeply involved in the social world of the communities, the association workers closely observe the problems of their fellow countrymen.

This possibility of interacting directly with their needs allows associations to build competence with respect to what can be defined (according to the World Health Organization) as a 'community health profile'.[6]

Volunteers from the ANGI association, for example, began to take an interest in the issue of health because many so people were asking for their help to access visits and treatments. In particular, they noticed that they were receiving numerous requests from pregnant women, and this prompted them to question what the major problems were in the relationship between women and hospitals:

> In Turin, the Chinese have a high birth rate; about one hundred Chinese children are born every year. We held several interviews with hospitals such as Sant'Anna and Maria Vittoria, and we have found that only 30 per cent of these women follow the standard protocol, with classes and scheduled visits. This is a risk because it can cause problems in childbirth. We decided to interview Chinese women to understand why, and we realized that there is difficulty in accessing the service even if the service is there. ... Language difficulties, problems with working hours, difficulty in finding people to accompany them who understand the language. ... In speaking with people, a wider health issue emerged that also involves men, the elderly, children, etc. ... We asked ourselves what we could do. We could not close our eyes. (Association representative, ANGI)

Following this phase, the association opened an information desk on health and, at the same time, set up institutional contacts with the municipality of Turin (to whom situations requiring action are reported), with the College of Midwives[7] (with whom they have established a training course on Chinese culture), and with a private facility, where a health day dedicated to the Chinese people living in Turin has been organized.

> We have made an arrangement with a private, contracted organization.[8] We have activated our own health desk, which means that for any health problem people come to us first, we see their situation (if they are workers, with documents, without documents, etc. ...).[9] With documents we make appointments for the public facilities, but without documents we send them to the private facility with an amount more or less equal to the bill.[10] The organization sends us all the various forms and consents, and we translate everything into Chinese. Since it is compulsory when they make a visit to declare and sign forms, the people will have a copy in Italian and in Chinese; they know what is written, they sign and they proceed to the visit or the exam. (Association representative, ANGI)

Although the first attempt is to enrol users in the national health service, referrals to the private sector represent a resource in the event that the person in need of care does not have a health card, when the public service is not deemed to be effective or when the wait is too long. The solution offered by the association thus protects the right to health, and can be considered as an attempt to stem other types of responses, such as the incorrect use of accident and emergency, the use of traditional medicine for self-medication,[11] the appearance of traditional doctors who are non-accredited and the search for a more 'acceptable' cure elsewhere, with the consequent appearance of transnational therapeutic itineraries. These types of responses, which often coexist and can represent resources within a context characterized by medical pluralism, can generate two unwanted consequences: firstly – as we shall see later – the lack of access to hospital care can be detrimental to the sick, especially in cases of serious illnesses; and secondly, they can prevent the need for health care from being expressed in the public institution responsible.

A similar experience is that of A.M.E.C.E., an association created with the intention of working in the educational field, but which has encountered health issues among the demands of its users and has therefore been pushed to act in this area and, subsequently, to formalize its work:

> Interest in health starts at the help desk. ... Many are looking for information on family reunification and on school for the children. They also come to ask about evictions, economic difficulties, and help finding work. We welcome everyone, we cannot do much but at least we support them, we direct them to the agencies. This is an informal step. Over time, a small collaboration with ASL[12] was born, for the translation of vaccine certificates in the countries of origin. As a help desk, we always looked for external resources that could better respond to health questions, and then we managed to formalize and be recognized by the city, putting us into the project with Prisma. (Association manager, A.M.E.C.E.)

The Prisma project is the fruit of a collaboration between the Office for the Disabled in Turin and a nonprofit organization that has created a network for integrating services for disabled people, promoting the complementarity of the activities carried out by volunteers with the general objectives pursued by the public administration. The network also includes some associations for non-Italians, which act as mediators.

> When they have meetings with Moroccans, they give out appointments according to the availability of the trainees or mediators. They rely on

us for mediation; we rely on them when cases that need to be certified come in, because they work with doctors who can evaluate the clinical documentation and know if the person can ask for civil disability. With Prisma we follow the people from the first visits until recognition of their INPS-paid disability right,[13] through the booking of visits and examinations; we accompany them on their visits. ...

So many people trust us more than a fellow countryman; they tell us more, because they don't understand the role of different services. So we divide the tasks with Prisma, and each one takes care of his/her own field – we do the medical accompaniment and they handle the legal part. (Volunteer, A.M.E.C.E.)

An interesting route – because it is different from those previously reported – is that of the San Lorenzo dei Romeni Association, which offers a unique service in Turin because of its degree of formalization and organization. In 2011, the priest of the Romanian Orthodox Church advocated the opening of a counselling centre that could answer all the questions that he was fielding from his congregation. Exactly like the other gathering places mentioned above, the church was a point of reference for its Romanian visitors, one that many people turned to when they needed help. For the opening of the counselling centre it was necessary to establish the association, which relied on a pre-existing Romanian organization based in Rome, and also to mobilize the necessary resources: on the one hand, the volunteers from the community, and, on the other, the trainers,[14] who prepared them for the task of answering all the disparate questions they would encounter at the listening centre.

The counselling centre does not have a specialization but welcomes questions of all sorts. According to the workers, most of the people turn to them for job searches, but the centre also offers other services, such as a food bank,[15] and training for family assistants, given the high number of Romanian women who work in this field. When people access the centre, whatever their request, a detailed personal file is compiled that allows the detection of other existing needs as well. Regarding the topic of health, people are asked about their state of health and whether or not they have a health card – elements that sometimes bring out the need for help in the health sphere as well.

As these anecdotes show, none of these associations had been founded with an explicit mission in the health field. The episodes that led the organizations to take care of health and, in some cases, to formalize their commitment through agreements with public services, show that, thanks to their flexible nature and to being points of reference within certain communities, associations have become advocates for a need for health care that otherwise would risk remaining unexpressed. If it is true that these actions are initiated in an informal way, it is in fact equally true that sometimes they are formalized through a process of stabilizing bottom-up practices.

Bridging Ties

Much of the literature on migration and health is interested in, observes and denounces the social inequalities at the root of health inequalities (Leclerc et al. 2000; Farmer 2003; Fassin 2009). To locate my reflections within this line of studies, I have chosen to discuss relational inequality, referring to the distance between those who have social networks and those who, instead, are part of weak social networks, and to reflect on how the presence of networks can be translated into an element of protection of the fundamental right to health.

To do this, I use Farmer's concepts of structural violence and Putnam's analysis of social networks. The idea of structural violence is at the basis of my reflection, to the extent that disparities – and the resulting health problems – are structured by historical forces and processes that conspire to limit the capacity for the action of individuals (Farmer 2004). A corollary of this definition is therefore the reflection that not only do material conditions affect the health status of individuals, but also – and this is the point to which I turn my attention – their ability to act. If structural violence limits the agency of certain people, social networks can be a means to increase the possibility for action by connecting marginal individuals with others who are well integrated into the city and well connected with the services that offer assistance. Putnam reminds us that with regard to social capital, it is useful to distinguish between '"bonding" social capital (ties to people who are *like* you in some important way) and "bridging" social capital (ties to people who are *unlike* you in some important way)' (Putnam 2007: 143).

The relationship between individuals and associations is an element that increases social capital bridging, as it connects migrants who suffer from some form of marginality with their compatriots who possess greater skills and useful knowledge for moving in the urban context. Thus, it is important to underscore that the people involved in the organizations – the managers as well as the volunteers – often already possess a professionalism that they provide to the association; they are deeply rooted in the territory, an element that substantially differentiates them from people who turn to associations to ask for some form of support:

> For us it is not work, but volunteering. There are people who are skilled in the field, all social mediators, experts in immigration, all very up to date, who do research even though they are volunteers. (Association manager, A.M.E.C.E.)

> I came to the association through my personal experience. I worked as an Italian teacher for foreigners. I worked with the illiterate and especially with the Chinese, who nobody wanted. It was a new experience for me; I had to think about things, to study. Meanwhile, I met a Chinese girl who I took care of for a few years, and then I met a Chinese mediator. Together we started thinking about how to solve certain community problems. (Italian volunteer, Zhi Song)

Particularly significant in this regard is the example of the San Lorenzo dei Romeni Association, where volunteers serve as cultural mediators who work in various services of the city, such as hospitals, trade unions, and the third sector dealing with health. The networks of these people, and the fact that they themselves are part of the services that often must be contacted to meet the needs of those who access the counselling centre, make the work of the association fluid and effective. In fact, contact with the services is often direct and functional, even in the absence of agreement protocols.

The fact that vulnerable migrants find the associations, and that the associations are formed and run by individuals who are 'unlike them in some important way', means that this relationship increases their social capital and brings them closer to the services. In the following paragraphs we will see what positive effects this may have for the protection of the health of marginal individuals.

Access to Services

Silvia is a Romanian woman suffering from leukaemia, who has lived in irregular conditions for years. Acquiring work and a contract have allowed her to be regularized and, consequently, to have access to medical care. The Italian health system guarantees access to treatment for undocumented migrants, but Silvia did not know that. Her job as a domestic worker isolated her from her compatriots and from the surrounding social context; thus, Silvia did not know she was entitled to the ENI card.[16] She was unaware of the existence of the ISI Centre,[17] and consequently could not enjoy what would have been her right.

> Then I was already suffering from leukaemia. I had throat infections, but I didn't know because I couldn't get blood tests. I had no contract and so I had no doctor.
>
> *Have you ever visited the ISI centres?*
>
> No, I didn't know, no one ever told me they existed. In 2012 I got a contract and I finally got a doctor. The first thing that interested me was health; we started with blood samples. (Silvia, San Lorenzo dei Romeni user)

Many of the people I interviewed told me stories about not accessing the health service in the early stages of their stay in Italy.

> When I was pregnant with my first child, I didn't understand Italian and I didn't do anything, no exam. I swear. In China there are not so many exams – or at least at that time there were not; now the system is more advanced. At the time, language was a huge problem. I didn't know what to do. I went directly to give birth in the hospital. (Mei, ANGI user)

These two examples show that even in an inclusive health system such as the one in Italy, rights can be disregarded because people are often unaware of either possessing these rights or of how they can transform formal into substantive rights. These are the most difficult cases to intercept for both the services and the associations. The fact that Silvia, despite realizing that her health was deteriorating, did not look for a way to take care of herself until she had a job is a paradigmatic example of structural vulnerability (Quesada, Hart and Bourgois 2011). This embodiment of subordinated status – that of the undocumented migrant inserted into a niche of the labour market that deprives her of external contacts – produces a form of symbolic violence whereby the everyday violence of imposed scarcity and insecurity is understood as natural and deserved (Bourdieu 2000). Often, however, when these people are looking for help, the network of compatriots is an easy recourse:

> Many don't know about the services, and when they do know they exist, they don't trust them or fear they won't be heard properly. And so the user doesn't come, and the service offered fails at best. Many pass by us [associations] before they go to the service. They aren't integrated into the Italian community, so information doesn't reach them. Since they are in contact with their community, taking children to school and the mothers

talking to each other, they access information about the Moroccan associations better than the Italian services. (Volunteer, A.M.E.C.E.)

The associations involved in the study welcomed migrants who did not know how to access the service or migrants who had unsatisfactory access, often caused by linguistic incomprehension between users and workers. The language barrier continues to be a strong limitation on foreigners' access, and cultural mediators are not always available – certainly not in all services. When the causes of non-access are attributable to the structure of institutions (originally aimed at satisfying the needs of the native population, thus putting other groups at a disadvantage), we are talking about institutional discrimination (Williams 1999). The topic of linguistic accessibility certainly falls into this category, which is why foreigners often turn to associations of their compatriots.

> If there were no A.M.E.C.E., I would be looking for a person to translate. Sometimes if I don't find anyone I leave it and go back home, especially if I have to go to the hospital, and I look for another day [when] someone can come with me. (Hasna, A.M.E.C.E. user)

> When I have a problem, I don't go to my doctor because I cannot talk. The times I had to go I took a friend's son with me, but he's a child, he can't help me much. Now the first person I turn to when I have a problem is the girl from the association. (Ping, ANGI user)

It is quite common for linguistic problems to be circumvented by foreigners by referring to relatives or friends who speak Italian. In some communities there is even a phenomenon of payment between countrymen for these services (Sarli and Carrillo 2014).

These types of accompaniment infringe on people's rights as they do not guarantee a high-quality service and do not protect the patient's privacy; the patient might even omit part of the communication with the doctor so as not to spread news about their situation through their compatriot network. The work of the associations better protects people because it guarantees them anonymity and a certain quality of service (which can nevertheless vary depending on whether the association has cultural mediators or volunteers who have trained 'in the field' and who can relate to patients so as to make the care acceptable).

> Once a woman went to accident and emergency alone. Someone had tried to rape her, she asked for help and they called an ambulance. She was there alone; she could not explain and the doctors did not understand

anything until I arrived. When we entered the gynaecologist's room, she said she was still a virgin, because she was not married, and in front of me she could not say that she had had intercourse. When the gynaecologist examined her, he found out that it was not true; I knew it but I didn't say anything. (Volunteer, A.M.E.C.E.)

In addition to being contacted by users, associations are sometimes called for assistance even by doctors who, having met them previously, consider them a resource to be activated if needed:

My husband had done tests in China. When we came back to Italy we brought the translations and I talked to the doctors, but the translation was wrong and the situation was getting worse. The doctor advised us to talk with the association; he was the one who booked the appointment with the mediator of the association because he wanted to explain himself better. (Suzi, ANGI user)

When I went to the tuberculosis centre, they didn't understand what I had and what I wanted, and they called social services. The social services called the A.M.E.C.E. association because there is a collaboration between the municipality of Turin and A.M.E.C.E. The association called my doctor who explained my problems, and then an A.M.E.C.E. mediator accompanied me when I returned to the centre. (Hasna, A.M.E.C.E. user)

Between services and associations, a sort of alliance is therefore created. It works in favour of the therapeutic alliance between user and doctor, and is often based on the goodwill and initiative of the individual professional, rather than on written agreements.

Another case linked to linguistic incommunicability in which associations can come into play is that of the transition from a service with mediation to one that lacks it. There was a case of a pregnant Chinese woman who, during a visit to a family clinic,[18] was told that her baby was in a breech position. She was referred to a gynaecologist who could rotate the child, and at the same time she was warned that she would not find mediation at that service and that she should therefore be accompanied by someone who spoke Italian. When asked by the clinic mediator, the patient replied that she would be accompanied by an ANGI mediator, thus using that association to solve the problem of being sent to a service that does not offer mediators.

The fear of not being understood and the absence of a cultural mediator can become obstacles to access, as well as causes of treatment failure. Medical anthropology has shown that the gaps in linguistic communication (both at the level of understanding, and at the level of comparison of different cultural constructions of clinical reality) are the main cause of noncompliance – that is, the failure of patients to adhere to therapies indicated by doctors (Quaranta 2006: xi) – and that communicative inefficiency is destined to manifest itself in terms of therapeutic practice (Eisenberg and Kleinman 1981). The difficulty of access due to language barriers, therefore, is only the tip of a much larger iceberg.

> We had a case of a gentleman with diabetes who did not understand anything they told him at the hospital. He went to the doctor and was happy, but when we brought him the Chinese translation of what the doctor had written and explained, he realized that he hadn't understood what the doctor had told him. He was not in bad condition, but explaining to him that he had to eat less food and not have three big meals a day was as fundamental as explaining when and how to take the tablets. People sometimes, even when they speak the language a little, don't understand what the disease is, how they should behave, how they can be helped, what tests they should do. We ourselves are hard pressed to understand the doctor, so if you have to work it out in another language and in a different logic from yours, then it becomes very complex. (Italian volunteer, Zhi Song)

Culturally Competent Assistance

The role of associations is not limited to facilitating encounters between the health system and foreign patients; it is more profound, because it follows people along the path of their illness. It is precisely when the patient meets the doctor, in fact, that the most important challenge begins – the therapeutic alliance and the success or failure of the treatment. At this stage, the concepts of compliance and trust come into play, and problems can arise that can also cause the abandonment of treatment.

> Usually the doctor prescribes the treatment and it seems that everything is fine, but then with time we discover that the person isn't following the treatment. Maybe he called China because he has a relative or a medical friend, and he consults with him on the phone. I don't normally accept this; in my opinion you go back to China to do the exams, otherwise you cannot ask for a treatment over the phone. (Italian volunteer, Zhi Song)

In this section, I will use two examples to show how associations can promote practices aimed at making assistance more culturally competent, and bringing it closer to users' expectations and sensibilities. The first example concerns the theme of truth; the second, the category of waiting. Truth and waiting are understood here as culturally conditioned categories (Kleinman 1978), with respect to which associations can act as mediators.

Regarding the theme of 'truth', a person in charge of the A.M.E.C.E. association reports:

> One thing I can say is that there is a different culture about health problems. There, when the person is in serious condition, they avoid telling the patient; but here they tell you, you become a participant, everything is spoken. Ahmed came to Italy seven months after his marriage. After a while he got sick. We helped him get a house, but after six months we found out he had a tumour. We wanted to bring his parents and his wife to Italy, but it was difficult – the bureaucracy was an obstacle that makes you angry. This person had to be with his parents, we told them about the disease but we didn't want to tell the young man. In our culture it is like that; in our view it makes the last days worse. The doctors insisted on telling him but then we convinced them not to say anything. … Ahmed changed bit by bit until we understood what he needed. He understood that he was waiting for death, but we discovered the secret: he wanted to have his wife with him. He found new strength when we discovered that the secret was in his family. (Association manager, A.M.E.C.E.)

The truth as a value in the doctor–patient relationship is not an absolute element, but changes according to the medical values of doctors and patients (Quagliariello 2016: 104). The variability of these health values explains why the right to information is implemented differently as the context changes (Bergman and Fiester 2014). What is interesting here is that within the same context, the coexistence of different faiths, cultures and sensibilities can lead to an encounter between different opinions on the role of truth and, ultimately, the coexistence of different values related to health. In the case of Ahmed, the mediator of the association considered that not informing him but only his family of the diagnosis was the best way to comfort Ahmed in the last stage of his life. This was not such a strange choice if we consider that even hospitals often opt for a similar solution (Quagliariello 2016: 123), because the patient is not an individual divorced from social relations (Charles, Gafni and Whelan 1999). To say whether, with this choice, his rights have been infringed or protected is an ethical dilemma with no easy solution. What is certain is that the intermediation of the association meant that Ahmed's family could reach him in Italy, and this undoubtedly proved to be of great value, confirming that during the experience of the disease the Western paradigm of individualism revealed its limitations (Carricaburu and Ménoret 2004).

With regard to 'waiting', on the other hand, I report on some reflections arising from observations of the work of the Chinese associations. A criterion by which users evaluate the national health service (SSN) is often that of timing. This applies to Italian and foreign users, but in dialogues with Chinese workers and users the 'time' variable emerged as crucial, as also revealed by other studies on the relationship between the Chinese and the Italian hospitals (Osteria, Carrillo and Sarli 2013; Sarli and Carrillo 2014). The 'time' variable is identified as the second reason that prevents Chinese people from using health services (Wu and Zanin 2009). The agreement between the ANGI association and the affiliated clinic, mentioned earlier, was designed for people who do not have access to the health services, such as Chinese students who enrol in Italian universities;[19] but it also proves useful for people who have not registered with the SSN, and for users who decide to turn to the private sector to get a faster service.

> I arrived at the association through a friend. I had a gynaecological problem and I had to have some check-ups, but I gave up on visits to the public hospital because the waits were too long. My friend gave me the phone number of the association and we spoke on the phone, they gave me my card and then we met in front of the hospital. (Li Ping, ANGI user)

It should be noted that for many Chinese users the 'time' variable is related to the type of treatment and its effectiveness. Traditional Chinese medicine, based on herbs and natural remedies, is widespread in both China and among the Chinese diaspora, and is used alongside Western medicine. In China, both medical traditions are accessible and, depending on the problem they have to solve, people decide which kind of treatment to turn to.

> Chinese medicine is not really specific to a disease. I use it in those cases when I don't feel well but I cannot say where; if I don't understand a specific problem. Or if they find kidney stones, with the traditional [medicine] it goes away. Another example is back pain: here they take care of it with tablets; in China no, they give you natural herbs and after six months or a year you have recovered. If you have a fever, however, use the European. If it is a serious problem that must be solved immediately, use European medicine. If it takes time, we use Chinese. (Volunteer, ANGI)

From these words it emerges that 'time' is a variable that comes into play when choosing between different medical systems: normally, when a rapid and immediate intervention is expected, it is common to turn to Western medicine, which acts directly on the symptoms. On the other hand, when a deeper cure is needed, one that treats the whole body and not just the symptoms, it is common to turn to Chinese medicine, which offers visible results, especially in the long run. This is the reason why one of the criteria guiding the orientation to a medical system is severity. Serious illnesses in which immediate action is needed because the patient is at an advanced stage are treated with Western medicine. This is reflected in a different hospital organization, consistent with the principle of the 'rapidity' of Western medicine compared to Chinese medicine:

> In China there are many hospitals. When you go in, they tell you: there is an island to receive information, you tell them what problem you have and they tell you where you should go, and on that day you decide, make visits and undergo exams; they never make you wait for months. You see the specialist right away, and 90 per cent of the time you can do everything in one day. (Suzi, ANGI user)

Such a conception of Western medicine and hospital organization makes long waits inconceivable; they are interpreted as 'malfunctioning' and 'lacking competence', and cause an increase in the distrust generally felt by the Chinese towards Italian doctors (Osteria, Carrillo and Sarli 2013: 511). Moreover, the dimension of work is often evoked to explain why the Chinese would like shorter waiting times and want to avoid the queue at a general practitioner's surgery. Often described in their own community as individuals who are totally dedicated to work, they appear to be people who do not 'have time to waste' and who put work before health.

> There are many Chinese who go to get a referral, but the doctor does not make an appointment and you have to wait in the waiting room. Sometimes just for the referral there is a half-day wait, they think that instead of losing half a day they can earn thirty euros more and leave it alone. Perhaps for this reason they agree to make visits that cost a little more. (Volunteer, ANGI)

The work dimension is clearly central to Chinese emigration – defined as 'emigration with capital' because they come in search of employment and economic success (Tassinari and Tomba 1996) – but being totally dedicated to work is also a consequence of the status of a migrant, rather than a cultural trait. Jobs that are often precarious and lack union protections require migrants to safeguard their jobs at the cost of renouncing their health (Sarli and Carrillo 2014: 6). In the case of the Chinese, this is added to a family-run production system in which the employer takes care of the food and accommodation of his employees, and so the work itself becomes a total institution (Wu and Zanin 2009).

Recently, the concept of cultural competence has been criticized by anthropologists, who underscore the risk that it suggests that culture can be reduced to a technical skill for which clinicians can be trained to develop expertise (Del Vecchio Good 1995; Taylor 2003; Kleinman and Benson 2006; Carpenter-Song, Nordquest Schwallie and Longhofer 2007). The examples discussed in this section alert us to the fact that associations also run the risk of simplification, as they too can be vested in a discourse based on the 'us–them' dichotomy and on operating instructions stating that 'the Chinese do so and so'. Nonetheless, the practices that are often put into play surpass these limits and provide examples of that 'mini-ethnography' that, according to Kleinman and Benson, should be the basis for understanding the patient's point of view. The case of Ahmed shows how the person is in the grasp of a holistic care and the search for a personal solution that answers the question 'What is at stake for patients?', whereas the solution proposed by the Chinese association, which considers the cultural variable as well as social and material difficulties, has the virtue of 'considering the ongoing stress and social supports that characterize people's lives' (Kleinman and Benson 2006).

Managing the Disease: Filling the Gap between Caring and Curing

The idea of the holistic care of the individual – viewed by the associations not as a patient, but as a person whose total needs must be considered – leads me to reflect on the fact that both the disease and the cure are social as much as physical events. Not infrequently part of the care activity is delegated outside the hospital institution, in particular to the parental contexts. In the case of foreign patients with weak parental networks, associations can represent the social capital that influences the management of the cure and the disease. One user was asked how they had got in touch with the association:

> While I was hospitalized, volunteers came by to ask if I needed anything. I said that my difficulty was going back from the hospital to home, because sometimes after the therapies I am weak and tired. They saw that I didn't understand, so they called the association mediator. When she came, she helped me get home and now she's helping me with other issues, like doing the civil disability application.[20] (Jiao, Zhi Song user)

Talking with some of the leaders of the associations about the differences between them and the mediation service offered by the hospitals, I was given a significant response that at the same time represented a critique of the mediation model:

> In Turin in the third sector there are experts who offer a service. We don't offer care, but we are cultural mediators or a channel or facilitator, not a substitution for a service. The mediator must be specialized in what he does, and must know 100 per cent of the situation before intervening. I'm against the fact that you call the mediator to mediate between doctor and patient. If mediation goes too far it is useless; you must follow the patient from the beginning, know the story, know how that person lives. From there, go and build an intervention; the person has to conquer it very slowly. (Association manager, A.M.E.C.E.)

The relative lack of formalization of the association's practices is transformed into a resource here, as it allows us to study the best approach for each individual to take their own health in hand – sometimes complete control. In this regard, the story of a volunteer from the San Lorenzo dei Romeni centre is touching and significant. This volunteer had welcomed Viorica to the counselling centre. Viorica was a Romanian woman who, at the time of access, had an advanced-stage tumour and was already very familiar with the treatment. She lived alone, and she no longer had any family in Romania. Her only son – whom she wanted to keep in the dark about her illness – lived in Belgium. When Viorica returned to ask for food aid, the centre's volunteers discovered that she had not worked for a long time and could no longer afford to shop or pay the rent.

> Through us, the landlord, who knew nothing, discovered that the lady was ill. Then we contacted her son, but we struggled because she didn't want him to know and said, 'When I'm better I'll call him'. We were able to contact her son because we hoped he would still be able to see her alive; in fact, when he arrived she was already in a coma. It took a long time to establish a relationship of trust for her to give us the keys to her house; and to contact her son we had to look at her phone in secret ... the nice thing was that in the end she began to trust us, called us her daughters. She had no one here – we took care of everything, even finding someone to fix the washing machine that was broken. (Mediator, San Lorenzo dei Romeni)

In these testimonies the role that associations can have in terms of care (or, to use the words of a volunteer from the Zhi Song association, 'social care') is evident. We can think of the concept of care as taking charge of the needs of the patient, as understood globally. The term 'care-mix' defines those situations in which care needs are met by subjects of a different nature, whether public or private (Ponzo 2014). The associations are shown to be a fundamental part of this mix, in which they not only function as glue for the network that moves around the user but can even replace the family in cases where it is not physically present alongside the patient. In the case of the San Lorenzo dei Romeni association, the social aspect is flanked by the religious one.

> Being listened to is important when one is ill; for those who are believers the religious aspect is very important. I believe that priests were the psychologists of the past; it was there that we talked about everything. For those who are not believers, maybe they can pour it out to a friend ... it even happens to me that I advise practitioners to go and talk to the father who will find words for them. People always thank us for having listened to them. (Mediator, San Lorenzo dei Romeni)

When they are ill, migrants are not just 'sick', but they become 'sick people out of place' – first of all in a geographical sense, because they are far from their primary socialization context, and secondly in a personal and existential sense, because becoming ill means that their migratory project will fail (Quaranta and Ricca 2012). By requesting services, and maintaining contact with doctors and various private social organizations, the associations try to satisfy the needs of the migrant as a person and not only as a patient.

Conclusions: Towards Community Welfare

The concepts of structural violence and of structural vulnerability shed light on the fact that agency – both in general and in relation to the state of health – is strongly conditioned by the material, social and political conditions in which an individual lives. As a consequence, it is common in the literature to find migrants described as subjects without agency and as victims who suffer and embody socio-economic inequalities (Farmer 2003).

In this chapter, I have looked at the concept of inequality, stemming from its meaning in terms of relational inequality, which is understood as the disparity between those who have social networks and those who do not. Starting with the observation that the absence of social networks can become a factor that increases risk, I have reflected on how the presence of social networks can instead be a factor for reducing health-related risks (Oliver 2017), in particular because having social networks can facilitate access to treatment and understanding – both linguistic and symbolic – in the relationship between doctor and patient.

In addition to having a positive impact on the practices of people who rely on them, the actions of the associations have collective repercussions because they overturn the perspective of migrants as victims. They shed light on the dynamics that lead us to think of foreigners not only as users of services but also as suppliers, and to think about associations not as 'representatives' of, but rather as 'instruments' of mediation between foreigners and institutions. The experience of a volunteer from the San Lorenzo dei Romeni listening centre is particularly significant in this regard. Her experience as a non-practising woman who decided to volunteer with a religious association sheds light on the fact that associations are not neutral, and above all they are not representative of national communities. In a context such as the Italian one, where the members of the associations are sometimes presented as 'representatives of the community', it is essential to underscore that the concepts of community and representativeness do not always overlap.

Traditionally, social capital is defined by accentuating two distinct profiles: first, its nature as a private good, which at the individual level allows people to mobilize certain relational resources they have to solve their problems (Van Der Gaag and Snijdersb 2005); and second, as a public good, which characterizes a given community, territory or set of subjects from which it is collectively produced and enjoyed (Barbieri 2005). After examining the role that some migrant associations play in the well-being of the members of their communities, one can conclude that their action increases either through the social capital of the individuals who access them, or through social capital understood as a public good, because of good practices and connections that they foster.

Acknowledgements

A previous version of this chapter was published as:

L. Ferrero. 2015. 'Dentro le reti per la salute dei migranti: tracce di welfare di comunità' [Inside the networks for migrants' health: Traces of community welfare], in E. Castagnone et al. (eds), *La salute come diritto fondamentale: esperienze di migranti a Torino* [Health as a fundamental right: Migrants' experiences in Turin]. Bologna: Il Mulino, pp. 201–30.

Laura Ferrero obtained her PhD in anthropology and has been a postdoctoral fellow at Turin University, where she teaches Anthropology of the Middle East; she is also research fellow at the Fundamental Rights Laboratory, Turin. She has conducted research in Italy, Egypt and Palestine. Her main research interests are: migration studies; migrants' access to health and housing; as well as gender and family in Arab-Muslim societies.

Notes

1. Data from the Statistics section of the Municipality of Turin, http://www.comune.torino.it/statistica/dati/2017/pdf/E12017.pdf, last accessed 14 August 2020.
2. Italy is noted for its inclusive health system in which the right to urgent care is guaranteed for everyone, both documented and undocumented.
3. All the interviews were conducted during the period January–June 2014.
4. For a critical reflection on cultural mediators, see Vargas, this volume.
5. Quotations are translated from Italian by the author.
6. The health profile is a description of the health status of a population. It is built by collecting useful information at the local level to make decisions about the relative priorities of health problems. This can be collected through interviews or focus groups with mediators or select witnesses in a certain social world. The final objective is to identify the priority problems and, on this basis, to build a 'health pact' between the health service and local administrations.
7. The College of Midwives is the institutionally recognized professional organization.
8. In Italy there are private facilities that have entered into an agreement with the Italian national health system, and therefore provide health services by asking citizens to pay the bill, or the amount that they would be asked to pay into the national system.
9. To access the SSN it is necessary to have a health card, issued to all Italian citizens and to foreigners residing legally. Foreigners without a residence permit can access via another card created for this category of people.
10. Each person assisted by the national health system must pay for medicines, clinical tests and other medical services. Citizens with very low income and the unemployed may request exemption from payment.
11. In the case of the Chinese, self-medication often takes place with traditional medicines. This should not be considered a 'traditional' attitude, or at least it is not from the perspective that the Chinese users with whom I spoke assess it. The principles that are used to justify self-medication are effectiveness (observing that the medicine has the desired effect) and speed (being able to act on the disease without having to wait for a health centre to open).

12. Local health authority centres that are part of the national health system and that organize health care in the territory for which they are responsible.
13. INPS is the national social security institution. Civil disability refers to difficulty performing the activities typical of daily life or of relationships due to a physical or mental impairment or an impairment of sight or hearing. The INPS, together with the health service, certifies the extent of civil disability and, depending on its seriousness, can provide a disability pension.
14. The priest had contacts with an important Turin association that had been working in the social field for years. Two workers from this association trained the listening centre volunteers, providing them with both practical information on the services of the territory, and with operational methods and advice on how to relate to the marginalized population.
15. The companies that adhere to this initiative belong to the ONLUS Food Bank Foundation, which organizes large collections of food at the national level and distributes it to charitable organizations, which in turn distribute it to people in need.
16. The ENI (non-registered European people) card is issued to non-EU citizens who do not have a residency permit. EU citizens in a state of poverty who are in the Italian territory but receive no assistance from their countries of origin, and have no coverage from a private insurance policy, are entitled to urgent and emergency services.
17. In the Piedmont region, the centre for public assistance for undocumented migrants is the ISI Centre (Immigrant Health Information Centre). These centres, which have been present experimentally since 1992, became fully operational in December 2004.
18. The local family counselling service is a prevention-oriented service for women and couples, with specific reference to issues of sexuality, procreation and contraception: it deals with pregnancy, the prevention of sexually transmitted diseases and the voluntary interruption of pregnancy.
19. Foreign students enrolled in Italian universities have the right to voluntary enrolment in the health service, after payment of an annual fee.
20. Citizens suffering from physical, mental or sensory impairments who have suffered a permanent reduction in their working capacity are considered to be civilly disabled. The disabled can get economic support from the state, provided they have obtained recognition of their disability.

References

Aïach, P. 2010. *Les inégalités sociales de santé*. Paris: Editions Economica.
Barbieri, P. 2005. 'Le fondamenta micro-relazionali del capitale sociale'. *Rassegna Italiana di Sociologia* XLVI(2): 345–84.
Beneduce, R. 2004. *Frontiere dell'identità e della memoria: Etnopsichiatria e migrazioni in un mondo creolo*. Milan: Franco Angeli.

Bergman, E., and A. Fiester. 2014. 'The Future of Clinical Ethics Education: Value Pluralism, Communication and Medication', in A. Akabayaski (ed.), *The Future of Bioethics: International Dialogues*. Oxford: Oxford University Press, pp. 703–11.
Biglino, I., and A. Olmo. 2014. *La salute come diritto fondamentale: una ricerca sui migranti a Torino*. Bologna: Il Mulino.
Bourdieu, P. 2000. *Pascalian Meditations*. Stanford, CA: Stanford University Press.
Carpenter-Song, E.A., M. Nordquest Schwallie and J. Longhofer. 2007. 'Cultural Competence Reexamined: Critique and Directions for the Future'. *Psychiatric Services* 58(10): 1362–65.
Carricaburu, D., and M. Ménoret. 2004. *Sociologie de la santé: Institutions, professions et maladies*. Paris: Armand Colin.
Charles, C., A. Gafni and T. Whelan. 1999. 'Decision Making in Physician–Patient Encounter: Revisiting the Shared Treatment Decision-Making Model'. *Social Science & Medicine* 49: 651–61.
Del Vecchio Good, M.J. 1995. *American Medicine: The Quest for Compentence*. Berkeley and Los Angeles: University of California Press.
Eisenberg, L., and A. Kleinman. 1981. 'Clinical Social Science', in L. Eisenberg and A. Kleinman (eds), *The Relevance of Social Science for Medicine*. Dordrecht: Reidel Publishing Company, pp. 1–23.
Farmer, P. 2003. *Pathologies of Power: Health, Human Rights and the New War on the Poor*. Berkeley: University of California Press.
———. 2004. 'An Anthropology of Structural Violence'. *Current Anthropology* 45(3): 305–25.
Farmer, P., et al. 2013. *Reimagining Global Health*. Berkeley: University of California Press.
Fassin, D. 2009. *Inégalités et santé*. Paris: La Documentation française.
Ferrero, L. 2015. 'Dentro le reti per la salute dei migranti: tracce di welfare di comunità', in E. Castagnone et al. (eds), *La salute come diritto fondamentale: esperienze di migranti a Torino*. Bologna: Il Mulino, pp. 201–30.
Geyer, S., and R. Peter. 2000. 'Income, Social Position, Qualification and Health Inequalities – Competing Risks?' *Journal of Epidemiology and Community Health* 54: 299–305.
Good, B.J. 1994. *Medicine, Rationality, and Experience: An Anthropological Perspective*. Cambridge: Cambridge University Press.
Kawachi, I. 1999. 'Social Capital and Community Effects in Population and Individual Health'. *Annals of the New York Academy of Sciences* 896: 120–30.
Kleinman, A. 1978. 'Concepts and a Model for the Comparison of Medical Systems as Cultural Systems'. *Social Science & Medicine* 12: 85–93.
Kleinman, A., and P. Benson. 2006. 'Anthropology in the Clinic: The Problem of Cultural Competency and How to Fix It'. *PLoS Med* 3(10).
Leclerc, A., et al. 2000. *Les inégalités sociales de santé*. Paris: La Découverte.

Lynch, J., et al. 2004. 'Is Income Inequality a Determinant of Population Health? Part 2. US National and Regional Trends in Income Inequality and Age and Cause Specific Mortality'. *The Milbank Quarterly* 82(2): 355–400.

Marmot, M. 2005. 'Social Determinants of Health Inequalities'. *Lancet* 365(9464): 1099–1104.

Minelli, M. 2007. *Capitale sociale e salute: Una bibliografia ragionata*. Perugia: Morlacchi University Press.

Oliver, C. 2017. 'Peer-Led Care Practices and "Community" Formation in British Retirement Migration'. *Nordic Journal of Migration Research* 7(3): 172–80.

Osteria, T., D. Carrillo and A. Sarli. 2013. *The Health Dimension of Asian Migration to Europe*. Manila: De La Salle University Publishing House for the Asia–Europe Foundation.

Ponzo, I. (ed.). 2014. *Il nuovo care mix: Realtà e prospettive della cura agli anziani, tra pubblico (locale) e privato (transnazionale)*. Turin: Fieri. Retrieved 21 December 2017 from http://fieri.it/wp-content/uploads/2014/04/Il-nuovo-care-mix_prefazione.pdf.

Putnam, R.D. 2007. '*E Pluribus Unum*: Diversity and Community in the Twenty-First Century. The 2006 Johan Skytte Prize Lecture'. *Scandinavian Political Studies* 30(2): 137–74.

Quagliariello, C. 2016. 'Quanto e chi informare? Autonomia del paziente e autodeterminazione delle scelte terapeutiche', in C. Quagliariello and C. Fin, *Il consenso informato in ambito medico*. Bologna: Il Mulino, pp. 103–36.

Quaranta, I. 2006. *Antropologia medica, i testi fondamentali*. Milan: Raffaello Cortina Editore.

Quaranta, I., and M. Ricca. 2012. *Malati fuori luogo, medicina interculturale*. Milan: Raffaello Cortina Editore.

Quesada, J., L.K. Hart and P. Bourgois. 2011. 'Structural Vulnerability and Health: Latino Migrant Laborers in the United States'. *Medical Anthropology* 30(4): 339–62.

Rocco, L., and M. Suhrcke. 2012. *Is Social Capital Good for Health? A European Perspective*. Copenhagen: WHO Regional Office for Europe.

Sarli, A., and D. Carrillo. 2014. 'Unasked Questions and Missing Answers: The Italian National Health System and Chinese Migrants in Milan', MPC Analytical and Synthetic Note, 1. Retrieved 21 December 2017 from http://cadmus.eui.eu/handle/1814/31977.

Sayad, A.M. 1999. *La double absence*. Paris: Editions du Seuil.

Tassinari, A., and L. Tomba. 1996. 'Zhejiang-Pechino, Zhejiang-Firenze: Due esperienze migratorie a confronto'. *La Critica Sociologica* 117–118: 27–38.

Taylor, J. 2003. 'Confronting "Culture" in Medicine's "Culture of No Culture"'. *Academic Medicine* 78(6): 555–59.

Tognetti Bordogna, M. 2008. *Disuguaglianze di salute e immigrazione*. Milan: Franco Angeli.

Van Der Gaag, M., and T.A.B. Snijdersb. 2005. 'The Resource Generator: Social Capital Quantification with Concrete Items'. *Social Networks* 27: 1–29.

Williams, D.R. 1999. 'Race, Socioeconomic Status, and Health: The Added Effects of Racism and Discrimination'. *Annals of the New York Academy of Sciences* 896: 173–88.

Wu, B., and V. Zanin. 2009. 'Healthcare Needs of Chinese Migrant Workers in Italy: A Survey Report on Chinese-Owned Workshops in Veneto'. University of Nottingham, China Policy Institute, discussion paper no. 48.

Afterword

Forced Migration, State Violence and the Right to Health

Daniela DeBono

The Right to Health and the State

> What is important for us to develop is an anthropology of affliction that can move easily from the local to the large-scale, tying together the ethnographically visible with the deeper structures that generate or perpetuate poverty and inequality, and with the meanings these events and processes are given. (Farmer 2004: 323)

The highest attainable standard of health is a fundamental human right. Defined by WHO in its 1946 Constitution as 'a state of complete physical, mental and social well-being, and not merely the absence of disease or infirmity', health is not reducible to a medical concept but encompasses a broader, social dimension. The loss of health entails the loss of capacity/capability to conduct various daily activities that constitute and give meaning to life, such as work, social networks, family, time and leisure activities. The ownership, control or possession of one's health contributes towards a life of dignity. Inversely, the loss or dispossession of health is of great harm to an individual and can constitute one of the gravest affronts to human dignity. It is for this reason that the right to health is recognized as a fundamental human right in all major international human rights conventions, and is part of customary international law.

Structural violence is often deep seated and well hidden, but the contributors to this volume have all, to a greater or lesser degree, been led to uncover and denounce it (see, in particular, Goldberg et al., Quagliarello, Ferrero, this volume). Structural violence – defined as a cause of inequality with direct effects on a person's health (Farmer 1999) – can be produced, sustained or challenged by state action. The investigation of the right to health of migrants needs to include the identification of the 'social fault lines' that produce structural violence (ibid.: 45). Farmer asserts that instances of structural violence are 'not the result of accident or a force majeure; they are the consequence, direct or indirect, of human agency' (Farmer 2003: 40). Human agency is implicated through structures that reflect an unequal distribution of power. The inequalities that exist in terms of disproportionate life chances due to disease or poverty are directly caused by an unequal distribution of resources; but the underlying problem is that 'the power to decide over the distribution of resources is unevenly distributed' (Galtung 1969: 171). The state is one of the most powerful institutions that is involved in the (re)production of historically established structures such as racism, sexism and poverty that constrain individual agency. Conversely, the state is also a foremost institution that could challenge these structures. Therefore, health and well-being, particularly of migrants in positions of social disadvantage, are largely dependent on the action or inaction of states. This inextricable relationship between state action, access to human rights and a person's health and well-being is at the heart of our discussion.

Some contributions show the prevalence of situations in which migrants' health is negatively impacted as a result of state laws and provisions, or the lack of them (Kline, Quagliarello, this volume). In line with Galtung's work, which distinguished between personal, cultural and structural violence, much of the work presented in this volume discusses the difficulty of differentiating between migrants' health as the embodiment of structural violence, and migrants' health as the individual's well-being (Cingolani, Kerbage and Marranconi, this volume). The contributors to this volume touch upon the difficulties of discussing the positive right to health when migrants demonstrate the embodiment of structural violence, which is a result of state activity or omission – this can range from state laws directly impinging on migrant health (Kline, this volume) to the lack of systemic recognition of the importance of the cultural mediator (Vargas, this volume). Another concern that Kline mentions explicitly, and that emerges from other contributions too, is that there appears to be a paradigm shift against the conceptualization of health as a human right.

In this Afterword I will be focusing on two issues that arise out of my own ethnographic work, in which the contradictions and complexities of the problematic access to the right to health are very evident. These are two tools/approaches to migration management, common across the Global North, that are a source of ill health to forced migrants. First is the 'humanitarian border'. This refers to the manner in which migration control strategies have engaged with humanitarian activities, and where 'care', including health care, functions as a technology of border enforcement and biopolitical power (Walters 2011; Williams 2015). Second is the evermore globally pervasive practice of 'immigration detention' (Silverman and Massa 2012; Flynn 2014). Both tools are closely interlinked, and guide policy to 'care, control and contain' (cf. Bloch and Schuster 2005 on the British migration regime; Campesi 2018 on the Italian migration regime) the movement of different population groups, and limit to varying degrees people's freedom of movement. This lack of access or even the violation of their right to health has severe consequences and repercussions on the well-being of migrants, making these issues, despite their statistical 'smallness', significant from a moral and political point of view. This reflection will offer a brief discussion on how they relate to the topic and discussions in this book. The aim is not to provide an exhaustive discussion of either, but to provoke further thinking on the impact on people's health – in other words, on the way they serve, directly or indirectly, to limit or violate forced migrants' access to their right to health at a particularly vulnerable period during their trajectory.

Forced Migration

The concept of 'forced migrants' refers to people who have been compelled to move because of conflict, development or disaster. The term itself suggests that the forced migrant is constantly on the move, which is not always the case since forced migrants often end up in situations of protracted immobility. It also suggests that the decision that leads to a person to becoming a forced migrant might be taken autonomously, but certainly not willingly. The decision is therefore a consequence or an effect of external conditions over which the migrant has little control. The contemporary use of the term 'forced migrants' often falls into the dualisms that are so typical of migration studies – and forced migrants often fall into the 'helpless victim', as opposed to the 'powerful villain', category. This is rather misleading, and obscures the fact that, despite powerful structural conditions, migrants retain agency and some decision-making powers as seen in the creative strategies they employ to resist migration controls (Mainwaring 2016).

Possibly a better description of forced migrants, stemming not from their mobility but from their daily condition, is that forced migrants have joined other groups of people who cannot enjoy their right to free movement – that is, those whose mobility is limited, coerced, controlled or at times even impeded (i.e. forced immobility) during parts of the journey. One example is border control in Italy and the treatment of forced migrants crossing the Mediterranean Sea. Tazzioli shows that although the Italian border control system claims to exclude, it is constructed to control (Tazzioli 2017). This comes out clearly in the management of migrant reception where people are subject to a policy of dispersal, without choice, from one reception centre to another, depending on their asylum application and other personal criteria (Campesi 2018). The EU's system of relocation operates on a similar 'dispersal' logic under the justification of burden-sharing, with migrants being either immobilized or moved and generally controlled through various legal, political and economic means. Australia's policy of offshore 'processing' and incarceration on Manus Island and Nauru has proven to be an effective means of forcing immobility on migrants who are trying to reach its shores.

Intrinsic to the conceptualization of forced migration is the 'state'. A person might experience a natural disaster but they become forced migrants when the state does not provide an alternative means of livelihood, when the state fails to protect, when the state persecutes, or when the state's economic system does not provide opportunities for people to make a livelihood. Beyond the actual kinetic movement, the original impetus of forced migration can be addressed or further induced by states. Therefore, forced migration is, either by omission or direct action, the outcome of state in/action. And even though the idea of the state is admittedly difficult to define, that of the liberal democratic state includes the safeguarding of human rights within its territory. Turton argues that the concept of forced migration obliges us to consider issues of membership, citizenship and democratic liberalism. They require us to ask 'what our responsibilities are to the stranger in distress' and, therefore, they require us 'to consider who we are – what is or should be our moral community and, ultimately, what it means to be human' (Turton 2003: 8). In practice, therefore, states are responsible for constructing systems that ensure that minimal standards of protection, empowerment and the basic conditions for livelihood are met.

Given that forced migration is the result of state failure to protect or empower, forced migration can be taken to be a 'social fault', a form of structural violence effected by states. Through exploitation and oppression/exclusion, discrimination and control, people experience the power of the state on a daily basis, and this becomes visible in their bodies as illness or death. Disease and illness, Farmer argues, are the manifestation of violence on the human body, and as such constitute the 'biological reflections of social fault lines' (Farmer 1999: 5). And yet despite its ugliness and visibility, structural violence – unlike direct violence – has no perpetrator or victim, and it is seen as being 'about as natural as the air around us' (Galtung 1969: 173). Unfortunately, forced migration as a result of state failure is rarely discussed in academia, with research opting to study mostly the effects and outcomes of forced migration. And yet, the imprint of structural violence is found not only in bodies and biographies but also, as Fassin has argued, in public policy and discourse (Fassin 2007, 2009).

Forced migration is therefore both an example and an outcome of the embodied experience of structural and state violence. Phenomena such as global inequality, injustice and exploitation are what force people to migrate. Viewed in this manner, forced migrants are the unwitting victims of a silent, normalized global system. In this respect, the right to health is both a poignant reminder of the intimate nature of oppression and exploitation, and also critically of the fundamental role of the state in perpetrating structural violence and its potential to address it.

Control as Care: The Humanitarian Border

Closely connected to the complexities of the relationship between forced migration and the state is the concept of the humanitarian border. The enactment of the humanitarian border, as Walters argues, 'goes hand in hand with the move [that] has made state frontiers into privileged symbolic and regulatory instruments within strategies of migration control' (Walters 2011: 138).

The emergence of the humanitarian border is thus intimately linked to what Düvell (2011) has called 'the legal and political construction of irregular migration', as he argues that irregular migration is a result of the enactment of state borders. But it is also, as Walters points out, a consequence of how border crossing – in particular to access the territories of the Global North – has become a matter of life and death. The humanitarian border thus 'crystallises as a way of governing this novel and disturbing situation … compensating for the social violence embodied in the regime of migration control' (Walters 2011: 139). In turn, the territorial border becomes a convenient site for the 'crisisification' of irregular migration.

The dynamics of humanitarianism in the realm of migration have been explored by several academics. One example is Khosravi (2009), who argues that the narrative of humanitarianism in immigration detention in Sweden gives the impression of a person-centred and caring approach, but it masks strategies of surveillance and control. In a similar vein, Williams (2015), writing about irregular migrants crossing the Mediterranean, shows how they are paradoxically exposed to dehumanizing border control mechanisms by humanitarian policies and practices. Cuttitta (2014) shows how the enactment of the humanitarian border is very closely connected to the crisisification of irregular migration through an analysis of border spectacles on the small island of Lampedusa. Humanitarianism, border control and migration management are now inextricably connected.

Health services are central to the enactment of the humanitarian border. The role they play is twofold: they serve to present the humanitarian border as one concerned with 'care', while at the same time preventing people's health from degenerating to a level where questions start being asked. But what does health-care provision look like in humanitarian emergencies? First of all, health care provision in emergencies is different in that it is based on addressing ailments in the short term, rather than on taking a longer-term approach. Second, health-care providers are working in highly politicized spaces. Asgary (2015), in discussing the shrinking of the humanitarian space and the increasing shelling of hospitals in conflict areas, calls on health professionals and provocatively asks, 'Where is the outrage'? His argument is that the neutrality and impartiality of medicine ought to be prioritized, and recognized by all, but acknowledges that this is difficult in this neo-humanitarian era. He places paramount emphasis on the importance of medical provision remaining neutral and impartial. The same dynamics and concerns are found in health-care provision on the humanitarian border.

On Europe's Mediterranean border, Médecins Sans Frontières (MSF) has been particularly vocal in denouncing that offering health services to people whose health problems are a result of state detention amounts to hypocrisy at best, and to a human rights violation at worst. In some known publicized situations in 2009 in Malta and in 2015 in Italy, MSF took the controversial decision to suspend or even completely withdraw their services, despite knowing that the withdrawal of services would inevitably lead to greater suffering. Indeed, NGOs running services outsourced by states find it difficult to sustain the cooperation if they want to avoid co-option by the state. In such cases, the dilemma is often on how to continue being of service to vulnerable people without being used by the state to maintain a system that is creating hardships for the same vulnerable people they are serving (DeBono 2019b).

An interesting concept that is widely used in humanitarian settings to prioritize needs is the concept of vulnerability. In neo-humanitarian settings, policy design generally includes vulnerability gauging or the preset identification of vulnerable groups. Viladrich (this volume) shows how vulnerability, rather than being a symbol of a caring border, denotes the discriminatory nature of the border which indulges in 'selective inclusion'. There are several other examples of these dynamics in this book. Apart from Viladrich, the most incisive is Quaglieriello's (this volume) on the treatment of pregnant women. This type of special treatment presents itself as a mechanism of inclusion and care, masking the mass exclusion and violence that is inherent in the system.

Forced migrants are particularly vulnerable during border crossing, and affording dignified treatment in line with minimal human rights at the border – which are part of customary international law and numerous international conventions – is an obligation of receiving states. The concept of the humanitarian border might convey the idea that it is based on these principles, but in practice it does not follow a rights-based, person-centred approach. Instead, it employs a charity and crisis approach through which control can be exerted over people. The humanitarian border is an example of how the state, under the ambiguous yet often convenient smoke screen of humanitarianism, provides medical services to address a crisis situation that not only could have been averted but that was constructed by states themselves. Humanitarianism is not oriented towards helping, caring or empowering migrants, but rather occupies a self-serving role of allowing the state to exclude or control the mobility of a group of people. In this regard, the provision of emergency health services critical to humanitarianism are not a solution to an emergency, but a strategy aimed at controlling people. The negative role of the state – which not only fails to uphold the right to health, but constructs systems that lead to the violation of the right to health – needs to be exposed and challenged.

Compulsion as Containment: Immigration Detention

The deprivation of liberty for immigration-related purposes is one of the most aggressive forms of state action, and has a negative effect on a person's physical and mental health (Rijks et al. 2016; DeBono 2017). Immigration detention is an administrative or punitive measure used by states to control and contain non-citizens for the purposes of realizing an immigration-related goal (Silverman and Massa 2012). Globally, immigration detention is on the increase (Silverman and Massa 2012; Turnbull 2017). Even where immigration-related offences have been decriminalized, for example in European Union member states, the increase in administrative detention has resulted in much higher numbers of people in detention (Flynn 2014).

As a result of a decriminalization turn that has taken place in the last two decades, immigration-related offences are no longer crimes in European Union member states. Yet, even though criminal detention of migrants is on the decrease, administrative detentions today far outnumber criminal detentions ten years ago. Apart from this, the fact that immigration detention manifests itself in different ways may easily elude statistics – for example, the Global Detention Project Observatory, which maps detention centres across the world, does not include detentions of asylum-seekers and migrants at first reception centres in Italy, Greece or Spain, the three main entry points for irregular migrants taking the Mediterranean maritime routes. The EU's 2015 Agenda on Migration legitimized detention of newly arrived migrants for the purposes of registration and medical clearance (under the hotspot approach). As a result, since autumn 2015 all new migrants, including asylum seekers, in Italy were detained for periods ranging from a few hours to a few months (DeBono 2019b). Apart from running counter to any hospitality principles or 'reception logic' this system in Italy inhibits the enactment of human rights safeguards by civil society by not allowing NGOs to act as independent human rights monitors, despite known risks that migrants face at the border and in immigration detention (DeBono, 2018, 2019a). A similar situation can be found in Greece, although in some cases migrants are not detained in a facility as such but are instead barred from leaving an island – constituting, albeit to a different degree, deprivation of liberty and forced immobility. The increasing use of administrative and punitive immigration detention globally is of great concern. Whilst in principle the two are different, studies show that migrants experience punitive and administrative detention in similar ways (JRS Europe 2010; DeBono et al. 2015; Barker 2017).

Research shows that immigration detention is a growing threat to the physical and mental well-being of migrants (JRS Europe 2010; Sampson 2013). For instance, in research I conducted in Sweden, a country known for its comparatively humane policies, the psychosocial, mental and physical health of people threatened with deportation nosedived definitively once they were placed in immigration detention (DeBono 2017). This confirms the conclusions of previously conducted studies in other countries, which identified the risks to the physical and mental health of migrants posed by detention, irrespective of the presence of safeguarding policies (see, for example, the pan-European study 'Becoming Vulnerable in Detention' (JRS Europe 2010; also, Rijks et al. 2016). Robjant, Hassan and Katona's (2009) study of the mental health outcomes of detaining asylum seekers found high levels of mental health problems in detainees. These included anxiety, depression and post-traumatic stress disorder, as well as self-harm and suicidal ideation. Among the contributing factors identified were the deprivation of liberty, the conditions of detention, the institutional rhythm and also – indicatively – a deep sense that their detention was unjust, irrespective of whether it was of an administrative or a punitive nature (JRS Europe 2010; DeBono et al. 2015; Turnbull 2017). Another noteworthy study is Hasselberg's (2016) monograph on migrants convicted of criminal offences in England and Wales, and who are appealing their deportation. Hasselberg gives a moving account of the frustrations and difficulties, of which a critical part are their experiences of state surveillance and control through detention. Tellingly, a recent study conducted by Hynie (2018) on the determinants of mental health amongst migrants concludes that whilst pre-migration trauma does predict mental disorders and PTSD, the post-migration context can be an equally powerful determinant of mental health. Significantly, it also shows that post-migration factors may moderate the ability of refugees to recover from pre-migration trauma. In line with these findings, Robjant, Robbins and Senior (2009) conclude, that migrant detention results in much higher and more severe mental health problems among immigration detainees as compared to asylum seekers living in the community. Irrespective of what a migrant has been through, immigration detention is a source of physical and mental health problems.

These results are similar to my findings on migrant detention in Malta. A small island state in the Mediterranean Sea, it is on the central Mediterranean route of irregular migration since it lies between Libya and Italy. Until recently, Malta implemented a blanket policy of detention of up to eighteen months for all asylum seekers and irregular migrants arriving from Libya. The appalling conditions of detention, the lack of legal remedies and the uncertainty produced spaces of cruelty, frustration and despair that, I have argued, rendered migrants 'less than human' (DeBono 2013). The other EU destination state on this route is Italy. The reception conditions here are different, but particularly since the 2015 European Agenda on Migration migrants have been deprived of liberty in order to implement the 'hotspot approach', part of the larger humanitarian border policy framework discussed earlier. Migrants are placed in a position of vulnerability, which can be due to one or more of the following factors: their irregular entry, the reason for their departure, the experiences of their journey and their request for asylum. In such a situation, where one would expect a state to implement human rights safeguards, as also advised by the Council of Europe, we find that Italy, for example, has very problematically not allowed the presence of NGOs as human rights monitors (DeBono 2018). The disregard of the need to enact human rights safeguards is part of an ongoing global movement of exclusion and structural violence enacted through border control, and it is telling that the editors of this volume have chosen to open their Introduction with a mention of this.

Health Denied: The Absence of Human Rights at the Border

In the tradition of medical anthropology, the contributions in this volume have directed our attention to the evidence of how the social, bodily and historical are all intertwined. This is an approach that is particularly important when discussing the perpetration of structural violence by the state. It allows us to reveal and dwell upon the effects of power and social inequality on people's health, rather than to study the body as detached from the social and political environment that it inhabits. Kerbage and Marranconi (this volume) make a very pertinent comment: professionals, they write, agree on their role in helping refugees to 'adapt' to reinforce their coping skills, but, they ask, 'what does it mean to adapt to the context when this same context forces the person into a perpetual struggle for survival, from which the only way out appears to be resettlement to a third country?'

I started this reflection by alluding to, on one hand, the central role of the state in ensuring access to the right to health, and, on the other hand, to the contemporary understanding of the right to health. The contributions in this book are testament to the various initiatives that demonstrate an awareness of the centrality of this human right, and bring to the fore various attempts aimed at ensuring migrants' access to health-care services. In this Afterword I have chosen to develop a thread that runs through the various contributions in this volume. It shows the detrimental effects of structural violence on people's health, and the grave consequences that ensue whenever states directly produce and sustain structural violence and inequality, instead of minimizing their effects.

In the case of forced migrants, the irony of states not offering adequate access to health care is even greater because people become forced migrants as a result of state failure. They are then being forced to travel irregularly because of other states' border control policies. So apart from the oft-discussed importance of solidarity between citizens, inter-state solidarity is particularly apt in this case. States need to recognize that in their own design and in the political power they yield lies a tremendous risk of violence on people, and as such, 'as compensation' or by way of redemption they have an obligation towards forced migrants. As such, states are under an obligation to address structural violence and to avoid creating situations where the state, proactively or indirectly, is the source of violence against people.

The picture that emerges is grave. Using the excuse of irregular legal status or irregular border crossing, states are constructing situations in which people are disregarded, contained and coerced. In these scenarios, bodies are uncared for and/or subject to violence. The neocolonial idea of the 'sick diseased body', abhorred by the slave abolitionists, but also by other rights-based movements like the disability rights movement, becomes a reality ironically through the active efforts of the state. The humanitarian border and migrant detention have a detrimental impact on people's health. They are tantamount to structural violence insofar as they constitute 'avoidable' harm (Galtung 1969). The ironic paradox is that the state not only fails to live up to its role as protector but becomes the perpetrator of such violence. The question that naturally follows is: which other institutions can introduce the structural interventions necessary to bring about change and alter the processes that encourage structural violence?

Daniela DeBono is an associate professor at Malmö University (Sweden), and Marie Curie COFAS research fellow at the Malmö Institute for the Studies of Migration, Welfare and Diversity, and at the European University Institute (Italy). She has conducted three long-term ethnographic projects on irregular migration in Malta, deportation from Sweden, and hospitality at the external borders of the EU, with a focus on Sicily, Lampedusa and Malta. In relation to these projects, she has published on irregular migration in the Mediterranean, on hospitality at state borders, on return and deportation from the EU, on citizenship and on children's rights.

References

Asgary R. 2015. 'Direct Killing of Patients in Humanitarian Situations and Armed Conflicts: The Profession of Medicine is Losing Its Meaning'. *The American Journal of Tropical Medicine and Hygiene* 92(4), 678–80.

Barker, V. 2017. 'Penal Power at the Border: Realigning State and Nation'. *Theoretical Criminology* 21(4): 441–57.

Bloch, A., and L. Schuster. 2005. 'At the Extremes of Exclusion: Deportation, Detention and Dispersal'. *Ethnic and Racial Studies* 28(3): 491–512.

Campesi, G. 2018. 'Between Containment, Confinement and Dispersal: The Evolution of the Italian Reception System before and after the "Refugee Crisis"'. *Journal of Modern Italian Studies* 23(4): 490–506.

Cuttitta, P. 2014. '"Borderizing" the Island Setting and Narratives of the Lampedusa "Border Play"'. *ACME – An International Journal for Critical Geographies* 13(2): 196–219.

DeBono, D. 2013 '"Less than Human": The Detention of Irregular Immigrants in Malta'. *Race and Class* 55(2): 60–81.

———. 2017. '"Burning without Fire" in Sweden: The Paradox of the State's Attempt to Safeguard Deportees' Psychosocial Wellbeing', in Z. Vathi and R. King (eds), *Return Migration and Psychosocial Wellbeing: Discourses, Policy-Making and Outcomes for Migrants and their Families*. London: Routledge, pp. 129–47.

———. 2018. 'In Defiance of the Reception Logic: The Case for Including NGOs as Human Rights Monitors in the EU's Policies of First Reception of Irregular Migrants'. *Peace and Conflict: Journal of Peace Psychology* 24(3): 291–95.

———. 2019a. 'Plastic Hospitality: The Empty Signifier at the EU's Mediterranean Border'. *Migration Studies* 7(3): 340–361.

---. 2019b. 'Narrating the Humanitarian Border: Moral Deliberations of Territorial Borderworkers on the EU's Mediterranean Border'. *Journal of Mediterranean Studies* 28(1): 55–73.
DeBono, D., et al. 2015. *Humane and Dignified? Migrants' Experiences of Living in a 'State of Deportability' in Sweden*. Malmo: Malmo University.
Düvell, F. 2011. 'Paths into Irregularity: The Legal and Political Construction of Irregular Migration'. *European Journal of Migration and Law* 13(3): 275–95.
Farmer, P. 1999. *Infections and Inequalities: The Modern Plagues*. Berkeley: University of California Press.
---. 2003. *Pathologies of Power: Health, Human Rights, and the New War on the Poor*. Berkeley: University of California Press.
---. 2004. 'An Anthropology of Structural Violence'. *Current Anthropology* 45(3): 305–25.
Fassin, D. 2007. *When Bodies Remember: Experiences and Politics of AIDS in South Africa*. Translated by Amy Jacobs and Gabrielle Varro. Berkeley: University of California Press.
---. 2009. 'A Violence of History: Accounting for AIDS in Post-apartheid South Africa', in B. Rylko-Bauer, L. Whiteford and P. Farmer (eds), *Global Health in Times of Violence*. Santa Fe: School for Advanced Research Press, pp. 113–35.
Flynn, M. 2014. 'How and Why Immigration Detention Crossed the Globe'. Global Detention Project Working Paper No. 8.
Galtung, J. 1969. 'Violence, Peace, and Peace Research'. *Journal of Peace Research* 6(3):167–91.
Hasselberg, I. 2016. *Enduring Uncertainty: Deportation, Punishment and Everyday Life*. New York: Berghahn Books.
Hynie, M. 2018. 'The Social Determinants of Refugee Mental Health in the Post-migration Context: A Critical Review'. *Canadian Journal of Psychiatry* 63(5): 297–303.
Jesuit Refugee Service (JRS), Europe. 2010. 'Becoming Vulnerable in Detention'. Retrieved 20 September 2018 from http://www.refworld.org/docid/4ec269f62.html.
Khosravi, S. 2009. 'Sweden: Detention and Deportation of Asylum Seekers'. *Race & Class* 50(4): 38–56.
Mainwaring, Ć. 2016. 'Migrant Agency: Negotiating Borders and Migration Controls'. *Migration Studies* 4(3): 289–308.
Robjant, K., R. Hassan and C. Katona. 2009. 'Mental Health Implications of Detaining Asylum Seekers: Systematic Review'. *The British Journal of Psychiatry* 194(4): 306–12.
Robjant, K., I. Robbins and V. Senior. 2009. 'Psychological Distress amongst Immigration Detainees: A Cross-sectional Questionnaire Study'. *British Journal of Clinical Psychology* 48(3): 275–86.

Rijks, B., et al. 2016. 'Immigration Detention and Health in Europe', in B. Elger, C. Ritter and H. Stöver (eds), *Emerging Issues in Prison Health*. Dordecht: Springer, pp. 217–36.

Sampson, R. 2013. 'Thinking Outside the Fence'. *Forced Migration Review* 44: 42–43.

Silverman, S.J., and E. Massa. 2012. 'Why Immigration Detention is Unique'. *Population, Space and Place* 18(6): 677–86.

Tazzioli, M. 2017. 'Containment through Mobility: Migrants' Spatial Disobediences and the Reshaping of Control through the Hotspot System'. *Journal of Ethnic and Migration Studies* 44(16): 2764–779.

Turnbull, S. 2017. 'Immigration Detention and Punishment', in *Oxford Research Encyclopedia of Criminology*. Oxford: Oxford University Press.

Turton, D. 2003. 'Conceptualising Forced Migration'. RSC Working Paper No. 12. University of Oxford.

Walters, W. 2011. 'Foucault and Frontiers: Notes on the Birth of the Humanitarian Border', in U. Bröckling, S. Krasmann and T. Lemke (eds), *Governmentality: Current Issues and Future Challenges*. New York: Routledge, pp. 138–64.

WHO. 1946. 'Constitution of the World Health Organisation'. Retrieved 29 June 2020 from https://www.who.int/governance/eb/who_constitution_en.pdf

Williams, J. 2015. 'From Humanitarian Exceptionalism to Contingent Care: Care and Enforcement at the Humanitarian Border'. *Political Geography* 47: 11–20.

Index

287(g) programme, 65–66

ACA (Affordable Care Act) 36–39, 46, 50–52, 59
accident and emergency department, 140
American Dream, 44, 47
anti-immigrant, 40, 72
asylum, 171, 238, 244, 247
asylum seekers, 6–12, 14–16, 21, 27, 113, 116, 242–44
   detention, 110, 237, 240, 242–44
   offshore processing, 238
austerity policies, 15, 186
   impact on intercultural mediation, 30, 182, 184
awareness session, 162, 164–66

barriers
   to health care/health services, 49
Beirut, 159–60, 170–73
Bekaa valley, 159–60
biomedical, 14, 16, 45, 68, 127, 142, 189, 196, 199
biomedicine, 99, 143, 196, 202
Black migrant women, 104, 109
bodies, subject to violence, 245
Bolivian Immigrants, 23, 80, 81, 84–85, 88–89, 95, 97–98
border
   concept of, 8–10
   control, 102, 110, 237–38, 240–41, 243–45
   Southern Europe, 23, 103
   Southern Italian, 106, 115

Buenos Aires, 23, 80, 81, 83–89, 90, 91, 95–98
bureaucratic
   procedures, 112, 175, 187
   situation, 153–154

camp, 9, 10, 12, 114, 129–48, 160, 164, 167
care-mix, 228
childbirth, 114, 116, 214
Chinese immigrants, 213
   and national health system, 213, 215, 225
   and pregnancy, 213, 219, 221
   and traditional medicine, 224
citizen/s, 42, 43–44, 48–49, 51, 53, 69, 71–73
citizenship, 41, 61, 63–64, 71–73, 105, 118, 132, 238
civil society, 211, 242
   and irregular migration, 242
communities, 10, 21, 24, 42, 60, 127, 129, 176, 195, 213, 217, 220, 229
community clinics, 187, 191
   intercultural mediation in, 191–94
community health agents, 95–96
   program community health workers, 95–96, 99
community health profile, 214
community welfare, 228
community-based intervention, 155, 57, 162–63, 168
companies (major brand export, clothing, foreign multinational), 81, 86

continuum of violence, 117
cost-effective frame, 37, 42, 46–48, 50, 53
cost-saving frame, 37, 42, 46–48, 50, 53
counter-frame, 40
cultural barriers, 116, 194
cultural competence, 18, 201, 202–3, 226
cultural difference, 24, 139, 200, 202, 204
cultural mediators, 18, 20, 183–84, 187, 191, 195, 200, 212, 216, 218, 220, 227. *See also* Intercultural mediators
culturalism, 196–97, 203
  Fassin, Didier on, 7, 172, 196–197

DACA (Deferred Action for Childhood Arrivals), 23, 37–39, 41–43, 45–46, 49–50, 52–53
deportation, 37, 44–45, 61, 62, 65–69, 73, 243, 246
depression, 12, 24, 44, 89, 114, 131, 154, 158, 162, 164–65
deserving, 14, 18, 37, 43, 48, 50–51
deservingness, 35, 37, 50, 52, 60–64, 66–70, 72, 74
detention, 240, 242, 243–24
  administrative detention, 110, 242, 243 (*see also* administrative detention centres)
  criminal, 242,
  immigration detention, 237, 240, 242–43,
  incarceration, 47, 238,
determinants of health, 4, 146, 210, 243. *See also* determinants of mental health
differentialist approach, 131, 146
discriminations, 3, 5, 13–14, 16, 18, 23, 84–85, 104–5, 115, 153, 172, 196, 220, 239
distrust, 134, 140, 213, 225
DREAM Act, 38, 53
dreamers, 38, 42, 44–47, 53

effortful immigrant, 37, 42–45, 50
embodiment, 219, 236

concept of, 10–11
and consequences of immigration laws, 62, 64, 67, 68, 72, 73
emergency
  context, 165–167
  room, 35, 48–49, 213
ENI card (Italy), 134, 219
entitlement, 22, 36, 40–41, 46, 50, 52, 63
ethno-psychology
  Franz Fanon Centre (Turin), 194
  intercultural mediation in, 187, 194
  Mamre Centre (Turin), 194
European Agenda on Migration, 244
European Union, 2, 9, 24, 109, 132, 140, 182, 242
Evidence-based mental health intervention, 155, 161–63, 167, 175, 177
exploitation, 5, 13, 81, 84–87, 96, 127, 172, 239

Farmer, Paul, 116, 196, 217, 236, 239
first reception
  centres, 125, 242
  logic, 242
forced immobility, 238, 242
forced migrants, 238, 241, 245
  as a concept, 237–39
forced migration, 235, 237–39
forced prostitution market, 107, 109, 117
foreign-born, 36, 42, 51

Gap Action Programme (mhGAP), 158, 161
gender and migration, 117, 188, 230
gender-based violence, 23, 104, 108
General Security Office (Lebanon), 152
Georgia (US State of), 10, 23, 61, 64–67, 70
GLAHR, 66–67, 73
global inequality, 239
government-sponsored health care, 37–39, 48

hard-working, 37, 42–43, 50
HB, 65–66, 68

health, 5, 11, 18, 182, 236
  insurance/coverage, 36–39, 44,
    46–49, 53
  mental, 24, 105, 118, 154–90,
    242–43
  physical, 81, 102, 105, 118, 167, 198,
    242–43
  in post-migration context, 243
  and pre-migration trauma, 243
  psychosocial, 242–43
  conditions, 43, 49, 95, 127–28, 131,
    146–48, 164, 176, 209
  inequalities, 13, 16, 81, 217
  literacy, 21, 163, 213
  outcomes, 35, 42, 46, 243
  policy/policies, 36, 41, 43, 49, 154
  rights, 7, 11–12, 37, 52, 128
  safety net, 37, 43, 50
health-care, 6, 35–39, 41–44, 46, 48,
    50–52, 54
  disparities, 197
  health-care reform in USA, 35,
    36–37, 41–42, 51
  workers, 11, 91, 129, 134, 136–39,
    186–89, 193
  access, 14–16, 52, 81, 153–54
Hispanic, 43
hospital/s, 35, 41, 47–49, 53, 67,
    112–15, 133, 135–37, 140–44,
    214–18, 225–27
  intercultural mediation in, 183,
    187–91
housing precariousness, 131
human rights, 236, 244
  and anthropology, 3–4
  at the border, 242
  charity approach, 241
  and deprivation of liberty, 35, 37,
    51, 54
  dignified treatment, 241
  'less than human', 241
  person-centred approach, 241
  safeguards, 244
humanitarian
  actors, 166
  agencies, 170, 172, 174–75
  aid, 172
  assistance, 153, 167
  attitude, 169

  discourse, 102, 104
  field, 154–55, 168
  organizations, 172–73
  reasons, 103, 174
  regime, 175
  response, 161
  setting, 156, 175, 178
  space, 174–175, 240
  system, 156, 167
humanitarian border, 237, 239, 240,
    244
  and vulnerability, 241
humanitarianism, 177, 240, 241

idioms of distress, 158, 168
illegal/illegality, 5, 22 40, 42, 44–45,
    47–48, 51, 70–72
illness, 4, 11–12, 17–18, 44, 80–82,
    91–96, 129, 156–57
immigration policies, 64, 69, 185
  and intercultural mediation in Italy,
    183, 185
  Turco-Napolitano law on immigra-
    tion (Italy), 184
immigration Status, 6, 23, 47–48,
    61–62, 71–72
inequalities, 81, 88– 89, 95, 128, 147,
    168
inequality, 183–85, 196, 209–10, 217,
    228, 235–39, 244–45
informed consent, and intercultural
    mediation, 187, 193
  and linguistic barrier, 198–99
injustice, 239
institutional discrimination, 220
institutional violence, 105, 113, 118,
    185
insurance, 15, 36–39, 46–50, 61, 69,
    71, 135
Inter-Agency Standing Committee
    (IASC), 154, 157, 162, 176
intercultural mediation, 24, 182–208
  A.M.M.I. Multiethnic Association
    of Intercultural Mediators, 184
  D.I.S.Co.R.S.I. Migranti project on,
    197
  informal mediation, 188, 194
  intercultural mediator (mediatore
    interculturale), 182–208

Italian State-Regions Conference's guidelines, 186
Luatti, Lorenzo on, 185
misunderstandings about, 17, 146, 185
Piedmont Region policies on, 186
International Medical Corps (IMC), 154–55, 166–67
International Organization for Migration (IOM), 5–6, 103, 176
Inter-Personal Therapy (IPT), 161, 163, 166, 177
intersectionality theories, 14, 23, 105
ISI Centre (Italy), 219
Italian national health system, 211, 218–19, 224
Italy, 23, 103–19, 128–47, 182–208, 209–29, 238, 241–42

Lampedusa, 9, 15, 17, 23, 102–19, 240
Latin America, 2, 10–12, 22, 60, 88
Latino, 36, 38, 42, 60
Latinx, 60–61, 64, 66, 70
legal status, 6, 15, 35, 39, 45, 48, 65, 130, 134, 153, 205, 245
Libya, 8, 11, 108–11, 114, 119, 244, 224
linguistic, 184, 197
   barriers, 5, 95, 116, 187, 194, 204, 220–22
   code, 200
   competence, 188
   comprehension, 199
   exchange, 200
   interpretation, 182
   Linguistic-cultural mediator, 18, 184–85
   translation, 200 (*see also* translation)
lying, 156, 168–71, 174

Malta, 240, 243
manipulation, 1, 168, 170, 174
Manus Island, 238
maternity care services, 104, 106
media
   analysis, 37, 41, 43
   coverage, 39, 45, 50

frames, 37, 40, 41, 48
framing, 36–37, 40, 50–51
Medicaid, 38–39, 53, 61, 69, 71
medical
   bills, 43
   care, 4, 16, 35, 49, 63, 72, 99, 189, 218
   consultations, 112, 115
   insurance/coverage, 35, 48
   services, 15, 35–36, 52, 230, 241
Medi-Cal (US), 39, 43, 49
medical pluralism, 16, 196, 215
Medicare, 38, 61
Mediterranean Sea, 102–5, 109, 113, 238, 240, 243–44
mental health
   disorder, 164–65, 167–68
   donors, 158, 165–66, 173
   education, 163, 168
   funding, 165–67
Mexico, 2, 8, 36, 38, 60, 64, 68–69
migrant/s
   defining migrant/s, 5
   as helpless victim, 237
   as human agency, 236
   as powerful villain, 237
migrant associations, 19–20, 25, 211, 217, 222, 224, 229
   A.M.E.C.E. (Moroccan association), 211, 215–16, 218–21, 223, 227
   ANGI (Chinese association), 212, 214, 219–21, 224–25
   and health, 216–17, 222
   San Lorenzo dei Romeni (Romanian association), 212, 216, 218–19, 227–29
   and social capital, 218
   Zhi Song (Chinese association), 212–13, 218, 222, 226–27
migrant reception, 238
   centers, 9, 113–15
   hospitality, 242
   hotspot approach, 242, 244
migrant women, 103–6, 110–11, 113–15, 117, 123
migration

definition, 5
Ministry of Public Health (MoPH)
– Lebanon, 153–55, 159, 160, 162–64
Ministry of Social Affairs (MoSA) – Lebanon, 153–54, 160, 164
model immigrant, 45, 53
multi-drug-resistant tuberculosis (MDR-TB), 92–94, 98

narrative interview, 183, 204
National Mental Health Program (NMHP), 154–155, 161–62, 166
Nauru, 238
neoliberal
  capitalist globalization, policies, hegemony, 2, 8, 81, 83, 84, 95, 96
  positions/paradigm, 35, 38, 41, 52, 72
Neo-Pentecostal evangelical church, 91–93, 95, 98, 99
news, 23, 37, 39–42, 49
Nigeria, 106–11, 115–16, 118
Nigerian
  girls, 105–7, 109, 117, 121
  migrants, 104, 106, 107, 112, 113
  women, 104–9, 112–13, 117–18
nomadism, 129, 131
noncompliance, and linguistic barrier, 221–22
non-governmental organisations, 1, 4, 15, 19, 152, 154–55, 159–60, 162, 164–68, 170, 172–73, 177, 178, 241
  as independent human rights monitors, 242, 244
non-profit organizations, 211

Obama, Barack, 23, 36, 38, 44, 65
obstetrical consultations, 112–13
otherness, 11, 63, 196

Palermo (Italy), 104–6, 112, 117, 119
paradigm shift, 41, 52, 236
participant observation, 67, 81, 105, 183
participative knowledge, 183

physical violence, 109–10
pool risks, 47–8
post-traumatic stress disorder (PTSD), 24, 68, 154, 156–58, 164, 243
power
  Brigg, Morgan on power, mediation and conflict, 195
  and decision making, 198–99
  and intercultural mediation, 195–97
pregnancy, 15, 91, 102–3, 105, 110–12, 114–15, 119, 135, 148, 188, 231
pregnant migrants, 14–5, 102–3, 114, 118
premiums (insurance), 37, 47–50
private health sector, 141, 153, 167, 176, 185, 187, 191, 224
private insurance, 36, 38, 231
privatization, 96, 135, 190, 203
professionals, 11, 15, 17–18, 24, 106, 115, 135–36, 138, 140, 146, 155–56, 159, 161–70, 172–77, 182–83, 197, 199, 201–2, 240, 244
psychiatric categories, 156, 161
  consultation, 157, 159, 162, 165–67, 176
  diagnosis, 158–59, 163
  discourse, 175
  disorder, 156–59, 163, 178
  intervention, 156
  knowledge, 164
psychological
  category, 156, 159
  condition, 161–62, 169
  counselling, 156, 159, 168
  distress, 18, 165
  first aid, 161
  traumas, 109, 117
Psychosocial Support services (MHPSS services), 154–60, 162–64, 167–68, 172, 174
Psychosocial Support Task Force (MHPSS-TF), 155, 162, 166–67
public health, 3, 11, 15, 42, 48–49, 51, 53, 80, 89, 92, 96, 99, 134–36, 153, 157, 159, 191, 211
public opinion, 36–37, 40

Putnam, Robert, 217

qualitative, 22, 24, 37, 41–42, 105, 131, 154

racialization, 18
   of labour process, 84–85
relational inequality, 210, 217, 228
reproductive rights, 112, 118–19
resettlement, 169–72, 174–75, 244
right to health, 3–4, 7, 11–12, 14–16, 20–22, 26, 127, 146–47, 182, 215, 217, 235–39, 241, 245
right to health care, 35–36, 54, 81, 134
rights-based approach, 241
risk, 19, 20, 80, 82, 89, 96
Roma, 10, 12, 16–17, 21, 24, 128–48, 201
Romania, 128–29, 132–35, 137, 139–48, 227

São Paulo, 23, 80–91, 95–98
sexual violence, 108, 110–11
Shanty town, 132, 136. *See also* spontaneous settlement
Sicily, 104–5, 112–20
sick diseased body, 245
slavery, 23, 81, 85, 87, 90, 95
social capital, 5, 21, 209–10, 217–19, 226, 228–29
   loss of, 210,
social determinants of health, 4, 146, 210
social fault lines, 236, 239
social inclusion
   policies, 185
   projects, 183
social inequality, 96, 127–28, 196, 244. *See also* social marginality
social marginality, 10, 13, 136, 146, 188, 190, 194, 204
social network, 18–20, 24, 154, 157, 196, 209–10, 213, 217–18, 235
   absence of, 19, 210, 217, 226, 227–28
   and health, 210, 217, 219, 229–30
social worker, 106, 133, 137, 140, 143, 145, 160, 164–65, 173–74, 177–78, 205
solidarity, 193, 212, 245

spontaneous settlement, 130, 132. *See also* shanty town
state
   action, 236, 238, 242
   surveillance, 132, 243
   violence, 235, 239 (*see also* institutional violence)
stereotypes
   on Arab women, 201
   and intercultural mediation, 17–18, 105, 117, 156, 178, 200–1
stigma, 13, 18, 44, 84–85, 93, 165, 177
Stranieri Temporaneamente Presenti (STP, Italy), 134, 148, 187, 205
structural violence, 13–14, 23, 80–82, 85, 95–96, 105, 113, 116, 118, 196, 217, 228, 235–36, 239, 244–45
structural vulnerability, 13–14, 22, 54, 127–128, 146–47, 203, 219, 228
students, 42, 46–47, 53, 65, 205, 224, 231
suffering (social suffering), 13, 81–83, 87, 90–93, 158, 175, 194, 196
sweatshops, 80–82, 85–86, 88–90, 95–98
Sweden, 144, 240, 243

tactic of avoidance and adaptation, 173
taxes, 46–47
therapeutic encounter, 175, 209, 222
   relationship, 138, 155, 168–169, 174, 199
   setting, 169–70
Third sector, 184, 212–13, 218, 227
traditional medicine, 93, 139, 142, 215, 230
translation, 191, 197, 199, 200, 215, 221–22
   Giordano, Cristiana on, 199
transnational
   mobility, 127–28, 139
   ties, 144–45, 210–11
trauma therapy, 156, 161, 166
trauma-focused Services, 157
Trump, Donald, 2, 39, 41, 44–45, 60–62, 66, 73
tuberculosis (TB), 12, 23, 80–83, 88–99, 190, 221

Turin, 21, 25, 132–133, 136, 139–141, 144, 147–48, 182–83, 186, 194, 205, 211–16, 221, 227, 230–31

unauthorized
immigrant/s, 35–37, 41, 48, 50
youth, 35, 37–39, 44–45, 47, 50–51, 53
undeservingness, 23, 60–62, 64, 67–70, 72–73. *See also* deservingness
undocumented youth, 36–39, 41, 46–47, 49–50, 52
uninsured, 36, 38, 42, 47, 49, 52, 61, 135
United Nations Children's Fund (UNICEF), 154–155
United Nations High Commissioner for Refugees (UNHCR), 152–54, 158–60, 162–64, 166, 168–72, 176–78
registration, 153–54, 163
United States, 2, 10, 12, 14–15, 21–22, 35–39, 41, 44–48, 50–53, 60–65, 69, 71–73, 84, 127, 156, 177
economy, 43, 49, 51
media, 36, 40, 48, 50, 51

violence, 5, 23, 60, 156, 170–171, 175. *See also* institutional violence, state violence and structural violence
voluntary termination of pregnancy (VTP), 23, 105, 112–13
volunteers, 138, 145, 204, 211–12, 214–18, 220, 226–27, 231
vulnerability (social vulnerability, context of), 13–14, 22, 54, 61, 81–82, 95, 98, 104, 127–28, 139, 142, 146–47, 176, 203, 219, 228, 241, 244
vulnerable groups/populations, 38–39, 47, 51–52, 241

welfare, 6–7, 18–19, 21, 41, 47, 50–51, 63, 103, 186, 192, 203, 209, 213
well-being, 14, 85, 118, 157, 185, 189, 206, 210, 212, 229, 236–37, 243
World Health Organization (WHO), 144, 154–55, 177, 210, 214, 236

young immigrants, 37, 44–45, 48, 50

www.ingramcontent.com/pod-product-compliance
Lightning Source LLC
Chambersburg PA
CBHW051534020426
42333CB00016B/1927